Computer Graphics Handbook

Computer Graphics Handbook

Geometry and Mathematics

Michael E. Mortenson

Industrial Press Inc.

Library of Congress Cataloging-in-Publication Data

Mortenson, Michael E., 1939–
    Computer graphics handbook : geometry and mathematics/Michael
E. Mortenson.
       p.   cm.
    ISBN 0–8311–1002–3
    1. Computer graphics—Handbooks, manuals, etc. I. Title.
T385.M6683   1990
006.6–dc20   89-27664 CIP

INDUSTRIAL PRESS INC.
200 Madison Avenue
New York, New York 10016-4078

First Printing

2   4   6   8   7   5   3

Preface

Successful computer graphics applications depend on skill in using certain basic geometric and mathematical principles and concepts. These principles and concepts are presented in this *Computer Graphics Handbook*. Each page contains a single concept or related group of concepts, often with examples and with commentary in the margins. Emphasis is on understanding and using vector and matrix algebra and a variety of transformations as they apply to constructing and displaying geometric objects.

Although *Computer Graphics Handbook* is not written in the usual textbook style, you can read it that way, from beginning to end, since independent and simpler concepts generally appear earlier in the sequence, and more complex concepts and those that depend on the simpler concepts appear later. This handbook can also serve as a concise, but nonetheless comprehensive, supplement to college-level textbooks on computer graphics or any of the popular-application programming guides.

Whether you are a novice in computer graphics or an expert or whether you are a student, professional, or hobbyist, you will find *Computer Graphics Handbook* to be a useful reference for a broad range of applicable geometric and mathematical topics. The topics are presented in a simple, straightforward way, and the nomenclature and symbol format are consistent with the most popular textbooks and technical literature in the field.

If your educational experience includes the standard four years of high school mathematics (algebra, geometry, and trigonometry), then you will have little trouble understanding the concepts presented here. Although some subjects depend in part on elementary calculus, most of them can be understood as they stand, without recourse to a calculus textbook.

Computer Graphics Handbook is divided into 14 chapters, each presenting a major topic on geometry or mathematics in computer graphics:

1. Vectors	8. Surfaces
2. Matrices	9. Solids
3. Numerical Methods	10. Transformations
4. Boolean Operators	11. Intersections
5. Elementary Geometry	12. Local Properties
6. Polygons and Polyhedra	13. Global Properties
7. Curves	14. Display Geometry

Vectors and Matrices: The general properties are summarized. Vector equations for the line and plane are also explained, setting the stage for the application of these concepts to subjects in later chapters. *Numerical Methods*: Horner's Rule, the forward difference method, Newton's method for computing roots, and quadrature are presented. *Boolean Operators*: The union, difference, and intersect operators are defined, including many examples of their application to shape definition and point classification. *Elementary Geometry*: The standard analytic definitions of lines, planes, and conics are given, with commentary. *Polygons and Polyhedra*: Here you will find the definition and properties of the regular and semiregular polyhedra, including a discussion of rotational symmetry groups, Euler's formulas for simple and nonsimple polyhedra, the convex hull, half-spaces, and other related topics. *Curves, Surfaces, and Solids*: Vector parametric formulation is the underlying concept, including Hermité, Bézier, and *B*-spline definitions in both rational and integer forms. *Transformations*: All principal modes of transformation are presented, as well as projections and nonlinear deformations. *Intersections*: A variety of geometric intersections is described, along with their computation. *Local Properties and Global Properties*: Computation techniques yielding tangents, curvatures, and normals, as well as length, area, and volume are defined. Computing distance between various combinations of geometric objects is also discussed. *Display Geometry*: Much of the earlier material is focused and recast into the more specialized formulations for generating computer graphic displays, including projections, clipping, filling, scene transformations, and visibility.

Gaining access to the most current literature in a field like computer graphics is a necessity for compiling a book such as this. Thanks to Beverly Lamb, Director, and the staff of the Port Townsend library for their help in obtaining the articles and texts underlying much of this book. Thanks also to Woodrow Chapman, Editorial Director, James Geronimo, Senior Editor, and others at Industrial Press for their skills and support that made this project work. Finally, thanks to my wife Janet, for her support, encouragement, and editorial talents. If I have learned the value of directness and clarity, I learned it from her.

Symbols and Conventions

		Greek Alphabet
Scalars	$a, b, c, \ldots$ (Lower case letters)	
Vectors	$\mathbf{a}, \mathbf{b}, \mathbf{p}, \mathbf{q}, \ldots$ (Bold face lower case letters)	A α Alpha
Unit vectors	$\hat{\mathbf{a}}, \hat{\mathbf{p}}, \hat{\mathbf{r}}, \ldots$	B β Beta
Vector magnitude	$\lvert \mathbf{a} \rvert, \lvert \mathbf{p} \rvert, \ldots$	Γ γ Gamma
Matrices	$\mathbf{A}, \mathbf{B}, \mathbf{M}, \mathbf{T}, \ldots$ (Bold face upper case letters)	Δ δ Delta
Matrix inverse	$\mathbf{A}^{-1}, \mathbf{B}^{-1}, \mathbf{M}^{-1}, \ldots$	E ε Epsilon
Matrix transpose	$\mathbf{A}^{T}, \mathbf{B}^{T}, \mathbf{M}^{T}, \ldots$	Z ζ Zeta
Inverse of matrix transpose	$\mathbf{A}^{T-1}, \mathbf{B}^{T-1}, \mathbf{M}^{T-1}, \ldots$	H η Eta
Transpose of inverted matrix	$\mathbf{A}^{-T}, \mathbf{B}^{-T}, \mathbf{M}^{-T}, \ldots$	Θ θ Theta
Transformed vector or matrix	$\mathbf{p}^{*}, \mathbf{r}^{*}, \mathbf{M}^{*}, \ldots$	I i Iota
Determinants	$\lvert A \rvert, \lvert \mathbf{A} \rvert, \ldots$ or $\det A$	K κ Kappa
Parametric variables	$s, t, u, v, w, \ldots$	Λ λ Lambda
Cartesian coordinates	$x, y, z, x^1, x^2, \ldots x^i_j \ldots$	M μ Mu
Union	$A \cup B$	N ν Nu
Intersect	$A \cap B$	Ξ ξ Xi
Difference	$A - B$	O o Omicron
a is an element of b	$a \in b$	Π π Pi
For all	$\forall$	P ρ Rho
Closed interval	$[a, b]$ (continuous values)	Σ σ Sigma
Closed interval	$[a : b]$ (integral or discrete values)	T τ Tau
Open interval	(a, b) (continuous values)	Υ υ Upsilon
Differentiation	$y^x = dy/dx$	Φ ϕ Phi
	$y^{xx} = d^2 y/dx^2$	X χ Chi
	$x^u = dx/du$	Ψ ψ Psi
	$x^{uw} = \partial^2 x/\partial u \partial w$	Ω ω Omega

Summation notation

$$\sum_{i=1}^{n} a_i = a_1 + a_2 + a_3 + \cdots + a_n$$

$$\sum_{i=1}^{m} \sum_{j=1}^{n} a_i b_j = a_1 b_1 + a_1 b_2 + \cdots + a_1 b_n + a_2 b_1 + \cdots + a_m b_n$$

"... real mathematics, that which is good for something ..."

Henri Poincaré

Contents

6. Polygons and Polyhedra

7. Curves

11. Intersections

12. Local Properties

13. Global Properties

14. Display Geometry

Vector Definition

Definition: **A vector** is a geometric object represented by an ordered set of numbers to which are assigned certain properties: **direction** and **magnitude**.

It is usually visualized as a directed line segment, or arrow.

Standard Form:

$$\mathbf{p} = p_x \mathbf{i} + p_y \mathbf{j} + p_z \mathbf{k} \qquad (1.1)$$

i, j, k are unit **basis vectors**, usually, but not necessarily, mutually orthogonal.

p_x, p_y, p_z are vector components, representing displacements in the x, y, and z directions.

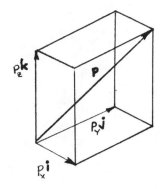 

A **free vector** is not necessarily associated with any point in space.

A **position** or **radius vector** has its initial point fixed at the origin, so that its components are the coordinates of a point.

Alternative Forms:

$$\mathbf{p} = [p_x \ p_y \ p_z] \quad \text{or} \quad [x \ y \ z] \quad \text{or} \quad \begin{bmatrix} x \\ y \\ z \end{bmatrix}$$

Matrix form: to simplify, **i, j, k** are omitted.

$$\mathbf{p} = (x, y, z)$$

Coordinate form.

$$\mathbf{x} = \sum_{i=1}^{3} x^i \mathbf{e}_i = x^i \mathbf{e}_i$$

$$= x^1 \mathbf{e}_1 + x^2 \mathbf{e}_2 + x^3 \mathbf{e}_3$$

Tensor form: the superscript on x identifies the component (x, y, z), where $\mathbf{e}_i$ is the corresponding unit basis vector. The repetition of the index i indicates summation. This is the Einstein convention used in tensor analysis.

W.R. Hamilton (1805–1865) and H. Grassman (1809–1877) developed the foundations of vector analysis in the mid-nineteenth century. J.W. Gibbs (1839–1903) made important contributions to the present form of vector analysis.

Vector Magnitude

The magnitude of a vector $\mathbf{p} = [p_x \ p_y \ p_z]$ is the real number $|\mathbf{p}|$, where

$$|\mathbf{p}| = \sqrt{p_x^2 + p_y^2 + p_z^2} \tag{1.2}$$

$|\mathbf{p}| \geq 0.$

To change the magnitude of a vector, multiply by a scalar, k:

$$k\mathbf{p} = [kp_x \ kp_y \ kp_z]$$

$$|k\mathbf{p}| = k\sqrt{p_x^2 + p_y^2 + p_z^2} = k|\mathbf{p}|$$

$|\mathbf{p}| = 0$, if and only if $\mathbf{p} = 0$; i.e., $\mathbf{p} = [0 \ 0 \ 0]$, the null vector.

If $k < 0$, the direction of $\mathbf{p}$ is reversed.

The magnitude of a vector is invariant under rigid-body transformations; that is, magnitude is independent of direction.

Two vectors are equal if they have the same direction and magnitude.

Example:

Let $\mathbf{p} = [6 \ -2 \ 1]$ and $\mathbf{q} = [-1 \ -6 \ 2]$; then

$$|\mathbf{p}| = 6.403$$
$$|\mathbf{q}| = 6.403$$

But $\mathbf{p} \neq \mathbf{q}$, since they are not in the same direction.

"Mathematics is the queen of the sciences."

Carl Friedrich Gauss

Vector Direction

The direction of a vector is given by its **direction cosines**:

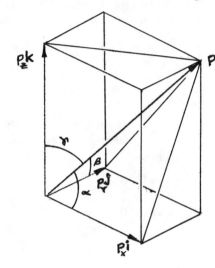

$$\cos \alpha = \frac{p_x}{|\mathbf{p}|}$$

$$\cos \beta = \frac{p_y}{|\mathbf{p}|} \qquad (1.3)$$

$$\cos \gamma = \frac{p_z}{|\mathbf{p}|}$$

cos α, cos β, cos γ.

Two vectors are parallel if they differ only by a scalar multiplier, k (i.e., if $\mathbf{p} = k\mathbf{q}$).

If $k > 0$, then $\mathbf{p}$ and $\mathbf{q}$ are in the same direction. If $k < 0$, then they are in the opposite directions.

Since $|\mathbf{p}| = \sqrt{p_x^2 + p_y^2 + p_z^2}$, then

$$\left(\frac{p_x}{|\mathbf{p}|}\right)^2 + \left(\frac{p_y}{|\mathbf{p}|}\right)^2 + \left(\frac{p_z}{|\mathbf{p}|}\right)^2 = 1$$

so that

$$\cos^2 \alpha + \cos^2 \beta + \cos^2 \gamma = 1 \qquad (1.4)$$

Two direction cosines are sufficient to determine the direction of a vector.

Example:

Let $\mathbf{p} = [6 \ \ 2 \ \ 4]$ and $\mathbf{q} = [9 \ \ 3 \ \ 6]$, then for $\mathbf{p}$: $\cos \alpha = 0.802$, $\cos \beta = 0.267$, $\cos \gamma = 0.535$; and for $\mathbf{q}$: $\cos \alpha = 0.802$, $\cos \beta = 0.267$, $\cos \gamma = 0.535$. Therefore, $\mathbf{p}$ and $\mathbf{q}$ have the same direction; furthermore, $\mathbf{q} = 1.5\mathbf{p}$.

"For us, whose shoulders sag under the weight of the heritage of Greek thought and who walk in the paths traced out by the heroes of the Renaissance, a civilization without mathematics is unthinkable."

André Weil

Unit Vector

The **unit vector, u,** in the direction of **p** is a vector having a magnitude equal to one; $|\mathbf{u}| = 1$. It is given by

$$\mathbf{u} = \frac{\mathbf{p}}{|\mathbf{p}|} \qquad (1.5)$$

Thus

$$u_x = \frac{p_x}{|\mathbf{p}|}$$

$$u_y = \frac{p_y}{|\mathbf{p}|}$$

$$u_z = \frac{p_z}{|\mathbf{p}|}$$

So that

$$|\mathbf{u}| = \sqrt{u_x^2 + u_y^2 + u_z^2} = 1$$

From Eq. (1.3)

$$u_x = \cos \alpha$$
$$u_y = \cos \beta$$
$$u_z = \cos \gamma$$

The following notation convention is useful: If **p** is any vector, then $\hat{\mathbf{p}}$ denotes its unit vector.

i, j, k are unit vectors in the x, y, z directions, respectively. Thus

$$\mathbf{i} = [1 \ \ 0 \ \ 0]$$
$$\mathbf{j} = [0 \ \ 1 \ \ 0]$$
$$\mathbf{k} = [0 \ \ 0 \ \ 1]$$

$$u_x^2 + u_y^2 + u_z^2 = 1.$$

The components of a unit vector are also its direction cosines.

A set of vectors $\mathbf{e}_i$ is a **basis** if every vector can be expressed as a linear combination of them and if the $\mathbf{e}_i$ are linearly independent. In three-dimensional Cartesian coordinate space any three linearly independent vectors form a basis.

i, j, k form such a basis; since $\mathbf{i} = [1 \ \ 0 \ \ 0]$, $\mathbf{j} = [0 \ \ 1 \ \ 0]$, and $\mathbf{k} = [0 \ \ 0 \ \ 1]$, they are linearly independent.

The components of a vector depend on the basis chosen, and, in general, the components change if the basis changes (i.e., in location or orientation).

Vector Addition

Given two vectors $\mathbf{p} = [p_x \; p_y \; p_z]$ and $\mathbf{q} = [q_x \; q_y \; q_z]$, their sum is the vector

$$\mathbf{p} + \mathbf{q} = [(p_x + q_x) \; (p_y + q_y) \; (p_z + q_z)] \qquad (1.6)$$

The difference of two vectors $\mathbf{p}$ and $\mathbf{q}$ is

$$\mathbf{p} - \mathbf{q} = [(p_x - q_x) \; (p_y - q_y) \; (p_z - q_z)] \qquad (1.7)$$

Order is not important. If $\mathbf{d} = \mathbf{a} + \mathbf{b} + \mathbf{c}$, then it is also true that $\mathbf{d} = \mathbf{a} + \mathbf{c} + \mathbf{b}$. Vector addition is *commutative*.

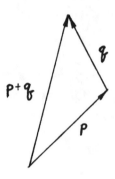

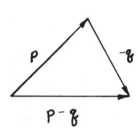

Graphic Interpretation: To add two or more vectors (drawn as arrows), join the tail of each succeeding vector to the head of the preceding one. The resultant vector is represented by an arrow from the tail of the first vector to the head of the last.

Example:

Let $\mathbf{p} = [5 \;\; -3 \;\; -2]$ and $\mathbf{q} = [1 \;\; 7 \;\; 4]$, then

$$\mathbf{p} + \mathbf{q} = [6 \; 4 \; 2]$$

Scalar Product

The **scalar product** of two vectors **p** and **q** is the sum of the products of their corresponding components:

$$\mathbf{p} \cdot \mathbf{q} = p_x q_x + p_y q_y + p_z q_z \tag{1.8}$$

If $\mathbf{p} = \mathbf{q}$, then $\mathbf{p} \cdot \mathbf{p} = |\mathbf{p}|^2$.

Alternative form:

The scalar product is also called the "inner product," written in tensor notation as

$$\mathbf{p} \cdot \mathbf{q} = p^j q^k \delta_{jk}$$

where δ_{jk} is the Kronecker delta.

$$\mathbf{i} \cdot \mathbf{i} = \mathbf{j} \cdot \mathbf{j} = \mathbf{k} \cdot \mathbf{k} = 1$$
$$\mathbf{i} \cdot \mathbf{j} = \mathbf{j} \cdot \mathbf{k} = \mathbf{k} \cdot \mathbf{i} = 0$$
$$\mathbf{i} \cdot \mathbf{k} = \mathbf{j} \cdot \mathbf{i} = \mathbf{k} \cdot \mathbf{j} = 0$$

If $\mathbf{p} \cdot \mathbf{q} = 0$, they are perpendicular.

$$\delta_{jk} = \begin{cases} 1 \text{ if } j = k \\ 0 \text{ if } j \neq k \end{cases}$$

The angle θ between two vectors **p** and **q** satisfies the following equation:

$$\mathbf{p} \cdot \mathbf{q} = |\mathbf{p}||\mathbf{q}| \cos \theta$$

$$\theta = \cos^{-1} \frac{\mathbf{p} \cdot \mathbf{q}}{|\mathbf{p}||\mathbf{q}|}$$

The scalar product of two vectors is independent of the coordinate system in which they are expressed.

Example:

If $\mathbf{p} = [3 \quad 1 \quad 4]$ and $\mathbf{q} = [-2 \quad 0 \quad 6]$, then

$$\mathbf{p} \cdot \mathbf{q} = -6 + 0 + 24 = 18$$
$$\theta = \cos^{-1}(0.558)$$
$$\theta = 56°$$

Vector Product

The **vector product** of two vectors **p** and **q** is another vector, **r**.

$$\mathbf{p} \times \mathbf{q} = \mathbf{r} \qquad\qquad (1.9)$$

$$\mathbf{r} = [(p_y q_z - p_z q_y)\ (p_z q_x - p_x q_z)\ (p_x q_y - p_y q_x)]$$

Alternative form:

$$\mathbf{p} \times \mathbf{q} = \begin{vmatrix} \mathbf{i} & \mathbf{j} & \mathbf{k} \\ p_x & p_y & p_z \\ q_x & q_y & q_z \end{vmatrix}$$

$$|\mathbf{p} \times \mathbf{q}| = |\mathbf{p}|\,|\mathbf{q}|\sin\theta$$

Vector division is not defined.

$\mathbf{p} \times \mathbf{p} = 0$.

If $\mathbf{p} \times \mathbf{q} = 0$, they are parallel.

The vector product can be obtained as the expansion of the **determinant**.

θ is the angle between **p** and **q**.

The **right-hand rule** gives an intuitive sense of the vector **r** resulting from **p** × **q**. Think of rotating **p** into **q**, curling the fingers of your right hand in this angular direction. Then the extended thumb of your right hand will point in the direction of **r**.

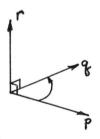

$$\mathbf{i} \times \mathbf{j} = \mathbf{k}$$
$$\mathbf{j} \times \mathbf{k} = \mathbf{i}$$
$$\mathbf{k} \times \mathbf{i} = \mathbf{j}$$

$$\mathbf{i} \times \mathbf{i} = \mathbf{j} \times \mathbf{j} = \mathbf{k} \times \mathbf{k} = 0$$

The area of the triangle ABC is

$$\text{Area} = \tfrac{1}{2}\,|\mathbf{a} \times \mathbf{b}|$$

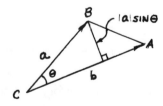

Triple Product

The **triple scalar product** $\mathbf{p} \cdot \mathbf{q} \times \mathbf{r}$ is given in terms of a determinant:

$$\mathbf{p} \cdot \mathbf{q} \times \mathbf{r} = \begin{vmatrix} p_x & q_x & r_x \\ p_y & q_y & r_y \\ p_z & q_z & r_z \end{vmatrix} \qquad (1.10)$$

$$\mathbf{p} \cdot \mathbf{q} \times \mathbf{r} = \mathbf{p} \times \mathbf{q} \cdot \mathbf{r}.$$

Alternative form:

$$\mathbf{p} \cdot \mathbf{q} \times \mathbf{r} = \mathscr{E}_{ijk} p^i q^j r^k$$

$$\mathscr{E}_{ijk} = \begin{Bmatrix} 1 \\ -1 \\ 0 \end{Bmatrix} \text{ if } i, j, k \text{ is}$$

$$\text{an} \begin{Bmatrix} \text{even} \\ \text{odd} \\ \text{other} \end{Bmatrix} \text{ permutation of 1, 2, 3}$$

The **triple vector product** yields

$$\mathbf{p} \times (\mathbf{q} \times \mathbf{r}) = (\mathbf{p} \cdot \mathbf{r})\mathbf{q} - (\mathbf{p} \cdot \mathbf{q})\mathbf{r}$$

$\mathbf{p} \times (\mathbf{q} \times \mathbf{r})$ is in the plane of $\mathbf{q}$ and $\mathbf{r}$.

"Not only Newton's laws, but also the other laws of physics, so far as we know today, have the two properties which we call invariance (or symmetry) under translation of axes and rotation of axes [coordinate systems]. These properties are so important that a mathematical technique has been developed to take advantage of them in writing and using physical laws . . . called vector analysis."

R.P. Feynman

Vector Properties

   Given vectors **p**, **q**, **r** and scalars k and l, then

1. $\mathbf{p} + \mathbf{q} = \mathbf{q} + \mathbf{p}$

2. $\mathbf{p} + (\mathbf{q} + \mathbf{r}) = (\mathbf{p} + \mathbf{q}) + \mathbf{r}$

3. $k(l\mathbf{p}) = kl\mathbf{p}$

4. $(k + l)\mathbf{p} = k\mathbf{p} + l\mathbf{p}$

5. $k(\mathbf{p} + \mathbf{q}) = k\mathbf{p} + k\mathbf{q}$

6. $\mathbf{p} \cdot \mathbf{r} = |\mathbf{p}||\mathbf{r}| \cos \theta$

7. $\mathbf{p} \cdot \mathbf{p} = |\mathbf{p}|^2$

8. $\mathbf{p} \cdot \mathbf{r} = \mathbf{r} \cdot \mathbf{p}$

9. $\mathbf{p} \cdot (\mathbf{r} + \mathbf{q}) = \mathbf{p} \cdot \mathbf{r} + \mathbf{p} \cdot \mathbf{q}$

10. $(k\mathbf{p}) \cdot \mathbf{r} = \mathbf{p} \cdot (k\mathbf{r}) = k(\mathbf{p} \cdot \mathbf{r})$

11. If $\mathbf{p} \cdot \mathbf{r} = 0$, they are perpendicular

12. $\mathbf{p} \times \mathbf{q} = \mathbf{r}$; **r** is perpendicular to both **p** and **q**

13. $\mathbf{p} \times \mathbf{r} = \begin{vmatrix} \mathbf{i} & \mathbf{j} & \mathbf{k} \\ p_x & p_y & p_z \\ q_x & q_y & q_z \end{vmatrix}$

14. $\mathbf{p} \times \mathbf{r} = -(\mathbf{r} \times \mathbf{p})$

15. $\mathbf{p} \times (\mathbf{q} + \mathbf{r}) = \mathbf{p} \times \mathbf{q} + \mathbf{p} \times \mathbf{r}$

16. $(k\mathbf{p}) \times \mathbf{r} = \mathbf{p}(k\mathbf{r}) = k(\mathbf{p} \times \mathbf{r})$

17. If $\mathbf{p} \times \mathbf{r} = 0$, they are parallel

18. $\mathbf{p} \times \mathbf{p} = 0$

Fixed vectors (or radius or position vectors) are equal if and only if their respective end points coincide. Free vectors are equal if they can be made to coincide by a translation.

Solution of Vector Equations

The vector equation

$$\mathbf{a} + u\mathbf{b} + w\mathbf{c} = \mathbf{d} + t\mathbf{e}$$

represents a system of three linear equations in three unknowns: u, w, and t. In nonvector form these equations are

$$a_x + ub_x + wc_x = d_x + te_x$$
$$a_y + ub_y + wc_y = d_y + te_y$$
$$a_z + ub_z + wc_z = d_z + te_z$$

Use the vector form to solve for u, w, and t by isolating each in turn. To isolate t apply $(\mathbf{b} \times \mathbf{c})$ as follows:

$$(\mathbf{b} \times \mathbf{c}) \cdot (\mathbf{a} + u\mathbf{b} + w\mathbf{c}) = (\mathbf{b} \times \mathbf{c}) \cdot (\mathbf{d} + t\mathbf{e})$$

Since $(\mathbf{b} \times \mathbf{c})$ is perpendicular to both $\mathbf{b}$ and $\mathbf{c}$, then

$$(\mathbf{b} \times \mathbf{c}) \cdot \mathbf{a} = (\mathbf{b} \times \mathbf{c}) \cdot \mathbf{d} + (t\mathbf{b} \times \mathbf{c}) \cdot \mathbf{e}$$

Solve for t:

$$t = \frac{(\mathbf{b} \times \mathbf{c}) \cdot \mathbf{a} - (\mathbf{b} \times \mathbf{c}) \cdot \mathbf{d}}{(\mathbf{b} \times \mathbf{c}) \cdot \mathbf{e}}$$

Similar calculations yield expressions for u and w:

$$u = \frac{(\mathbf{c} \times \mathbf{e}) \cdot \mathbf{d} - (\mathbf{c} \times \mathbf{e}) \cdot \mathbf{a}}{(\mathbf{c} \times \mathbf{e}) \cdot \mathbf{b}}$$

$$w = \frac{(\mathbf{b} \times \mathbf{e}) \cdot \mathbf{d} - (\mathbf{b} \times \mathbf{e}) \cdot \mathbf{a}}{(\mathbf{b} \times \mathbf{e}) \cdot \mathbf{c}}$$

Vector Projection

The scalar projection s of $\mathbf{p}$ onto $\mathbf{q}$ is

$$s = \mathbf{p} \cdot \left(\frac{\mathbf{q}}{|\mathbf{q}|} \right) \qquad (1.11)$$

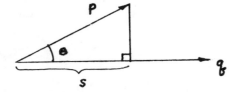

$s = |\mathbf{p}| \cos \theta.$

The vector projection $\mathbf{v}$ of $\mathbf{p}$ onto $\mathbf{q}$ is

$$\mathbf{v} = s \left(\frac{\mathbf{q}}{|\mathbf{q}|} \right)$$

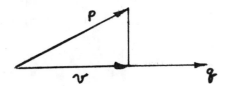

If $\mathbf{p}$ is perpendicular to $\mathbf{a}$ and $\mathbf{b}$, then

$$\mathbf{p} \cdot \mathbf{a} = 0 \quad \text{and} \quad \mathbf{p} \cdot \mathbf{b} = 0$$

so that $p_x a_x + p_y a_y + p_z a_z = 0$ and $p_x b_x + p_y b_y + p_z b_z = 0$. From these equations derive the ratios

$$\frac{p_x}{a_y b_z - a_z b_y} = \frac{p_y}{a_z b_x - a_x b_z} = \frac{p_z}{a_x b_y - a_y b_x}$$

The vector $[(a_y b_z - a_z b_y)\,(a_z b_x - a_x b_z)\,(a_x b_y - a_y b_x)]$ is proportional to $\mathbf{p}$ and therefore is perpendicular to $\mathbf{a}$ and $\mathbf{b}$. QED.

Find a vector perpendicular to two given vectors.

Vector Equation of a Line

The vector equation of a line through point p_0 and parallel to vector **t** is

$$\mathbf{p} = \mathbf{p}_0 + u\mathbf{t} \qquad (1.12)$$

$$x = x_0 + ut_x$$
$$y = y_0 + ut_y$$
$$z = z_0 + ut_z$$

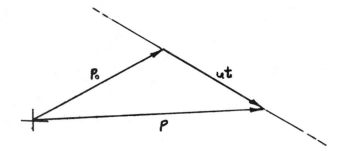

If $\mathbf{q} = \dot{\mathbf{q}}_0 + w\mathbf{s}$ and $\mathbf{s} = k\mathbf{t}$, then the lines through $\mathbf{p}_0$ and $\mathbf{q}_0$ are parallel.

Alternative form:

$$\mathbf{p} = \mathbf{p}_0 + u(\mathbf{p}_1 - \mathbf{p}_0) \qquad (1.13)$$

If $u \in [0,1]$, then (1.13) defines a line segment from $\mathbf{p}_0$ to $\mathbf{p}_1$.

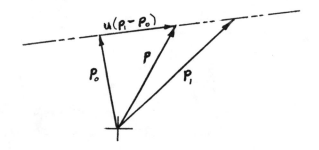

Vector Equation of a Plane

The vector equation of a plane through $\mathbf{p}_0$ and parallel to two independent vectors $\mathbf{s}$ and $\mathbf{t}$ is

$$\mathbf{p} = \mathbf{p}_0 + u\mathbf{s} + v\mathbf{t} \tag{1.14}$$

$\mathbf{s} \neq k\mathbf{t}$, where $\mathbf{s}, \mathbf{t}$ are unit vectors.

$$x = x_0 + us_x + vt_x$$
$$y = y_0 + us_y + vt_y$$
$$z = z_0 + us_z + vt_z$$

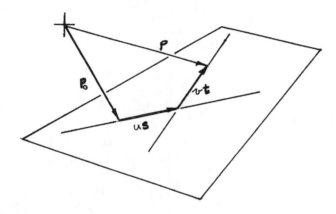

$\mathbf{n} = \mathbf{s} \times \mathbf{t}$
where $\mathbf{n}$ is the unit normal to the plane.

Alternative form:

$$\mathbf{p} = \mathbf{p}_0 + u(\mathbf{p}_1 - \mathbf{p}_0) + v(\mathbf{p}_2 - \mathbf{p}_1) \tag{1.15}$$

Three noncollinear points are sufficient to uniquely define a plane.

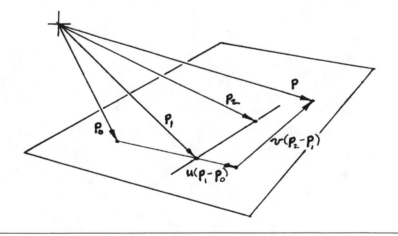

$\mathbf{n} = (\mathbf{p}_1 - \mathbf{p}_0) \times (\mathbf{p}_2 - \mathbf{p}_1)$

"There is no royal road to geometry," said to Ptolemy I, who asked Euclid if there was any shorter way to a knowledge of geometry other than by a study of his **Elements**.

Vector Equation of a Plane: Normal Form

Define a plane by giving the vector **d** from the origin and perpendicular to the plane. Then any point **p** on the plane must satisfy

$$(\mathbf{p} - \mathbf{d}) \cdot \mathbf{d} = 0 \tag{1.16}$$

Expand (1.16) to obtain

$$(x - d_x)d_x + (y - d_y)d_y + (z - d_z)d_z = 0$$

or

$$d_x x + d_y y + d_z z - (d_x^2 + d_y^2 + d_z^2) = 0$$

which reduces to

$$x \cos \alpha + y \cos \beta + z \cos \gamma - d = 0 \tag{1.17}$$

$d^2 = (d_x^2 + d_y^2 + d_z^2)$
$\cos \alpha = d_x/d$, etc.

$\cos \alpha$, $\cos \beta$, $\cos \gamma$ are the direction cosines of **d**.

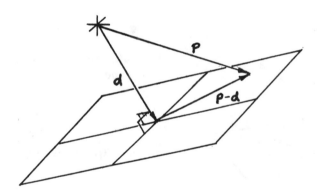

15

2. Matrices

Matrix Definition

A **matrix** is a rectangular array of numbers or other mathematical elements arranged in m rows and n columns. For example:

$$A = \begin{bmatrix} a_{11} & a_{12} & a_{13} & a_{14} \\ a_{21} & a_{22} & a_{23} & a_{24} \\ a_{31} & a_{32} & a_{33} & a_{34} \end{bmatrix} = a_{ij}$$

The **order** of a matrix is determined by the number of rows (m) and columns (n). A matrix of m rows and n columns is of order $m \times n$. Then $i \in [1:m]$ and $j \in [1:n]$.

Two matrices **A** and **B** are equal if corresponding elements are equal.

$$A = B \text{ if } a_{ij} = b_{ij} \text{ for all } i,j$$

A square matrix: $\begin{bmatrix} 3 & -4 & 5 \\ 7 & 3 & 2 \\ 1 & 8 & -6 \end{bmatrix}$

A row matrix: $[2 \quad 8 \quad 5 \quad -9]$

A column matrix: $\begin{bmatrix} x \\ y \\ z \end{bmatrix}$

A matrix is a complex number, with a unique "algebra" to govern operations between and upon matrices.

i,j identify element row and column.

The order of the largest square submatrix whose determinant has a nonzero value is called the **rank** of the matrix.

$m = n$

$m = 1$

$n = 1$

Row and column matrices are sometimes called vectors.

The English mathematician Arthur Cayley (1821–1895) developed and refined the algebra of matrices.

Special Matrices

A **diagonal matrix** is a square matrix that has zero elements everywhere except on the main diagonal.

$$A = \begin{bmatrix} a_{11} & 0 & 0 & 0 \\ 0 & a_{22} & 0 & 0 \\ 0 & 0 & a_{33} & 0 \\ 0 & 0 & 0 & a_{44} \end{bmatrix}$$

$a_{ij} = 0$ if $i \neq j$

If all the a_{ii}'s are equal, then the diagonal matrix is called a **scalar matrix**.

A null matrix is one whose elements are all zero.

Denoted by $\varnothing$.

A diagonal matrix that has unit elements on the main diagonal is called a **unit matrix** or **identity matrix**.

$$I = \begin{bmatrix} 1 & 0 & 0 \\ 0 & 1 & 0 \\ 0 & 0 & 1 \end{bmatrix} = \delta_{ij}$$

δ_{ij} is the **Kronecker delta**

A square matrix whose elements are symmetrical about the main diagonal is a **symmetric matrix**.

$$B = \begin{bmatrix} 5 & 3 & 7 \\ 3 & 1 & 4 \\ 7 & 4 & -2 \end{bmatrix}$$

$b_{ij} = b_{ji}$

A square matrix is **antisymmetric** or **skew symmetric** if $a_{ij} = -a_{ji}$

$$A = \begin{bmatrix} 0 & -9 & -3 \\ 9 & 0 & 1 \\ 3 & -1 & 0 \end{bmatrix}$$

Note: $a_{ij} = -a_{ij}$ implies that $a_{ii} = 0$.

Matrix Transpose

Obtain the **transpose** of a matrix $\mathbf{A}$, denoted by $\mathbf{A}^T$, by interchanging the rows and columns of $\mathbf{A}$.

$$\text{If}\quad \mathbf{A} = \begin{bmatrix} 3 & 1 & 2 \\ 0 & -1 & -2 \\ -3 & 0 & 4 \end{bmatrix}$$

$$\text{Then}\quad \mathbf{A}^T = \begin{bmatrix} 3 & 0 & -3 \\ 1 & -1 & 0 \\ 2 & -2 & 4 \end{bmatrix}$$

All matrices have a transpose, not just square ones. Thus,

$$\text{if}\quad \mathbf{B} = \begin{bmatrix} x & y & z \end{bmatrix}$$

$$\text{then}\quad \mathbf{B}^T = \begin{bmatrix} x \\ y \\ z \end{bmatrix}$$

The product of any matrix and its transpose is a symmetric matrix, that is, $(\mathbf{A}\mathbf{A}^T)^T = \mathbf{A}\mathbf{A}^T$

$$a_{ij}^T = a_{ji}$$

$$\mathbf{I}^T = \mathbf{I}$$

"I have resolved to quit only abstract geometry, that is to say, the consideration of questions that serve only to exercise the mind, and this, in order to study another kind of geometry, which has for its object the explanation of the phenomena of nature."

René Descartes

Matrix Addition

Adding two matrices **A** and **B** produces a third matrix, **C**, whose elements are equal to the sum of the corresponding elements of **A** and **B**.

A + **B** = **C**

A and B must be of the same order.

or $a_{ij} + b_{ij} = c_{ij}$

The resulting matrix is of the same order as the original matrices.

The difference of two matrices **A** and **B** is another matrix **D** whose elements are equal to the difference of corresponding elements of **A** and **B**.

A − **B** = **D**

or $a_{ij} - b_{ij} = d_{ij}$

Example:

$$A = \begin{bmatrix} 3 & 1 & -6 \\ 5 & 0 & 2 \end{bmatrix} \quad B = \begin{bmatrix} -2 & 1 & 3 \\ 2 & 0 & 0 \end{bmatrix}$$

$$A + B = \begin{bmatrix} 1 & 2 & -3 \\ 7 & 0 & 2 \end{bmatrix}$$

Scalar Multiplication

Multiply a matrix **A** by some scalar constant k to produce a new matrix **B** of the same order as **A**.

$$k\mathbf{A} = \mathbf{B}$$

or $\quad ka_{ij} = b_{ij}$

Example:

$$k = 3, \quad \mathbf{A} = \begin{bmatrix} 2 & -3 \\ 0 & 1 \end{bmatrix}$$

$$k\mathbf{A} = \begin{bmatrix} 6 & -9 \\ 0 & 3 \end{bmatrix}$$

Matrix Multiplication

Multiply two matrices **A** and **B** to produce a third matrix **C**, if and only if the number of columns of **A** is equal to the number of rows of **B**.

$$\mathbf{AB} = \mathbf{C}$$

The product of two matrices defined in terms of their elements is

$$c_{ij} = \sum_{k=1}^{n} a_{ik}b_{kj}$$

$$
\begin{bmatrix} b_{11} & b_{12} \\ b_{21} & b_{22} \\ b_{31} & b_{32} \end{bmatrix}
$$

$$
\begin{bmatrix} a_{11} & a_{12} & a_{13} \\ a_{21} & a_{22} & a_{23} \\ a_{31} & a_{32} & a_{33} \end{bmatrix}
\begin{bmatrix} c_{11} & c_{12} \\ c_{21} & c_{22} \\ c_{31} & c_{32} \end{bmatrix}
$$

A and B must be **conformable**:
If   **A**: $m \times n$
         B: $n \times p$
then   **C**: $m \times p$

A is **premultiplier**
B is **postmultiplier**

In general, $\mathbf{AB} \neq \mathbf{BA}$.

Given matrices **P** and **M**, then $\mathbf{P^*} = \mathbf{MP}$, **M** premultiplies **P**, $\mathbf{P'} = \mathbf{PM}$, **M** postmultiplies **P**, and $\mathbf{P^*} \neq \mathbf{P'}$ in general.

$\mathbf{AI} = \mathbf{A}$
$\mathbf{IA} = \mathbf{A}$

Example:

$$
\mathbf{A} = \begin{bmatrix} 2 & -1 \\ 1 & 4 \\ -3 & 0 \end{bmatrix} \qquad
\mathbf{B} = \begin{bmatrix} 2 & 3 \\ -5 & 1 \end{bmatrix}
$$

$$
\mathbf{C} = \begin{bmatrix} 9 & 3 \\ -18 & 7 \\ -6 & -9 \end{bmatrix}
$$

It is possible to construct matrices **A** and **B** such that $\mathbf{A} \neq 0$, $\mathbf{B} \neq 0$, but $\mathbf{AB} = 0$. A zero or null matrix is one for which all elements are zero.

Partitioned Matrices

It is often useful to subdivide a large matrix into a set of smaller matrices, like this:

$$M = \left[\begin{array}{c|c} M_{11} & M_{12} \\ \hline M_{21} & M_{22} \end{array}\right]$$

Let

$$A = \left[\begin{array}{c|c|c} A_{11} & A_{12} & A_{13} \\ \hline A_{21} & A_{22} & A_{23} \end{array}\right], \quad B = \left[\begin{array}{c|c|c} B_{11} & B_{12} & B_{13} \\ \hline B_{21} & B_{22} & B_{23} \end{array}\right]$$

Then

$$C = \left[\begin{array}{c|c|c} A_{11}+B_{11} & A_{12}+B_{12} & A_{13}+B_{13} \\ \hline A_{21}+B_{21} & A_{22}+B_{22} & A_{23}+B_{23} \end{array}\right]$$

where A_{ij} and B_{ij} are conformable.

Same number of rows:
M_{11} and M_{12},
M_{21} and M_{22}
Same number of columns:
M_{11} and M_{21},
M_{12} and M_{22}

Here is an example of the multiplication of partitioned matrices:

$$A = \left[\begin{array}{cc|cc|c} a_{11} & a_{12} & a_{13} & a_{14} & a_{15} \\ a_{21} & a_{22} & a_{23} & a_{24} & a_{25} \\ \hline a_{31} & a_{32} & a_{33} & a_{34} & a_{35} \\ a_{41} & a_{42} & a_{43} & a_{44} & a_{45} \end{array}\right] = \left[\begin{array}{ccc} A_{11} & A_{12} & A_{13} \\ A_{21} & A_{22} & A_{23} \end{array}\right]$$

$$B = \left[\begin{array}{cc|c} b_{11} & b_{12} & b_{13} \\ b_{21} & b_{22} & b_{23} \\ \hline b_{31} & b_{32} & b_{33} \\ \hline b_{41} & b_{42} & b_{43} \\ b_{51} & b_{52} & b_{53} \end{array}\right] = \left[\begin{array}{cc} B_{11} & B_{12} \\ B_{21} & B_{22} \\ B_{31} & B_{32} \end{array}\right]$$

$$AB = \left[\begin{array}{cc} A_{11}B_{11}+A_{12}B_{21}+A_{13}B_{31} & A_{11}B_{12}+A_{12}B_{22}+A_{13}B_{32} \\ A_{21}B_{11}+A_{22}B_{21}+A_{23}B_{31} & A_{21}B_{12}+A_{22}B_{22}+A_{23}B_{32} \end{array}\right]$$

Multiplication of partitioned matrices.

It is often computationally convenient to partition a matrix into submatrices and to treat it as a matrix whose elements are themselves these submatrices.

Note that the matrices must be conformable for multiplication before and after partitioning.

The computation is completed when the products $A_{11}B_{11}$, $A_{12}B_{21}$, . . ., etc., are determined and the indicated sums are performed.

Matrix Inversion

The inverse A^{-1} of a square matrix A is a matrix that satisfies the conditions

$$AA^{-1} = A^{-1}A = I$$

The elements of A^{-1} are

$$a_{ij}^{-1} = \frac{(-1)^{i+j}|A_{ij}^*|}{|A|}$$

where $|A_{ji}^*|$ denotes the determinant of the $(n-1) \times (n-1)$ matrix derived from A by deleting row j and column i from A.

Note subscript order on A_{ji}^*

If A^{-1} exists, then $|A| \neq 0$.

Example:

If
$$A = \begin{bmatrix} 2 & 1 & 0 \\ -1 & -1 & 2 \\ 2 & 1 & 3 \end{bmatrix}, \quad \text{then } |A| = -3$$

$\therefore A^{-1}$ exists

and
$$A^{-1} = -\tfrac{1}{3} \begin{bmatrix} -5 & -3 & 2 \\ 7 & 6 & -4 \\ 1 & 0 & -1 \end{bmatrix}$$

"The discipline of computational geometry arises from the desire to perform complex geometric calculations automatically on digital computers."

R.T. Farouki & J.K. Hinds

Scalar and Vector Products

Represent two vectors **p** and **q** as row matrices:

$$\mathbf{P} = [p_1 \ p_2 \ p_2] \quad \text{and} \quad \mathbf{Q} = [q_1 \ q_2 \ q_3]$$

Then the **scalar product** of **p** and **q** is

$$\mathbf{p} \cdot \mathbf{q} = \mathbf{PQ}^T \tag{2.1}$$

or

$$\mathbf{PQ}^T = [p_1 \ p_2 \ p_3] \begin{bmatrix} q_1 \\ q_2 \\ q_3 \end{bmatrix} = p_1 q_1 + p_2 q_2 + p_3 q_3$$

To represent the **vector product** of **p** and **q** as a matrix multiplication, use the components of **p** to form the anti-symmetric matrix

$$\begin{bmatrix} 0 & -p_3 & p_2 \\ p_3 & 0 & -p_1 \\ -p_2 & p_1 & 0 \end{bmatrix}$$

Then

$$\mathbf{p} \times \mathbf{q} = \begin{bmatrix} 0 & -p_3 & p_2 \\ p_3 & 0 & -p_1 \\ -p_2 & p_1 & 0 \end{bmatrix} \begin{bmatrix} q_1 \\ q_2 \\ q_3 \end{bmatrix}$$

Matrix Properties

1. $\mathbf{A} + \mathbf{B} = \mathbf{B} + \mathbf{A}$
2. $\mathbf{A} + (\mathbf{B} + \mathbf{C}) = (\mathbf{A} + \mathbf{B}) + \mathbf{C}$
3. $b(\mathbf{A} + \mathbf{B}) = b\mathbf{A} + b\mathbf{B}$
4. $(b + d)\mathbf{A} = b\mathbf{A} + d\mathbf{A}$
5. $b(d\mathbf{A}) = (bd)\mathbf{A} = d(b\mathbf{A})$
6. $(\mathbf{AB})\mathbf{C} = \mathbf{A}(\mathbf{BC})$
7. $\mathbf{A}(\mathbf{B} + \mathbf{C}) = \mathbf{AB} + \mathbf{AC}$
8. $(\mathbf{A} + \mathbf{B})\mathbf{C} = \mathbf{AC} + \mathbf{BC}$
9. $\mathbf{A}(k\mathbf{B}) = k\mathbf{AB} = (k\mathbf{A})\mathbf{B}$
10. $(\mathbf{A} + \mathbf{B})^T = \mathbf{A}^T + \mathbf{B}^T$
11. $(k\mathbf{A})^T = k\mathbf{A}^T$
12. $(\mathbf{AB})^T = \mathbf{B}^T\mathbf{A}^T$
13. If $\mathbf{AA}^{-1} = \mathbf{I}$ and $\mathbf{A}^{-1}\mathbf{A} = \mathbf{I}$, then $\mathbf{A}$ is nonsingular.
14. If $|\mathbf{A}| = 0$, then $\mathbf{A}$ is singular.
15. If $\mathbf{AA}^T = \mathbf{I}$, then $\mathbf{A}$ is orthogonal.

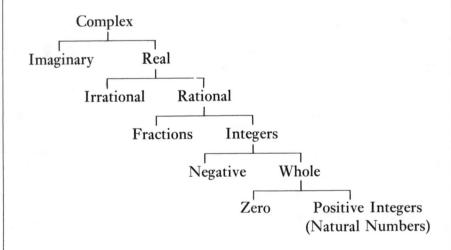

The Number System

Determinants

A **determinant** is a square array of elements that is reducible to a single value by following a well-defined procedure. Determinants facilitate many vector and matrix operations.

A matrix must be square to be associated with a determinant. Not every square matrix is associated with a determinant.

If
$$\mathbf{A} = \begin{bmatrix} a_{11} & a_{12} \\ a_{21} & a_{22} \end{bmatrix}$$

then
$$|\mathbf{A}| = \begin{vmatrix} a_{11} & a_{12} \\ a_{21} & a_{22} \end{vmatrix} = a_{11}a_{22} - a_{12}a_{21}$$

If
$$\mathbf{A} = \begin{bmatrix} a_{11} & a_{12} & a_{13} \\ a_{21} & a_{22} & a_{23} \\ a_{31} & a_{32} & a_{33} \end{bmatrix}$$

then
$$|\mathbf{A}| = a_{11}\begin{vmatrix} a_{22} & a_{23} \\ a_{32} & a_{33} \end{vmatrix} - a_{12}\begin{vmatrix} a_{21} & a_{23} \\ a_{31} & a_{33} \end{vmatrix} + a_{13}\begin{vmatrix} a_{21} & a_{22} \\ a_{31} & a_{32} \end{vmatrix}$$

The **cofactor** of element a_{ij} of determinant $|\mathbf{A}|$ is

$$c_{ij} = (-1)^{i+j}|\mathbf{A}_{ij}^*|$$

$$a_{ij}^{-1} = c_{ji}$$

where $|\mathbf{A}_{ij}^*|$ denotes the determinant of the $(n-1) \times (n-1)$ matrix derived from $\mathbf{A}$ by deleting row i and column j from $\mathbf{A}$. (See Matrix Inversion.)

Determinant Properties

1. The determinant of a square matrix is equal to the determinant of its transpose.

$$|\mathbf{A}| = |\mathbf{A}^T|$$

2. Interchanging any two rows (or columns) of $\mathbf{A}$ changes the sign of $|\mathbf{A}|$.

3. If you obtain $\mathbf{B}$ by multiplying one row (or column) of $\mathbf{A}$ by a constant, c, then

$$|\mathbf{B}| = c|\mathbf{A}|$$

4. If two rows (or columns) of $\mathbf{A}$ are identical, then

$$|\mathbf{A}| = 0$$

If every element of a row (or column) is zero, then the value of the determinant is zero.

5. If you derive $\mathbf{B}$ from $\mathbf{A}$ by adding a multiple of one row or column of $\mathbf{A}$ to another row or column of $\mathbf{A}$, then

$$|\mathbf{B}| = |\mathbf{A}|$$

6. If $\mathbf{A}$ and $\mathbf{B}$ are both $n \times n$ matrices, then the determinant of their product is

$$|\mathbf{AB}| = |\mathbf{A}||\mathbf{B}|$$

Augustin-Louis Cauchy (1789–1857) demonstrated that if A,B,C are the true lengths of three edges of a parallelipiped, and if the projections of A,B,C on the x,y,z coordinate axis are

A_1,B_1,C_1
A_2,B_2,C_2
A_3,B_3,C_3

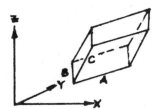

$$V = \begin{vmatrix} A_1 & B_1 & C_1 \\ A_2 & B_2 & C_2 \\ A_3 & B_3 & C_3 \end{vmatrix}$$

then the volume of the parallelipiped is $A_1(B_2C_3 - B_3C_2) + A_2(B_3C_1 - B_1C_3) + A_3(B_1C_2 - B_2C_1)$.

Horner's Rule

To evaluate a general polynomial of degree n,

$$p(u) = a_n u^n + a_{n-1} u^{n-1} + \cdots + a_1 u + a_0$$

use **Horner's rule**, an efficient way to compute $p(u)$.

For $n = 1$: $\quad p(u) = a_1 u + a_0$

For $n = 2$: $\quad p(u) = (a_2 u + a_1) u + a_0$

For $n = 3$: $\quad p(u) = [(a_3 u + a_2) u + a_1] u + a_0$

For $n = 4$: $\quad p(u) = \{[(a_4 u + a_3) u + a_2] u + a_1\} u + a_0$

and so on.

Combine Horner's rule with a straight-line program to obtain

$$
\begin{aligned}
\text{For } n = 1 \quad & t \leftarrow a_1 u \\
& p \leftarrow t + a_0 \\[1em]
\text{For } n = 2 \quad & t \leftarrow a_2 u \\
& t \leftarrow t + a_1 \\
& t \leftarrow tu \\
& p \leftarrow t + a_0 \\[1em]
\text{For } n = 3 \quad & t \leftarrow a_3 u \\
& t \leftarrow t + a_2 \\
& t \leftarrow tu \\
& t \leftarrow t + a_1 \\
& t \leftarrow tu \\
& p \leftarrow t + a_0
\end{aligned}
$$

"A mathematician knows how to solve a problem but he can't do it."

W.E. Milne

In more formal realms of mathematics a problem is solved when a formula is obtained or a theorem proved. Computing numerical results is often seen as being less glamorous.

Forward Difference Method

To evaluate a polynomial at equal intervals of the parametric variable use the **forward difference method**.

For the linear equation $p(u) = cu + d$, the difference between two successive values of $p(u)$ is constant: c/n for $n + 1$ equal increments of u (including $u = 0$).

For the cubic equation $p(u) = au^3 + bu^2 + cu + d$, initialize at $u = 0$ and begin with

$$p = d$$

$$d_1 = \frac{a}{n^3} + \frac{b}{n^2} + \frac{c}{n}$$

$$d_2 = \frac{6a}{n^3} + \frac{2b}{n^2}$$

$$d_3 = \frac{6a}{n^3}$$

To compute p at the next and each successive increment in u, three additions are required:

$$d_2 \leftarrow d_2 + d_3$$
$$d_1 \leftarrow d_1 + d_2$$
$$p \leftarrow p + d_1$$

"The aim of numerical analysis is to provide convenient methods for obtaining solutions to mathematical problems and for obtaining information from solutions not expressed in tractable form."

F.B. Hildebrand

Roots: Newton's Method

Given a function $f(u) = 0$, find its root(s). Here is an iterative technique (attributed to Newton) that works in certain controlled conditions. Isolate the root(s) u_r such that $u_j < u_r < u_k$, where there is only one root in this interval and the function (curve) is well-behaved (no discontinuities or inflections). Let $f'(u) = df(u)/du$. Then

$$u_{i+1} = u_i - \frac{f(u_i)}{f'(u_i)}$$

and $u_r = u_i$
when $u_{i+1} - u_i = 0$

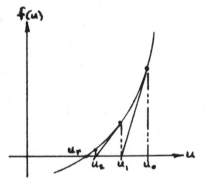

A better name might be "the sliding tangent method."

$|f'(u_i)| > 0$

If $f'(u_i)$ is zero or very small, then the shift or increment is very large, and convergence to a solution is doubtful.

For example:

$$f(u) = 30u^3 - 3u^2 + 9u - 15$$
$$f'(u) = 90u^2 - 6u + 9$$

$$u_{i+1} = u_i - \frac{30u^3 - 3u^2 + 9u - 15}{90u^3 - 6u + 9}$$

u_i	u_{i+1}
0.416 667	→ 0.850 596
0.850 596	→ 0.720 948
0.720 948	→ 0.698 190
0.698 190	→ 0.697 539
0.697 539	→ 0.697 539

$u_r = 0.697\,539.$

Algorithm: a set of procedures created to execute specific computations; derived from the name al-Khowarizmi. Mohamed ibn-Musa al-Khowarizmi was a ninth-century scholar who wrote many works on mathematics and astronomy.

Quadrature

Quadrature formulas are devised to evaluate integrals. The underlying assumption is that an integral represents the area under a curve defined by some function, say $f(u)$. Thus,

$$dA = \int_a^b f(u)\,du$$

Assume that $f(u)$ is given by an explicit formula that can be evaluated at any u in the range (a,b).

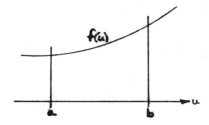

The Newton–Coates quadrature formulas assume equally spaced ordinates, including the bounding ones. The first four formulas are:

$$A_2 = \frac{w}{2}\left[f(u_a) + f(u_b)\right] \quad \text{(Trapezoidal rule)}$$

$$A_3 = \frac{w}{3}\left[f(u_a) + 4f(u_b) + f(u_c)\right] \quad \text{(Simpson rule)}$$

$$A_4 = \frac{3w}{8}\left[f(u_a) + 3f(u_b) + 3f(u_c) + f(u_d)\right]$$

$$A_5 = \frac{4w}{90}\left[7f(u_a) + 32f(u_b) + 12f(u_c) + 32f(u_d) + 7f(u_e)\right]$$

$$\vdots$$

(There is a continuing sequence of higher-order formulas.)

Another approach, Gaussian quadrature, abandons equal spacing and allows the function to be sampled (evaluated) at more optimal locations. And, of course, there are many other quadrature formulas. Each should be evaluated and selected for any particular problem based on its applicability.

A_i is the total area.

w is the width of a single quadrature division.

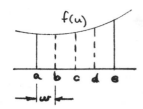

A_5 = total area between a,e.

Union

The **Union** operator $\cup$ unites or adds two shapes to form a third shape. If A and B are two shapes, then

$$A \cup B = C$$

where the shape C consists of all the points in A and B.

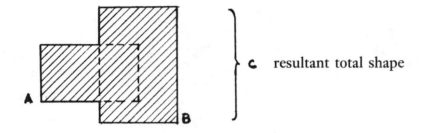

C resultant total shape

The order of a sequence of union operations is not important. Thus,

$$A = B \cup C \cup D = C \cup B \cup D$$

There are two kinds of points in any shape A: those that are inside it and those that are on its boundary. Let iA denote the set of points interior to A and bA the set of points on its boundary. Then the totality of points defining A consists of the union of the boundary points and the interior points:

$$A = bA \cup iA$$

All points exterior to A define the **complement** of A: written cA.

George Boole (1815–1864) published his classic work *Investigation into the Laws of Thought* in 1854 and established formal logic and a new algebra, known as Boolean algebra.

Difference

The **difference** operator subtracts one shape from another to form a third shape:

$$A - B = C$$

where the shape C (heavy outline) consists of all the points in A that are not in B.

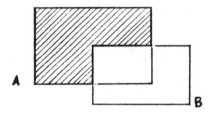

The order of the operands is **important**:

$$A - B \neq B - A$$

"But even while this creative activity of pure thought is going on, the external world once again reasserts its validity, and by thrusting new questions upon us through the phenomena that occur, it opens up new domains of mathematical knowledge; and as we strive to bring these new domains under the dominion of pure thought we often find answers to outstanding unsolved problems, and thus at the same time we advance in the most effective way the earlier theories. On this ever-repeated interplay of thought and experience depend, it seems to me, the numerous and astonishing analogies and the apparently pre-established harmony that the mathematician so often perceives in the problems, methods, and concepts of diverse realms of knowledge."

David Hilbert

Intersect

The **intersect** operator ∩ limits two shapes to form a third

$$A \cap B = C$$

where the shape C (heavy outline) consists of all points in A that are also in B:

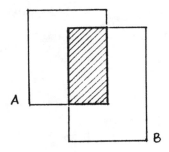

The order of the operands is not important:

$$A \cap B = B \cap A$$

and, in general,

$$A \cap B \cap C = A \cap C \cap B$$

Properties

---

1. $A \cup B = B \cup A$

2. $(A \cup B) \cup C = A \cup (B \cup C)$

3. $A \cup \varnothing = A$ $\varnothing = $ **null set**

4. $A \cup A = A$

5. $A \cup cA = E$ $E = $ **universal set**

6. $A \cap B = B \cap A$ $E = A \cup cA$

7. $A \cap E = A$

8. $A \cap A = A$

9. $A \cup (B \cap C) = (A \cup B) \cap (A \cup C)$

10. $A \cap (B \cup C) = (A \cap B) \cup (A \cap C)$

11. $cE = \varnothing$

12. $c\varnothing = E$

13. $c(cA) = A$

14. $c(A \cup B) = cA \cap cB$

15. $c(A \cap B) = cA \cup cB$

Half-Spaces: Two Dimensional

An unbounded straight line or curve divides a plane of two-dimensional space into two regions, called **half-spaces**, and denoted $h(x,y)$.

For a two-dimensional half-space bounded by a straight line, let

$$h(x,y) = ax + by + c$$

Observe the following conventions:

1. If the coordinates of a point produce $h(x,y) = 0$, then the point is on the boundary of the half-space.
2. If $h(x,y) > 0$, then the point is inside.
3. If $h(x,y) < 0$, then the point is outside.

Half-spaces can be combined using the Boolean operators: union, intersect, and difference.

Change the sign of $h(x,y)$ to reverse the inside/outside classification.

Example:

Let $h(x,y) = x - 2y - 6$; then point $(0,0)$ lies outside the half-space, since $h(0,0) = -6$.

Let $h(x, y) = -(x-2)^2 - (y-2)^2 + 1$; then point $(3,1)$ lies outside the circular half-space, since $h(3,1) = -1$.

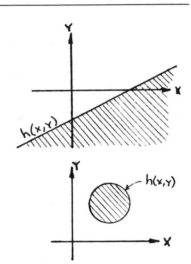

Half-Spaces: Three Dimensional

A plane or curved surface divides three-dimensional space into two regions called half-spaces, denoted by $h(x,y,z)$.

A three-dimensional half-space bounded by a plane is given by

$$h(x,y,z) = Ax + By + Cz + D$$

The point classification conventions are the same as those for two-dimensional half-spaces.

Example

Let $h(x,y,z) = 3x + 3y + 4z - 24$ (a half-space bounded by a plane); then the point $(0,0,0)$ is outside the half-space, since $h(0,0,0) = -24$.

Let $h(x,y,z) = -x^2 - z^2 + 9$ (a half-space bounded by a cylindrical surface); then the point $(2, -1,0)$ is inside the half-space, since $h(2, -1,0) = 5$.

Intersection of Two Half-Spaces: $h_1 \cap h_2$

Use Boolean operators to combine half-spaces to form more complex shapes.

Let $h_1 = -(x-2)^2 - (y-2)^2 + 4$ and $h_2 = -x + 3$; then express the intersections of these two half-spaces as

$$g = h_1 \cap h_2$$

Preserve dimensional homogeneity: combine half-spaces of like dimension.

There are nine possible point classifications with respect to the intersection of two half-spaces (two- or three-dimensional). These are best illustrated by means of the table below.

$$g = h_1 \cap h_2$$

	If						Then		
	ih_1	bh_1	oh_1	ih_2	bh_2	oh_2	ig	bg	og
1	1	0	0	1	0	0	1	0	0
2	1	0	0	0	1	0	0	1	0
3	1	0	0	0	0	1	0	0	1
4	0	1	0	1	0	0	0	1	0
5	0	1	0	0	1	0	0	1	0
6	0	1	0	0	0	1	0	0	1
7	0	0	1	1	0	0	0	0	1
8	0	0	1	0	1	0	0	0	1
9	0	0	1	0	0	1	0	0	1

i = inside
b = boundary
o = outside

1 = yes
0 = no

Interpret this table as in the following example (see No. 4): If a point is on the boundary of h_1 and inside h_2, then it is on the boundary of their intersection, bg.

Intersection of Multiple Half-Spaces

The general expression for the intersection of multiple half-spaces is:

$$g = \bigcap_{i=1}^{n} h_i$$

$$= h_1 \cap h_2 \cap h_3 \cdots \cap h_n$$

n = number of half-spaces

Listing all of the possible point classification conditions is cumbersome with more than two half-spaces, so, instead, follow these three general classification rules:

1. If and only if a point is inside all h_i, then it is inside g.
2. If and only if a point is outside at least one h_i, then it is outside g.
3. If and only if a point is on the boundary of at least one h_i and inside the remaining h_i, then it is on the boundary of g.

Combine half-spaces using both the intersect and union operators. First, perform sets of intersections, then combine the results with the union operator; thus,

$$g = \bigcup_{i=1}^{m} \bigcap_{j=1}^{n} h_{ij}$$

John Wallis (1616–1703), Professor of Geometry at Oxford, was the first to use the "love knot" symbol, ∞, for infinity.

Rectangle and Circle Classification

Let R denote a rectangle in the plane and C denote a circle. Determine the relationship between them by computing the rectangle's vertex point distribution relative to the circle.

$$R \langle \rangle C$$

	Vertex Point Distribution			
	iC	bC	oC	Classification
1	4	0	0	$R \langle$ inside $\rangle C$
2	3	1	0	$R \langle$ inside $\rangle C$
3	3	0	1	$R \langle$ intersect $\rangle C$
4	2	2	0	$R \langle$ inside $\rangle C$
5	2	1	1	$R \langle$ intersect $\rangle C$
6	2	0	2	$R \langle$ intersect $\rangle C$
7	1	3	0	See note
8	1	2	1	$R \langle$ intersect $\rangle C$
9	1	1	2	$R \langle$ intersect $\rangle C$
10	1	0	3	$R \langle$ intersect $\rangle C$
11	0	4	0	$R \langle$ inside $\rangle C$
12	0	3	1	See note
13	0	2	2	$R \langle$ intersect $\rangle C$
14	0	1	3	Indeterminate*
15	0	0	4	Indeterminate*

Note: 7 and 12 are the same as 11. In fact, if three vertex points are on the boundary of a circle, then the fourth must also be on it.

iC = inside circle
bC = boundary
oC = outside

* Vertex point distribution alone is not enough to determine the classification.

". . . mathematics in general and geometry in particular owe their existence to our need to learn something about the properties of real objects."

Albert Einstein

Rectangle$_1$ $\cup$ Rectangle$_2$ Point Classification

This table shows eight possible combinations of point classification for two rectangles, R_1 and R_2, joined by the union operator.

$$g = R_1 \cup R_2$$

	If				Then	
	bR_1	iR_1	bR_2	iR_2	bg	ig
1	1	0	0	0	1	0
2	1	0	1	0	Indeterminate	
3	1	0	0	1	0	1
4	0	1	0	0	0	1
5	0	1	1	0	0	1
6	0	1	0	1	0	1
7	0	0	1	0	1	0
8	0	0	0	1	0	1

i = inside
b = boundary

1 = yes
0 = no

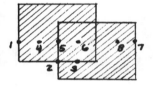

Points outside R_1 and R_2 are not included in the table, for they are also outside g. If a point is outside only one of the rectangles, then it is inside or on the boundary of g according to whether it is inside or on the boundary of the other rectangle.

Circle$_1$ $\cup$ Circle$_2$ Point Classification

This table shows eight possible combinations of point classification for two circles, C_1 and C_2, joined by the union operator.

$$g = C_1 \cup C_2$$

	If				Then	
	bC_1	iC_1	bC_2	iC_2	bg	ig
1	1	0	0	0	1	0
2	1	0	1	0	1	0
3	1	0	0	1	0	1
4	0	1	0	0	0	1
5	0	1	1	0	0	1
6	0	1	0	1	0	1
7	0	0	1	0	1	0
8	0	0	0	1	0	1

i = inside
b = boundary

1 = yes
0 = no

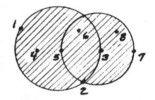

Rectangle ∪ Circle Point Classification

This table shows eight possible combinations of point classification for a rectangle and circle joined by the union operator.

$$g = R \cup C$$

	If				Then	
	bR	iR	bC	iC	bg	ig
1	1	0	0	0	1	0
2	1	0	1	0	1	0
3	1	0	0	1	0	1
4	0	1	0	0	0	1
5	0	1	1	0	0	1
6	0	1	0	1	0	1
7	0	0	1	0	1	0
8	0	0	0	1	0	1

i = inside
b = boundary

1 = yes
0 = no

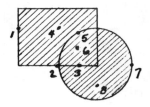

Rectangle$_1$ — Rectangle$_2$ Point Classification

This table shows eight possible combinations of point classification for the Boolean difference of two rectangles.

$$g = R_1 - R_2$$

	If				Then		
	bR_1	iR_1	bR_2	iR_2	bg	ig	og
1	1	0	0	0	1	0	0
2	1	0	1	0	Indeterminate		
3	1	0	0	1	0	0	1
4	0	1	0	0	0	1	0
5	0	1	1	0	1	0	0
6	0	1	0	1	0	0	1
7	0	0	1	0	0	0	1
8	0	0	0	1	0	0	1

i = inside
b = boundary
o = outside

1 = yes
0 = no

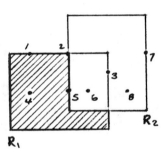

Circle$_1$ − Circle$_2$ Point Classification

This table shows eight possible combinations of point classification for the Boolean difference of two circles.

$$g = C_1 - C_2$$

	If				Then		
	bC_1	iC_1	bC_2	iC_2	bg	ig	og
1	1	0	0	0	1	0	0
2	1	0	1	0	1	0	0
3	1	0	0	1	0	0	1
4	0	1	0	0	0	1	0
5	0	1	1	0	1	0	0
6	0	1	0	1	0	0	1
7	0	0	1	0	0	0	1
8	0	0	0	1	0	0	1

i = inside
b = boundary
o = outside

1 = yes
0 = no

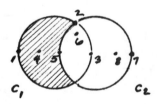

Circle — Rectangle Point Classification

This table shows eight possible combinations of point classification for the Boolean difference of a circle and a rectangle.

$$g = C - R$$

	If				Then		
	bC	iC	bR	iR	bg	ig	og
1	1	0	0	0	1	0	0
2	1	0	1	0	1	0	0
3	1	0	0	1	0	0	1
4	0	1	0	0	0	1	0
5	0	1	1	0	1	0	0
6	0	1	0	1	0	0	1
7	0	0	1	0	0	0	1
8	0	0	0	1	0	0	1

i = inside
b = boundary
o = outside

1 = yes
0 = no

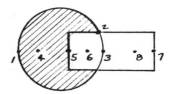

Rectangle$_1$ ∩ Rectangle$_2$ Point Classification

This table shows eight possible combinations of point classification for the intersection of two rectangles.

$$g = R_1 \cap R_2$$

	If				Then		
	bR_1	iR_1	bR_2	iR_2	bg	ig	og
1	1	0	0	0	0	0	1
2	1	0	1	0	1	0	0
3	1	0	0	1	1	0	0
4	0	1	0	0	0	0	1
5	0	1	1	0	1	0	0
6	0	1	0	1	0	1	0
7	0	0	1	0	0	0	1
8	0	0	0	1	0	0	1

i = inside
b = boundary
o = outside

1 = yes
0 = no

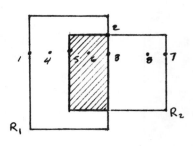

Circle$_1$ ∩ Circle$_2$ Point Classification

This table shows eight possible combinations of point classification for the Boolean intersection of two circles.

$$g = C_1 \cap C_2$$

	If				Then		
	bC_1	iC_1	bC_2	iC_2	bg	ig	og
1	1	0	0	0	0	0	1
2	1	0	1	0	1	0	0
3	1	0	0	1	1	0	0
4	0	1	0	0	0	0	1
5	0	1	1	0	1	0	0
6	0	1	0	1	0	1	0
7	0	0	1	0	0	0	1
8	0	0	0	1	0	0	1

i = inside
b = boundary
o = outside

1 = yes
0 = no

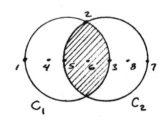

Rectangle ∩ Circle Point Classification

This table shows eight possible combinations of point classification for the Boolean intersection of a rectangle and circle.

$$g = R \cap C$$

	If				Then		
	bR	iR	bC	iC	bg	ig	og
1	1	0	0	0	0	0	1
2	1	0	1	0	1	0	0
3	1	0	0	1	1	0	0
4	0	1	0	0	0	0	1
5	0	1	1	0	1	0	0
6	0	1	0	1	0	1	0
7	0	0	1	0	0	0	1
8	0	0	0	1	0	0	1

i = inside
b = boundary
o = outside

1 = yes
0 = no

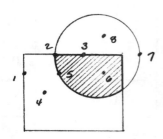

Plane Geometry: Straight Lines

Point–slope form:

$$y - y_1 = m(x - x_1)$$

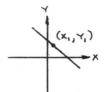

$m =$ slope
$m = \Delta y / \Delta x$

Slope–intercept form:

$$y = mx + b$$

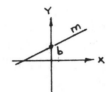

$b =$ intercept

Two-point form:

$$\frac{y - y_1}{x - x_1} = \frac{y_2 - y_1}{x_2 - x_1}$$

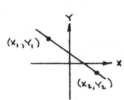

$$m = \frac{y_2 - y_1}{x_2 - x_1}$$

Intercept form:

$$\frac{x}{a} + \frac{y}{b} = 1$$

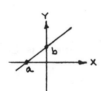

$a =$ intercept on x axis
$b =$ intercept on y axis

Angle between two lines:

$$\tan \theta = \frac{m_1 - m_2}{1 + m_1 m_2}$$

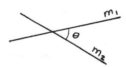

Parallel lines: $m_1 = m_2$
Perpendicular lines:
$m_1 m_2 = -1$

Perpendicular distance from line $Ax + By + C = 0$
to $\mathbf{p}_1(x_1, y_1)$

$$d = \frac{Ax_1 + By_1 + C}{\pm \sqrt{A^2 + B^2}}$$

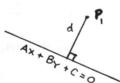

A two-dimensional half-space is defined by the implicit equation of a line. For example, if $f(x,y) = 2x - y + 2$, then $f(x,y) > 0$ and $f(x,y) < 0$ define two half-spaces, and $f(x,y) = 0$ defines their common boundary.

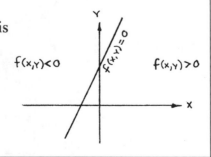

The concept of half-spaces extends to curves in the plane and to higher-dimension functions and spaces.

Intervals

Consider the continuous set of points defining the real line X. Let an interval on X be defined by $a < x < b$, where a and b are limiting points on the interval. This is an open interval because it does not contain its limit points. If $a \leq x \leq b$, then it is a closed interval because it does contain its limit points.

A closed interval is denoted $[a,b]$, using brackets, with the interval limits separated by a comma. An open interval is denoted (a,b), using parentheses, with the interval limits again separated by a comma. Write for a closed interval

$x \in [a,b]$

Read this as: x is an element (or member) of the interval $[a,b]$. The unit interval $x \in [0,1]$ is a special case and is often used in computer graphics and modeling.

These concepts are from set theory. Interpret the interval as a subset (open or closed), and x as a member of this subset if it falls within the interval.

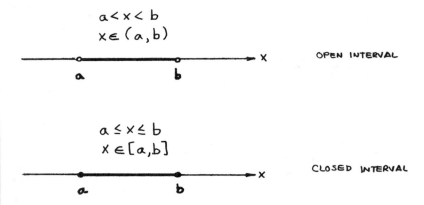

OPEN INTERVAL

CLOSED INTERVAL

$u \in [0,1]$ is a one-dimensional interval.

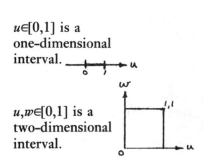

$u, w \in [0,1]$ is a two-dimensional interval.

An inequality states that two expressions are not equal.

i. If a and b are real numbers, then exactly one of the following is true: $a = b$, $a < b$, or $a > b$.
ii. If $a < b$ and $b < c$, then $a < c$.
iii. If $a < b$, then $a + c < b + c$.
iv. If $a < b$, and $c > 0$, then $ac < bc$.
v. If $a < b$, and $c < 0$, then $ac > bc$.

$a < b$: a is less than b.
$a \leq b$: a is less than or equal to b.
$a > b$: a is greater than b.
$a \geq b$: a is greater than or equal to b.

Planes

Cartesian form:

$$Ax + By + Cz + D = 0$$

A,B,C,D are the Cartesian coefficients of the plane.

Unit normal components:

$$\mathbf{n} = [n_x \ n_y \ n_z]$$
$$n_x = A/\sqrt{A^2 + B^2 + C^2}$$
$$n_y = B/\sqrt{A^2 + B^2 + C^2}$$
$$n_z = C/\sqrt{A^2 + B^2 + C^2}$$

Normal distance from origin to plane:

$$d = D/\sqrt{A^2 + B^2 + C^2}, \quad d = |\mathbf{d}|$$

Normal vector from origin to plane:

$$\mathbf{d} = [n_x d \ n_y d \ n_z d]$$

Given three points on a plane,

$$\mathbf{p}_1 = [a \ 0 \ 0]$$
$$\mathbf{p}_2 = [0 \ b \ 0] \quad \text{then:} \ \frac{x}{a} + \frac{y}{b} + \frac{z}{c} = 1$$
$$\mathbf{p}_3 = [0 \ 0 \ c]$$

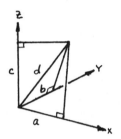

Direction numbers a,b,c
$$a^2 + b^2 + c^2 = d^2$$

Direction cosines $\cos \alpha$, $\cos \beta$, $\cos \gamma$
$$\cos^2 \alpha + \cos^2 \beta + \cos^2 \gamma = 1$$
$$\cos \alpha = a/d$$
$$\cos \beta = b/d$$
$$\cos \gamma = c/d$$

Given two planes $A_1x + B_1y + C_1z + D_1 = 0$ and $A_2x + B_2y + C_2z + D_2 = 0$; the direction numbers of their line of intersection are:

$$(B_1C_2 - C_1B_2), \ (C_1A_2 - A_1C_2), \ (A_1B_2 - B_1A_2)$$

If θ = angle between the planes, then

$$\cos \theta = \frac{A_1A_2 + B_1B_2 + C_1C_2}{\sqrt{A_1^2 + B_1^2 + C_1^2} \ \sqrt{A_2^2 + B_2^2 + C_2^2}}$$

This looks like the expansion of the vector product!

Planes and Linear Equations

A linear equation in three unknowns defines a plane in three-dimensional space. A system of three linear equations with three unknowns has six possible forms of solution:

1. No points in common; the planes are parallel.
2. Intersect in one point.
3. Intersect in one line.
4. Intersect in two lines.
5. Intersect in three lines.
6. All points in common; the planes are coincident.

Know the range of forms the solution to a particular problem can take.

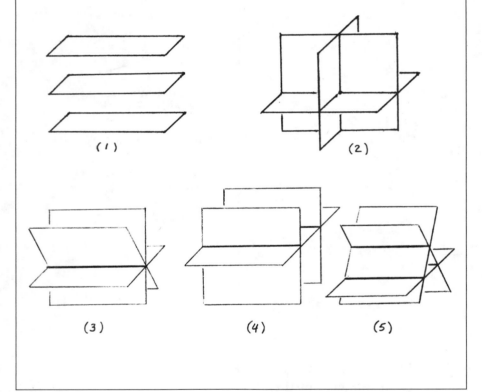

"Minus times minus is plus,
the reason for this we need not discuss."

W.H. Auden

Planes: Normal Form

Define a plane by giving its normal distance d from the origin, and the direction cosines of the line defined by d: $\cos\theta$, $\cos\beta$, $\cos\gamma$ (these are also the direction cosines of the plane). The angle $Op_d p_a$ is a right angle (since d is perpendicular to the plane, then any line in the plane through $\mathbf{p}_d$ is necessarily perpendicular to d). Thus

$$a = d/\cos\theta$$
$$b = d/\cos\beta$$
$$c = d/\cos\gamma$$

This yields $\mathbf{p}_a = [a\ 0\ 0]$, $\mathbf{p}_b = [0\ b\ 0]$, and $\mathbf{p}_c = [0\ 0\ c]$. Therefore, the equation of the plane is

$$x\cos\theta + y\cos\beta + z\cos\gamma - d = 0$$

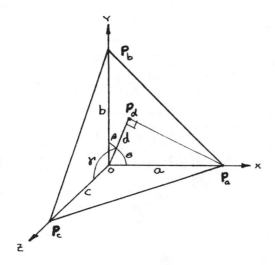

If two planes have the same direction cosines, then they are parallel.

Given $Ax + By + Cz + D = 0$,

$$d = \frac{D}{\sqrt{A^2 + B^2 + C^2}}$$

$$\cos\theta = \frac{A}{\sqrt{A^2 + B^2 + C^2}}$$

$$\cos\beta = \frac{B}{\sqrt{A^2 + B^2 + C^2}}$$

$$\cos\gamma = \frac{C}{\sqrt{A^2 + B^2 + C^2}}$$

Plane Defined by Three Points

Three noncollinear points in space are sufficient to define a plane. Given three points, p_1, p_2, and p_3, and the general equation of a plane, $Ax + By + Cz + D = 0$; rewrite the equation as

$$A'x + B'y + C'z + 1 = 0 \qquad\qquad A' = A/D,\ B' = B/D,\ C' = C/D$$

Use this equation and the three points to obtain

$$A'x_1 + B'y_1 + C'z_1 + 1 = 0$$
$$A'x_2 + B'y_2 + C'z_2 + 1 = 0$$
$$A'x_3 + B'y_3 + C'z_3 + 1 = 0$$

These three simultaneous linear equations are solved for A', B', and C'.

$$A' = \frac{(y_1 z_3 - y_3 z_1)(z_3 - z_2) - (y_2 z_3 - y_3 z_2)(z_3 - z_1)}{(x_1 z_3 - x_3 z_2)(y_2 z_3 - y_3 z_2) - (y_1 z_3 - y_3 z_1)(x_2 z_3 - x_3 z_2)}$$

$$B' = \frac{(x_1 z_3 - x_3 z_1)(z_3 - z_2) - (x_2 z_3 - x_3 z_2)(z_3 - z_1)}{(x_2 z_3 - x_3 z_2)(y_1 z_3 - y_3 z_1) - (x_1 z_3 - x_3 z_1)(y_2 z_3 - y_3 z_2)}$$

$$C' = \frac{(x_3 y_1 - x_1 y_3)(x_3 - x_2) - (x_3 y_2 - x_2 y_3)(x_3 - x_1)}{(x_3 y_2 - x_2 y_3)(x_3 z_1 - x_1 z_3) - (x_3 y_1 - x_1 y_3)(x_3 z_2 - x_2 z_3)}$$

Plane Geometry: Circles

Cartesian form:

$(x - h)^2 + (y - k)^2 = r^2$

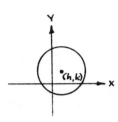

Parametric functions:

Center at $(0,0)$, $r = 1$

$\mathbf{p}(u) = [\cos u \quad \sin u]$

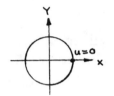

$u \in [0, 2\pi]$

$\mathbf{p}(u) = [(1 - u^2)/(1 + u^2) \quad 2u/(1 + u^2)]$

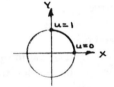

$u \in [0, 1]$

$\mathbf{p}(u) = [u \quad (1 - u^2)^{\frac{1}{2}}]$

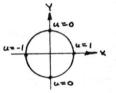

$u \in [-1, 1]$

$\mathbf{p}(u) = [(0.43u^3 - 1.466u^2 + 0.036u + 1) \\ (-0.43u^3 - 0.177u^2 + 1.607u)]$

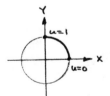

$u \in [0, 1]$

The efforts of Leonhard Euler (1707–1783) established the use of the Greek letter π for the ratio of the circumference of a circle to its diameter.

Plane Geometry: General Conic

A conic curve is described by a second-degree algebraic equation; and, conversely, any second-degree equation represents a conic.

$$Ax^2 + By^2 + 2Hxy + 2Fx + 2Gy + C = 0$$

In matrix form, this becomes

$$\mathbf{PQP}^T = 0$$

Certain characteristics of the quadratic equation are invariant under translation and rotation transformations; for example, $A + B$, $K = AB - H^2$, and the determinant $|\mathbf{Q}|$. Use K and $|\mathbf{Q}|$ to classify conic curves.

$$\mathbf{Q} = \begin{bmatrix} A & H & F \\ H & B & G \\ F & G & C \end{bmatrix}$$

$\mathbf{P} = [x \ \ y \ \ 1]$, where $\mathbf{P}$ is in homogeneous coordinates.

K	$\lvert\mathbf{Q}\rvert$	Other conditions	Curve type
0	$\neq 0$		Parabola
0	0	$B \neq 0, G^2 - BC > 0$	Two parallel real lines
0	0	$B \neq 0, G^2 - BC = 0$	Two parallel coincident lines
0	0	$B \neq 0, G^2 - BC < 0$	Two parallel imaginary lines
0	0	$B = H = 0, F^2 - AC > 0$	Two parallel real lines
0	0	$B = H = 0, F^2 - AC = 0$	Two parallel coincident lines
0	0	$B = H = 0, F^2 - AC < 0$	Two parallel imaginary lines
> 0	0		Point ellipse
> 0	$\neq 0$	$-B\lvert\mathbf{Q}\rvert > 0$	Real ellipse
> 0	$\neq 0$	$-B\lvert\mathbf{Q}\rvert < 0$	Imaginary ellipse
< 0	$\neq 0$		Hyperbola
< 0	0		Two intersecting lines

"Treat nature in terms of the cylinder, the sphere, the cone, all in perspective."

Paul Cézanne

Plane Geometry: Parabola

A parabola is the locus of a point **p** whose distance from a fixed point $\mathbf{p}_f$, called the focus, is equal to its distance from a fixed line, the directrix.

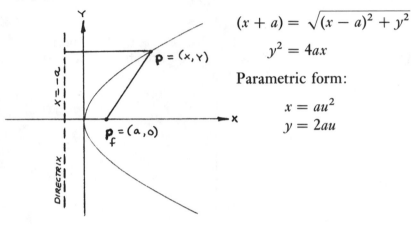

$$(x + a) = \sqrt{(x - a)^2 + y^2}$$

$$y^2 = 4ax$$

Parametric form:

$$x = au^2$$
$$y = 2au$$

Archimedes proved that the area of a parabolic segment is four-thirds the area of a triangle having the same base and equal height.

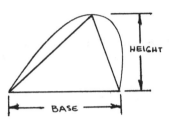

The Development of Geometry

Prehistoric:	Development of decorative forms
2000–1000 BC:	Egyptian surveyors use coordinates to lay out towns; practical rules for measurement of areas and volumes.
600 BC:	The study of lines and figures formed by lines (Thales); beginning of demonstrative geometry (if . . ., then . . .).
540 BC:	Development of geometric constructions (Pythagoras).
400 BC:	Idea of projecting lines onto a plane, intersections.
300 BC:	Euclid's *Elements*.
1637 AD:	René Descartes: Analytic geometry.
1650–1800:	Application of calculus to geometry begins.
1800:	Monge: theory of surfaces, descriptive geometry.
1822:	Poncelet: originates modern projective geometry.
1820–1860:	Recognition and development of new geometries by Lobachevsky, Riemann, *et al.* (noneuclidean geometry, topology).
1900–	Development of generalization, arithmetization, and axiomatic foundations of geometry (Hilbert *et al.*).
1916–	Geometrization of spacetime, general relativity (Einstein *et al*).
1960–	Computational geometry, application of digital computers, modeling, fractals.

Plane Geometry: Hyperbola

A hyperbola is the locus of a point **p** such that the difference of the distances of **p** from two fixed points, called foci, is constant. It is also a conic curve with eccentricity $e > 1$. There are two parameters, a and b, related by

$$b^2 = a^2(e^2 - 1)$$

The hyperbola is given by

$$\frac{x^2}{a^2} - \frac{y^2}{b^2} = 1$$

If $a = b$, the hyperbola is equilateral.

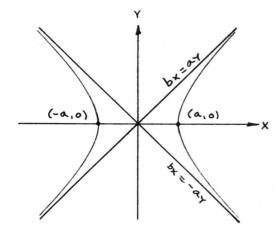

Parametric form:

$$x = a \sec u$$
$$y = b \tan u$$

$$u \in [-\pi, \pi]$$

Plane Geometry: Ellipse

An ellipse is the locus of a point **p** such that the sum of the distance from **p** of two fixed points, called foci, is constant. It is also a conic curve with eccentricity e such that $0 < e < 1$. There are two parameters, a and b, related by

$$b^2 = a^2(e^2 - 1)$$

The ellipse is given by

$$\frac{x^2}{a^2} + \frac{y^2}{b^2} = 1$$

If $a = b$, then a circle is produced.

a = semimajor axis
b = semiminor axis

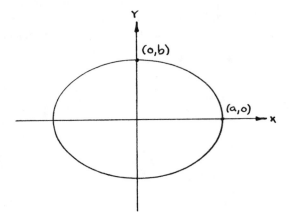

Area $= \pi a b$

Parametric form:

$$\begin{aligned} x &= a \cos u \\ y &= b \sin u \end{aligned} \qquad u \in [-\pi, \pi]$$

A superellipse is defined by

$$\frac{x^n}{a^n} + \frac{y^n}{b^n} = 1$$

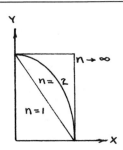

Superellipse

When $n = 2$, an ordinary ellipse is produced. As n increases, a fuller ellipse is produced, and as $n \to \infty$ the shape of the ellipse approaches that of a rectangle.

Plane Trigonometry

Relations:

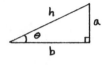

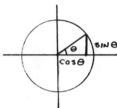

$$\sin \theta = a/h \qquad\qquad \csc \theta = 1/\sin \theta$$
$$\cos \theta = b/h \qquad\qquad \sec \theta = 1/\cos \theta$$
$$\tan \theta = a/b \qquad\qquad \cot \theta = 1/\tan \theta$$

$$\sin^2 \theta + \cos^2 \theta = 1$$
$$1 + \tan^2 \theta = \sec^2 \theta$$
$$1 + \cot^2 \theta = \csc^2 \theta$$

$$\sin \omega = \omega - \frac{\omega^2}{3!} + \frac{\omega^4}{5!} - \frac{\omega^6}{7!} + \cdots$$

The term "secant" is also used to denote any straight line cutting a curve in two or more points.

2π radians $= 360°$

It is not known exactly when the systematic use of the $360°$ circle became accepted, but Hipparchus' table of chords provided an impetus.

Functions of $(\theta + \phi)$ and $(\theta - \phi)$:

$$\sin (\theta + \varphi) = \sin \theta \cos \varphi + \cos \theta \sin \varphi \qquad \sin (\theta - \phi) = \sin \theta \cos \phi - \cos \theta \sin \phi$$
$$\cos (\theta + \phi) = \cos \theta \cos \phi - \sin \theta \sin \theta \qquad \cos (\theta - \phi) = \cos \theta \cos \phi + \sin \theta \sin \phi$$

$$\tan (\theta + \phi) = \frac{\tan \theta + \tan \phi}{1 - \tan \theta \tan \phi} \qquad\qquad \tan (\theta - \phi) = \frac{\tan \theta - \tan \phi}{1 + \tan \theta \tan \phi}$$

Functions of 2θ and $\theta/2$:

$$\sin 2\theta = 2 \sin \theta \cos \theta \qquad \sin (\theta/2) = \pm \sqrt{(1 - \cos \theta)/2} \qquad \sin^2 \theta = (1 - \cos 2\theta)/2$$

$$\cos 2\theta = \cos^2 \theta - \sin^2 \theta \qquad \cos (\theta/2) = \pm \sqrt{(1 + \cos \theta)/2} \qquad \cos^2 \theta = (1 + \cos 2\theta)/2$$

$$\tan 2\theta = \frac{2 \tan \theta}{1 - \tan^2 \theta} \qquad\qquad \tan (\theta/2) = \pm \sqrt{\frac{1 - \cos \theta}{1 + \cos \theta}}$$

Other functions:

$$\sin \theta + \sin \phi = 2 \sin \tfrac{1}{2}(\theta + \phi) \cos \tfrac{1}{2}(\theta - \phi)$$
$$\cos \theta + \cos \phi = 2 \cos \tfrac{1}{2}(\theta + \phi) \cos \tfrac{1}{2}(\theta - \phi)$$

$$\sin \theta - \sin \phi = 2 \cos \tfrac{1}{2} (\theta + \phi) \sin \tfrac{1}{2}(\theta - \phi)$$
$$\cos \theta - \cos \phi = - 2 \sin \tfrac{1}{2}(\theta + \phi) \sin \tfrac{1}{2}(\theta - \phi)$$

For any triangle:

Law of Sines: $\dfrac{a}{\sin A} = \dfrac{b}{\sin B} = \dfrac{c}{\sin C}$

Law of Cosines: $a^2 = b^2 + c^2 - 2bc \cos A$

Let $s = \tfrac{1}{2}(a + b + c)$, then

$$\text{Area} = \sqrt{s(s - a)(s - b)(s - c)}$$

"One must not always think that feeling is everything. Art is nothing without form."

Gustave Flaubert

Coordinate Systems

Rectangular

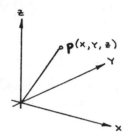

Right-hand system

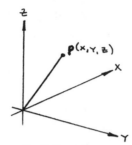

Left-hand system

Polar

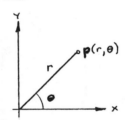

$x = r \cos \theta$
$y = r \sin \theta$
$r = \sqrt{x^2 + y^2}$
$\theta = \tan^{-1}(y/x)$

Cylindrical

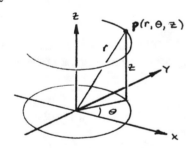

$x = r \cos \theta$
$y = r \sin \theta$
$z = z$
$r = \sqrt{x^2 + y^2 + z^2}$
$\theta = \tan^{-1}(y/x)$

Spherical

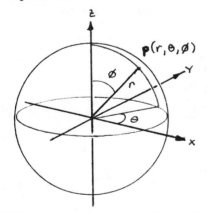

$x = r \sin \phi \cos \theta$
$y = r \sin \phi \sin \theta$
$z = r \cos \phi$
$r = \sqrt{x^2 + y^2 + z^2}$
$\theta = \tan^{-1}(y/x)$
$\phi = \cos^{-1}(z/\sqrt{x^2 + y^2 + z^2})$

6. Polygons and Polyhedra

Polygon Definition

A **plane polygon** is a many-sided two-dimensional figure bounded by a circuit of straight-line segments joining successive pairs of points. The line segments are **edges** and the points are **vertices**.

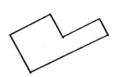

The number of vertices V equals the number of edges E.

$$V - E = 0.$$

Polygons are **convex, concave,** or **stellar** (left to right).

Convex: No straight lines that are prolongations of the bounding edges penetrate the interior, and edges intersect only at vertices.

Concave: Straight lines that are prolongations of edges penetrate the interior.

Stellar: Edges intersect at points in addition to vertex points.

A **regular polygon** lies in a plane, is convex, has straight-line edges all of equal length, and has all vertex angles equal.

Polygons whose edges are curve segments can be constructed on curved surfaces.

A plane polygon must have at least three edges to enclose a finite area.

Any plane polygon has a minimum triangulation of T triangles, where

$$T = V - 2$$

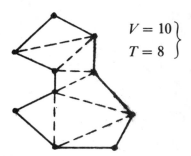

$$\left. \begin{array}{l} V = 10 \\ T = 8 \end{array} \right\}$$

The sum of the exterior angles of a plane (not a stellar) polygon is 2π.

The area of a regular polygon is

$$A = \frac{EL^2}{4} \cot\left(\frac{\pi}{E}\right)$$

E = number of edges,
L = length of edge

Area of a Plane Polygon

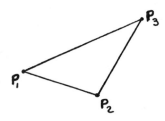

Select a reference vertex, say $\mathbf{p}_1$; then the area of the triangle is

$$A = \tfrac{1}{2}\left|(\mathbf{p}_2 - \mathbf{p}_1) \times (\mathbf{p}_3 - \mathbf{p}_1)\right|$$

Vertices are given by position vectors $\mathbf{p}_i$.

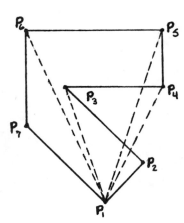

Select a reference vertex, say $\mathbf{p}_1$; then the area of a plane polygon with n vertices is

$$A = \tfrac{1}{2}\left|\sum_{i=1}^{n-2} (\mathbf{p}_{i+1} - \mathbf{p}_1) \times (\mathbf{p}_{i+2} - \mathbf{p}_1)\right|$$

Note: in general there are $n - 2$ "signed" (oriented) triangular areas. The vector product nicely accounts for triangle overlaps and thus holds for either convex or concave polygons.

"Had the early Greek mind been sympathetic to the algebra and arithmetic of the Babylonians, it would have found plenty to exercise its logical acumen, and might easily have produced a masterpiece of the deductive reasoning it worshipped, logically sounder than Euclid's greatly overrated *Elements*. The hypotheses of elementary algebra are fewer and simpler than those of synthetic geometry. The algebraic–analytic method in mensuration and geometry was well within the capacity of the Greek mathematicians, and they could have developed it with any degree of logical rigor they desired. Had they done so, Apollonius would have been Descartes, and Archimedes Newton."

E.T. Bell

Convex Hull of a Polygon

The **convex hull** of any polygon is the convex polygon that would be formed if a rubber band were stretched over the vertex points. The convex hull of a convex polygon corresponds identically to the shape of the polygon. The convex hull of a concave polygon always has fewer sides than the polygon and encloses a larger area.

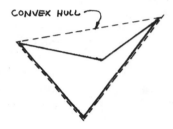

CONVEX HULL

Gauss proved that a regular convex polygon of n sides can be constructed using only a straight-edge and compass if, and only if,

    i. $n = 2^k$, where k is any integer, or
    ii. n is a prime number of the type $n = 2^k + 1$, or
    iii. n is a product of different factors of the type described in
       ii, where none are repeated.

For example, $n = 9$ or $n = 18$ cannot be constructed, since $9 = 3 \times 3$ and $18 = 2 \times 3 \times 3$, where 3 is repeated.

These can be constructed: 3, 4, 5, 6, 8, 10, 12, 15, 16, 17 . . . .

These cannot be: 7, 9, 11, 13, 14, 18, 19, 21, 22, 23, 25 . . . .

"Our notions of space are rooted in our physiological organism. Geometric concepts are the product of the idealization of physical experience of space. Systems of geometry, finally, originate in the logical classification of the conceptual materials so obtained. All three factors have left their indubitable traces in modern geometry."

Ernst Mach

Point Containment Test: Convex Polygons

Given a convex polygon and a test point $\mathbf{p}_T$, determine if $\mathbf{p}_T$ is inside the polygon. Establish a reference point $\mathbf{p}_R$, known to be inside the polygon; for example

$$\mathbf{p}_R = [(x_1 + x_3)/2 \quad (y_1 + y_3)/2]$$

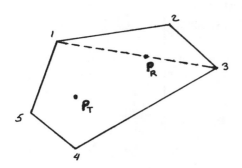

Write the implicit equation of each edge: $f_{1,2}(x,y), f_{2,3}(x,y),$ $f_{3,4}(x,y), \ldots,$ and so on. For each edge compute and compare $f_{ij}(x_T, y_T)$ and $f_{ij}(x_R, y_R)$. Then:

1. If the evaluated functions, in pairs, have the same sign, then $\mathbf{p}_T$ is inside the polygon.

2. If any $f_{ij}(x_T, y_T) = 0$ and if otherwise condition 1 holds, then $\mathbf{p}_T$ is on the boundary (an edge) of the polygon.

3. Otherwise $\mathbf{p}_T$ is outside the polygon.

This procedure will not work for concave polygons.

If the polygon has only three edges, then try

$$\mathbf{p}_R = [(2x_1 + x_2 + x_3)/4 \quad (2y_1 + y_2 + y_3)/4]$$

This is the midpoint of the line joining vertex 1 to the midpoint of edge 2,3.

If any two sequential f_{ij} both equal zero, then $\mathbf{p}_T$ is on the common vertex.

Given two convex polygons, if all the vertices of one are contained in the other, then the first polygon is inside the second.

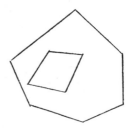

Point Containment Test:
Convex and Concave Polygons

Given a test point p_T determine if it is inside, outside, or on the boundary of a polygon (convex or concave). Do this in two steps:

1. Using the polygon vertex points, find the min–max box.
    i. If p_T is not inside the min–max box, then it is not inside the polygon.
    ii. If p_T is inside, proceed to the next step.

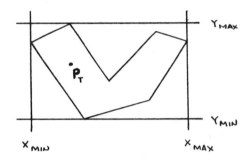

2. Compute the intersections of $y = y_T$ with the edges of the polygon. Consider only edges whose end points straddle y_T. There is always an even number of intersections. Pair the x coordinates of the intersections in ascending order; for example, (x_1, x_2), (x_3, x_4), and so on. Then
    i.   If x_T falls inside an interval, for example, $x_1 < x_T < x_2$, then p_T is inside the polygon.
    ii. If x_T is identically equal to one of the interval limits, then p_T is on the boundary.
    iii. Otherwise p_T is outside the polygon.

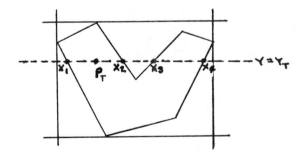

An analogous approach uses $x = x_T$.

Count intersections with a vertex as two.

"For he by geometric scale,
Could take the size of pots of ale."

Samuel Butler

Polyhedron Definition

A **polyhedron** is a multifaceted three-dimensional solid bounded by a finite, connected set of plane polygons such that every edge of each polygon belongs also to just one other polygon.

Three geometric elements characterize all polyhedra: vertices (V), edges (E), and faces (F).

1. Each vertex subtends an equal number of edges and faces.

2. Each edge is bounded by two vertices and two faces.

3. Each face is bounded by a closed loop of coplanar edges forming a polygon.

4. The angle between faces that intersect a common edge is called the **dihedral angle**.

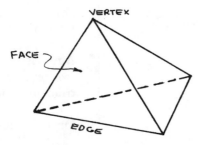

"Polytope is the general term of the sequence—point, segment, polygon, polyhedron . . ."

H.S.M. Coxeter

The sum of all face angles at any vertex of a convex polyhedron is always less than 2π.

Regular Polyhedra

A convex polyhedron is a **regular polyhedron** if its faces are regular polygons and equal, and if its vertices are surrounded alike. The cube is an example: all its faces are identical (equal size squares), and all its edges are of equal length.

In three-dimensional space there are only five regular polyhedra: tetrahedron, hexahedron (cube), octahedron, dodecahedron, and icosahedron. These are called the five **Platonic solids**.

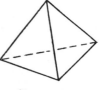

TETRAHEDRON

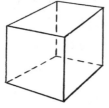

HEXAHEDRON

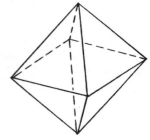

OCTAHEDRON

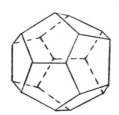

DODECAHEDRON

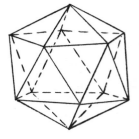

ICOSAHEDRON

Greek Roots

on	one
do	two
tri	three
tetra	four
penta	five
hexa	six
hepta	seven
octa	eight
enna	nine
deca	ten
dodeca	twelve
icosa	twenty
conta	thirty
triakis	three times
tetrakis	four times
pentakis	five times
poly	many
hedron	sided

Antiprism: a polyhedron having two regular N-gon faces and $2N$ triangular faces.

Dextro–: right-handed.

Enantiomorphic: having right- and left-handed forms.

Laevo–: left-handed.

Prism: a polyhedron consisting of two regular N-gon faces and N square faces.

Properties of Regular Polyhedra

	Face Polygons	V	E	F	$F@V$
Tetrahedron	Triangles	4	6	4	3
Cube	Squares	8	12	6	3
Octahedron	Triangles	6	12	8	4
Dodecahedron	Pentagons	20	30	12	3
Icosahedron	Triangles	12	30	20	5

	Area	Volume	D_c	D_i
Tetrahedron	$1.7321e^2$	$0.1178e^3$	1.2247	0.4082
Cube	$6e^2$	e^3	1.7321	1
Octahedron	$3.4641e^2$	$0.4714e^3$	1.4142	0.8165
Dodecahedron	$20.6458e^2$	$7.6632e^3$	2.8025	2.2270
Icosahedron	$8.6603e^2$	$2.1817e^3$	1.9021	1.5115

V = number of vertices
E = number of edges
F = number of faces

e = edge length

D_c = circumsphere diameter
D_i = in-sphere diameter

Note: D_c and D_i are tabulated for $e = 1$.

Read H.M.S. Coxeter's *Regular Polytopes*, Dover, New York, 1973, for a beautiful exposition on polytopes of many forms and dimensions.

There are 16 regular polytopes in four dimensions.

Semiregular Polyhedra

Only the five regular polyhedra, or Platonic solids, satisfy these four limiting conditions:

1. All face polygons are regular.
2. All face polygons are congruent.
3. All vertices are identical.
4. All dihedral angles are equal.

Vertices are identical if they are surrounded alike by edges and faces.

If conditions 2 and 4 are relaxed to allow two or more kinds of faces and two or more dihedral angles of differing value, then an infinite number of polyhedra is possible, including prisms and antiprisms, plus the 13 Archimedean semiregular polyhedra.

If conditions 1 and 3 are relaxed to allow nonregular faces and more than one kind of vertex, then another infinite set of polyhedra is possible, including the 13 Archimedean dual or vertically regular polyhedra, which are related to the Archimedean semiregular polyhedra through a correspondence between the faces in one group and the vertices in the other group.

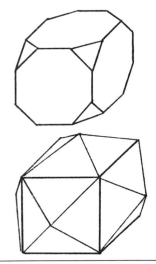

The truncated cube:

An Archimedean semiregular polyhedron.

Truncating the five Platonic polyhedra generates all the semiregular polyhedra except two snub forms. Truncating the thirteen Archimedean dual polyhedra generates the other polyhedra.

The tetrakis hexahedron:

An Archimedean dual polyhedron.

"We did not recognize the special character of our space until the non-Euclidean geometers of the nineteenth century and Einstein in the twentieth century showed that there are other spaces, and that patterns and forms in those other spaces differ from the ones we see in ours."

Peter S. Stevens
Patterns in Nature

Properties of Semiregular Polyhedra

	V	$E:V$	E	F and Type	
Truncated tetrahedron	12	3	18	8	4 triangles / 4 hexagons
Cuboctahedron	12	4	24	14	8 triangles / 6 squares
Truncated cube	24	3	36	14	8 triangles / 6 octagons
Snub cube	24	5	60	38	32 triangles / 6 squares
Truncated octahedron	24	3	36	14	6 squares / 8 hexagons
Small rhombicuboctahedron	24	4	48	26	8 triangles / 18 squares
Great rhombicuboctahedron	48	3	72	26	12 squares / 8 hexagons / 6 octagons
Truncated dodecahedron	60	3	90	32	20 triangles / 12 decagons
Snub dodecahedron	60	5	150	92	80 triangles / 12 pentagons
Icosidodecahedron	30	4	60	32	20 triangles / 12 pentagons
Truncated icosahedron	60	3	90	32	12 pentagons / 20 hexagons
Small rhombicosidodecahedron	60	4	120	62	20 triangles / 30 squares / 12 pentagons
Great rhombicosidodecahedron	120	3	180	62	30 squares / 20 hexagons / 12 decagons

V = number of vertices
$E:V$ = edges at each vertex
E = number of edges
F = number of faces

Dual Polyhedra

Two polyhedra are dual if the vertices of one can be put into one-to-one correspondence with the centers of the faces of the other. The cube and octahedron are dual polyhedra, with the six vertices of the octahedron corresponding to the six faces of the cube, and the eight vertices of the cube corresponding to the eight faces of the octahedron.

Here is how to generate the dual of any of the 5 regular and 26 Archimedean polyhedra:

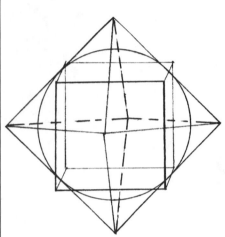

1. Inscribe a sphere in the polyhedron so that the surface of the sphere is tangent to every edge of the polyhedron. In the regular and Archimedean semiregular polyhedra, the sphere is tangent to the midpoint of each edge. In the Archimedean dual polyhedra, the sphere is tangent to each edge, but not necessarily at the midpoint.

2. At each point of tangency add another edge tangent to the sphere and perpendicular to the edge.

3. Extend the added edges until they meet to form the vertices and faces of the dual polyhedron.

Dual Pairs

Tetrahedron ↔ Tetrahedron

Cube ↔ Octahedron

Dodecahedron ↔ Icosahedron

Truncated tetrahedron ↔ Triakis tetrahedron

Cuboctahedron ↔ Rhombic dodecahedron

Truncated cube ↔ Triakis octahedron

Truncated octahedron ↔ Tetrakis cube

Small rhombicuboctahedron ↔ Trapezoidal icositetrahedron

Great rhombicuboctahedron ↔ Hexakis octahedron

Snub cube ↔ Pentagonal icositetrahedron

Icosidodecahedron ↔ Rhombic triacontahedron

Truncated dodecahedron ↔ Triakis icosahedron

Truncated Icosahedron ↔ Pentakis dodecahedron

Small rhombicosidodecahedron ↔ Trapezoidal hexacontahedron

Great rhombicosidodecahedron ↔ Hexakis icosahedron

Snub dodecahedron ↔ Pentagonal hexacontahedron

Tetrahedron

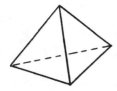

$V = 4$
$E = 6$
$F = 4$

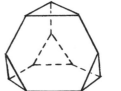

$V = 12$
$E = 18$
$F = 8$

Truncated tetrahedron

$V = 8$
$E = 18$
$F = 12$

Triakis tetrahedron

Dual: tetrahedron (self)
e = edge length
Area = $\sqrt{3}e^2 = 1.7321e^2$
Volume = $(\sqrt{2}/12)e^3 = 0.1178e^3$
Dihedral angle = $70°\,31'\,44''$
Angle subtended by an edge = $109°\,28'\,16''$
   (at center of tetrahedron)

If $e = 1$, then,
  Center of tetrahedron to
     center of face = $\sqrt{6}/12 = 0.2041$
     midedge   = $\sqrt{2}/4$ = 0.3536
     vertex   = $\sqrt{6}/4$ = 0.6124
  Center of face to
     vertex   = $\sqrt{3}/3$ = 0.5774
     midedge   = $\sqrt{3}/6$ = 0.2887

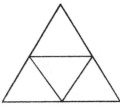

Net

$a = 60°$

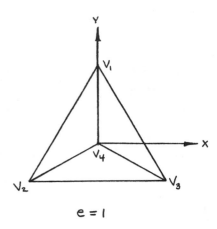

$e = 1$

V	x	y	z
1	0.0	0.5774	-0.2041
2	-0.5	-0.2887	-0.2041
3	0.5	-0.2887	-0.2041
4	0.0	0.0	0.6124

Cube (Hexahedron)

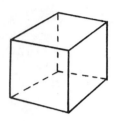

$V = 8$
$E = 12$
$F = 6$

For origin at the geometric center and $e = 1$

V	x	y	z
1	0.5	0.5	− 0.5
2	− 0.5	0.5	− 0.5
3	− 0.5	− 0.5	− 0.5
4	0.5	− 0.5	− 0.5
5	0.5	0.5	0.5
6	− 0.5	0.5	0.5
7	− 0.5	− 0.5	0.5
8	0.5	− 0.5	0.5

Dual: octahedron
e = edge length
Area = $6e^2$
Volume = e^3
Dihedral angle = $90°$
Angle subtended by an edge = $70° \, 31' \, 44''$
  (at center of cube)

If $e = 1$, then
  center of cube to
    center of face = 0.5
    midedge   = $\sqrt{2}/2 = 0.7071$
    vertex   = $\sqrt{3}/2 = 0.8660$
  center of face to
    vertex   = $\sqrt{2}/2 = 0.7071$
    midedge   = 0.5

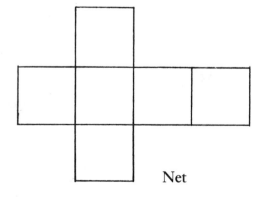

Net

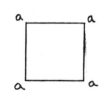

$a = 90°$

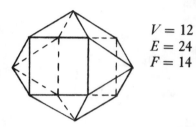

$V = 12$
$E = 24$
$F = 14$

Cuboctahedron

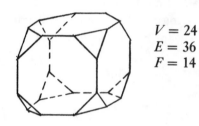

$V = 24$
$E = 36$
$F = 14$

Truncated cube

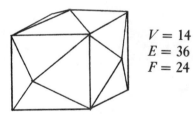

$V = 14$
$E = 36$
$F = 24$

Tetrakis cube

Octahedron

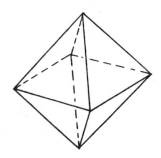

$V = 6$
$E = 12$
$F = 8$

For origin at the geometric center and $\overline{e = 1}$

V	x	y	z
1	0.5	0.5	0.0
2	-0.5	0.5	0.0
3	-0.5	-0.5	0.0
4	0.5	-0.5	0.0
5	0.0	0.0	0.7071
6	0.0	0.0	-0.7071

Dual: cube
e = edge length
Area = $2\sqrt{3}e^2 = 3.4641e^2$
Volume = $(\sqrt{2}/3)e^3 = 0.4714e^3$
Dihedral angle = $109°\,28'\,16''$
Angle subtended by an edge = $90°$
   (at center of octahedron)

If $e = 1$, then
  center of octahedron to
      center of face = $\sqrt{6}/6 = 0.4083$
      midedge   = 0.5
      vertex   = $\sqrt{2}/2 = 0.7071$
  center of face to
      vertex   = $\sqrt{3}/3 = 0.5774$
      midedge   = $\sqrt{3}/6 = 0.2887$

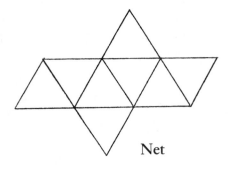

Net

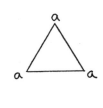

$a = 60°$

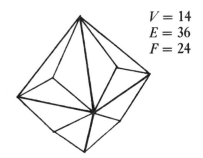

$V = 14$
$E = 36$
$F = 24$

Triakis octahedron

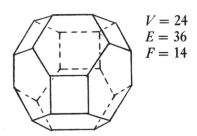

$V = 24$
$E = 36$
$F = 14$

Truncated octahedron

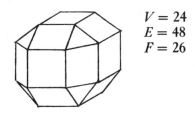

$V = 24$
$E = 48$
$F = 26$

Small rhombicuboctahedron

Dodecahedron

$V = 20$
$E = 30$
$F = 12$

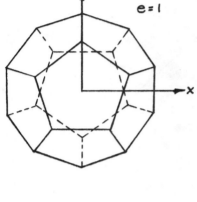

e = 1

Dual: icosahedron
e = edge length
Area = $3\sqrt{5(5 + 2\sqrt{5})}e^2 = 20.6458e^2$
Volume = $(15 + 7\sqrt{5})e^3/4 = 7.6632e^3$
Dihedral angle = $116° 33' 54''$
Angle subtended by an edge = $41° 28'$
    (at center of dodecahedron)

If $e = 1$, then
    center of dodecahedron to
        center of face = 1.1135
        midedge   = 1.3090
        vertex   = 1.4013
    center of face to
        vertex   = 0.8507
        midedge   = 0.6882

V	x	y	z
1	0.0	0.8507	1.1135
2	0.8090	0.2629	1.1135
3	0.5	− 0.6882	1.1135
4	− 0.5	− 0.6882	1.1135
5	− 0.8090	0.2629	1.1135
6	0.0	1.3769	0.2605
7	1.3095	0.4255	0.2605
8	0.8093	− 1.1139	0.2605
9	− 0.8093	− 1.1139	0.2605
10	− 1.3095	0.4255	0.2605
11	0.8093	1.1139	− 0.2605
12	1.3095	− 0.4255	− 0.2605
13	0.0	− 1.3769	− 0.2605
14	− 1.3095	− 0.4255	− 0.2605
15	− 0.8093	1.1139	− 0.2605
16	0.5	0.6882	− 1.1135
17	0.8090	− 0.2629	− 1.1135
18	0.0	− 0.8507	− 1.1135
19	− 0.8090	− 0.2629	− 1.1135
20	− 0.5	0.6882	− 1.1135

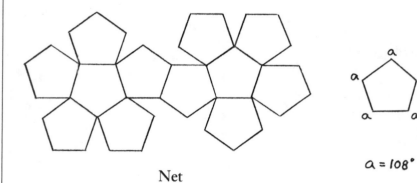

Net

a
a   a
a   a

$a = 108°$

Icosahedron

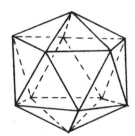

$V = 12$
$E = 30$
$F = 20$

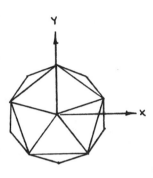

$e = 1$

Dual: dodecahedron
e = edge length
Area $= 5\sqrt{3}e^2 = 8.6603e^2$
Volume $= 2.1817e^3$
Dihedral angle $= 138°\,11'\,22''$
Angle subtended by an edge $= 63°\,26'$
   (at center of icosahedron)

If $e = 1$, then
  center of icosahedron to
     center of face $= 0.7558$
     midedge $= 0.8090$
     vertex $= 0.9511$
  center of face to
     vertex $= \sqrt{3}/3 = 0.5774$
     midedge $= \sqrt{3}/6 = 0.2887$

V	x	y	z
1	0.0	0.0	0.9512
2	0.0	0.8507	0.4253
3	0.8090	0.2629	0.4253
4	0.5	-0.6882	0.4253
5	-0.5	-0.6882	0.4253
6	-0.8090	0.2629	0.4253
7	0.5	0.6882	-0.4253
8	0.8090	-0.2626	-0.4253
9	0.0	-0.8507	-0.4253
10	-0.8090	-0.2629	-0.4253
11	-0.5	0.6882	-0.4253
12	0.0	0.0	-0.9512

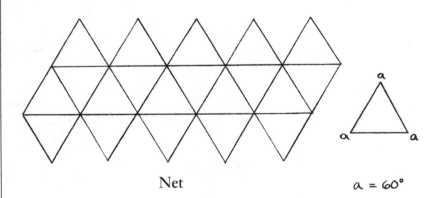

Net

$a = 60°$

Truncated Tetrahedron

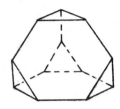

$V = 12$
$E = 18$
$F = 8$

Four hexagonal faces.
Four triangular faces.

Dual: triakis tetrahedron
e = edge length
Area $= 12.124e^2$
Volume $= 2.7102e^3$
Dihedral angle: 3–6: 109° 28′16″
               6–6: 70° 31′44″
Angle subtended by an edge $= 50° 28′$

If $e = 1$, then
  center of polyhedron to
      center of triangular face $= 5\sqrt{6}/12 = 1.0207$
      center of hexagonal face $= \sqrt{6}/4 = 0.6124$
      midedge $= 3\sqrt{2}/4 = 1.0607$
      vertex $= 1.1726$
  center of triangular face to
      vertex $= \sqrt{3}/3 = 0.5744$
      midedge $= \sqrt{3}/6 = 0.2887$
  center of hexagonal face to
      vertex $= 1$
      midedge $= \sqrt{3}/2 = 0.8660$

Net

$a = 120°$

Triakis Tetrahedron

$V = 8$
$E = 18$
$F = 12$

Only visible faces shown.

Four vertices are subtended by six edges; four are subtended by three edges.

Dual: truncated tetrahedron
Dihedral angle = 129° 31′ 16″

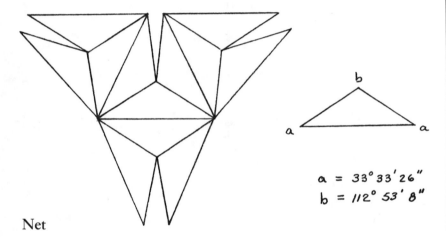

$a = 33° 33′ 26″$
$b = 112° 53′ 8″$

Net

Note: a concave version is possible.

Cuboctahedron

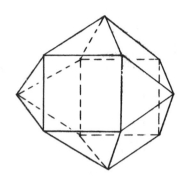

$V = 12$
$E = 24$
$F = 14$

Eight triangular faces.
Six square faces.

Dual: rhombic dodecahedron
e = edge length
Area = $9.4641e^2$
Volume = $2.3570e^3$
Dihedral angle = $125° 15' 51''$
Angle subtended by an edge = $60°$

If $e = 1$, then
  center of polyhedron to
      center of triangular face = $\sqrt{6}/3 = 0.8165$
      center of square face   = $\sqrt{2}/2 = 0.7071$
      midedge   = $\sqrt{3}/2 = 0.8660$
      vertex   = 1
  center of triangular face to
      vertex   = $\sqrt{3}/3 = 0.5774$
      midedge   = $\sqrt{3}/6 = 0.2887$
  Center of square face to
      vertex   = $\sqrt{2}/2 = 0.7071$
      midedge   = 0.5

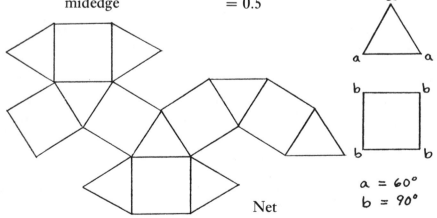

Net

$a = 60°$
$b = 90°$

Rhombic Dodecahedron

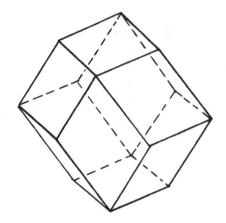

$V = 14$
$E = 24$
$F = 12$

Eight vertices with three edges.
Six vertices with four edges.

Dual: cuboctahedron
e = edge length
Area = $11.3137e^2$
Volume = $3.0792e^3$
Dihedral angle = $120°$
Angle subtended by an edge = $54° 44' 8''$

If $e = 1$, then
    center of polyhedron to
        center of face   = $\sqrt{6}/3 = 0.8165$
        tetraedge vertex = $2\sqrt{3}/3 = 1.1547$
        triedge vertex   = 1
    center of face to
        tetraedge vertex = $\sqrt{6}/3 = 0.8165$
        triedge vertex   = $\sqrt{3}/3 = 0.5774$

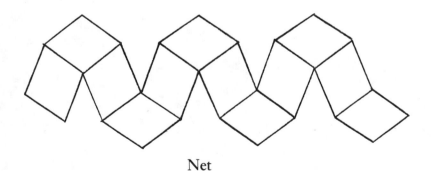

Net

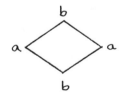

$a = 70° 31' 44''$
$b = 109° 28' 16''$

Truncated Cube

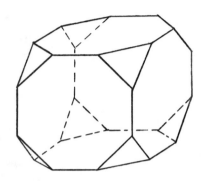

$V = 24$
$E = 36$
$F = 14$

24 3–8 edges.
12 8–8 edges.

Eight triangular faces.
Six octagonal faces.

Dual: Triakis octahedron
e = edge length
Area = $32.4320e^2$
Volume = $13.5988e^3$
Dihedral angle: 3–8: 125° 15′ 51″
                  8–8: 90°
Angle subtended by an edge = 32° 39′

If $e = 1$, then
   center of polyhedron to
      center of triangular face = 1.6825
      center of octagonal face = 1.2071
      midedge   = 1.7071
      vertex   = 1.7787
   center of triangular face to
      vertex   = 0.5774
      midedge   = 0.2887
   center of octagonal face to
      vertex   = 1.3066
      midedge   = 1.2071

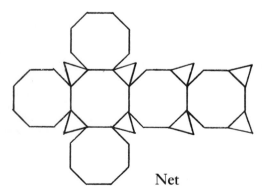

Net

$a = 135°$

$b = 60°$

Triakis Octahedron

$V = 14$
$E = 36$
$F = 24$

Dual: truncated cube
Dihedral angle $= 147°\,21'$

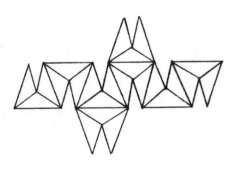

Net

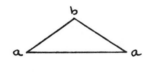

$a = 31°\,22'\,21''$
$b = 117°\,15'\,18''$

Truncated Octahedron

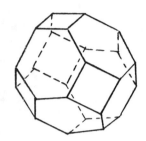

$V = 24$
$E = 36$
$F = 14$

Dual: tetrakis hexahedron
e = edge length
Area = $26.7846e^2$
Volume = $11.3137e^3$
Dihedral angle: 4–6: 125° 15′ 51″
                6–6: 109° 28′ 16″
Arc subtended by an edge = 36° 52′

If $e = 1$, then
  center of polyhedron to
        center of square face   = $\sqrt{2} = 1.4142$
        center of hexagonal face = $\sqrt{6}/2 = 1.2247$
        midedge   = 1.5
        vertex   = $\sqrt{10}/2 = 1.5811$
  center of square face to
        vertex   = $\sqrt{2}/2 = 0.7071$
        midedge   = 0.5
  center of hexagonal face to
        vertex   = 1
        midedge   = $\sqrt{3}/2 = 0.8660$

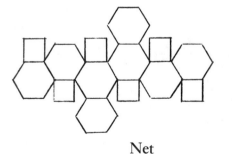

Net

$a = 120°$ $b = 90°$

Tetrakis Hexahedron

$V = 14$
$E = 36$
$F = 24$

Dual: truncated octahedron
Dihedral angle $= 143° 7' 48''$

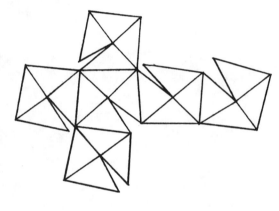

Net

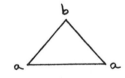

$a = 48° 11' 30''$
$b = 83° 37'$

Small Rhombicuboctahedron

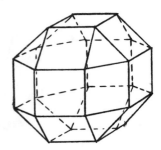

$V = 24$
$E = 48$
$F = 26$

Dual: trapezoidal icositetrahedron
e = edge length
Area $= 21.4641e^2$
Volume $= 8.7133e^3$
Dihedral angle: 3–4: $144°\,44'\,8''$
                          4–4: $135°$
Angle subtended by an edge $= 41°\,53'$

If $e = 1$, then
    center of polyhedron to
        center of triangular face $= 1.2743$
        center of square face $= 1.2071$
        midedge $= 1.3065$
        vertex $= 1.3989$
    center of triangular face to
        vertex $= 0.5774$
        midedge $= 0.2887$
    center of square face to
        vertex $= 0.7071$
        midedge $= 0.5$

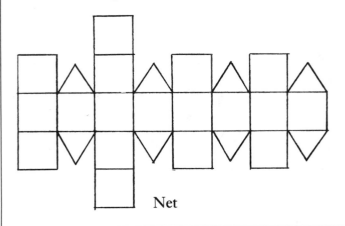

Net

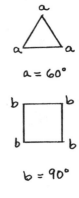

$a = 60°$

$b = 90°$

Trapezoidal Icositetrahedron

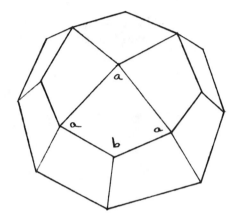

$V = 26$
$E = 48$
$F = 24$

$a = 81° 34' 44''$
$b = 115° 15' 48''$

Dual: small rhombicuboctahedron
Dihedral angle: $138° 6' 34''$

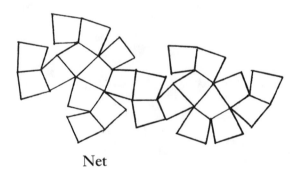

Net

"Jeremiah was a bullfrog . . . a good friend of mine . . . and I never understood a single word he said."

Hoyt Axton
Joy to the World

Great Rhombicuboctahedron

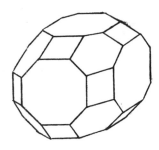

$V = 48$
$E = 72$
$F = 26$

Twelve square faces
Eight hexagonal faces
Six octagonal faces

Dual: hexakis octahedron
e = edge length
Area = $61.7551e^2$
Volume = $41.7942e^3$
Dihedral angle: 4–6: $144° 44' 8''$
　　　　　　　 4–8: $135°$
　　　　　　　 6–8: $125° 15' 1''$
Angle subtended by an edge $24° 55'$

If $e = 1$, then
　　center of polyhedron to
　　　　center of square face　　 = 2.2071
　　　　center of hexagonal face = 2.0908
　　　　center of octagonal face = 1.9142
　　　　midedge　　　　　　　　 = 2.2630
　　　　vertex　　　　　　　　　 = 2.3176
　　center of square face to
　　　　vertex　　　　　　　　　 = 0.7071
　　　　midedge　　　　　　　　 = 0.5
　　center of hexagonal face to
　　　　vertex　　　　　　　　　 = 1
　　　　midedge　　　　　　　　 = 0.8660
　　center of octagonal face to
　　　　vertex　　　　　　　　　 = 1.3066
　　　　midedge　　　　　　　　 = 1.2071

Rotational Symmetry Groups

The five Platonic and thirteen Archimedean semiregular polyhedra may be classified into one of three rotational symmetry families or groups: 3:2, 4:3:2, or 5:3:2.

The icosahedron belongs to the 5:3:2 rotational symmetry group.

The 3:2 symmetry group: the tetrahedron is the only polyhedron in this group.

The 4:3:2 symmetry group: the octahedron and its dual, the cube, are the principal members of this group.

The 5:3:2 symmetry group: the icosahedron and its dual, the dodecahedron, are the principal members of this group.

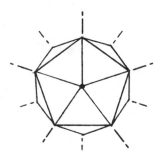

The fivefold axes, each passing through one of six pairs of vertices. On a fivefold axis there are five symmetry rotations.

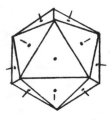

The threefold axes, each passing through the centers of one of ten pairs of faces. On a threefold axis there are three symmetry rotations.

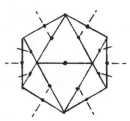

The twofold axes, each passing through the centers of one of fifteen pairs of opposite edges. On a twofold axis there are two symmetry rotations.

Euler's Formula for Simple Polyhedra

There is a mathematical relationship between the number of vertices (V), edges (E), and faces (F) of a simple polyhedron, called **Euler's Formula**. It is

$$V - E + F = 2 \qquad (6.1)$$

A simple polyhedron is one that can be continuously deformed into a sphere, assuming that its faces are treated as rubber sheets. Other conditions are:

1. All faces are bounded by a single ring of edges, and there are no holes in the faces.
2. The polyhedron has no holes through it.
3. Each edge adjoins exactly two faces and is terminated by a vertex at each end.
4. At least three edges meet at each vertex.

Pronounced "oiler."

Poincaré generalized this to n-dimensional space:

$$N_0 - N_1 + N_2 - \cdots = 1 - (-1)^n$$

where N_i is the number of i-dimension elements in the polytope.

Euler's formula provides proof that there are only five regular polyhedra, or Platonic solids. Every face of a regular polyhedra has the same number of edges, h; every vertex has the same number of edges radiating from it, k. Since every edge has two vertices and belongs to exactly two faces, it follows that $hF = 2E = kV$. Substituting into (6.1):

$$\frac{1}{E} = \frac{1}{h} + \frac{1}{k} - \frac{1}{2}$$

Assume $h, k \geq 3$. Both h and k cannot be larger than three. If $h = 3$, then $3 \leq k \leq 5$, and if $k = 3$, then $3 \leq h \leq 5$. Therefore, $(h,k,E) = (3,3,6), (4,3,12), (3,4,12), (5,3,30),$ and $(3,5,30)$, which describe the five regular polyhedra. QED.

$h, k > 3$ implies $\dfrac{1}{E} \leq 0$, which is impossible.

"The mathematician's patterns, like the painter's or poet's, must be beautiful . . . ."

G.H. Hardy

Euler's Formula for Nonsimple Polyhedra

If a polyhedron is subdivided into C polyhedral cells, then the vertices, edges, faces, and cells are related by

$$V - E + F - C = 1 \qquad (6.2)$$

This is demonstrated by adding a vertex $\mathbf{p}_9$ to the interior of a cube and joining it with edges to each of the other eight vertices, creating a six-celled polyhedron with $V = 9$, $E = 20$, $F = 18$, and $C = 6$.

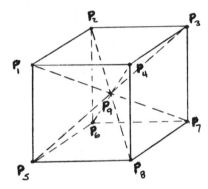

If a polyhedron has one or more holes (H) in its faces, passages (P) through it, and/or consists of disjoint bodies (B), then

$$V - E + F - H + 2P = 2B \qquad (6.3)$$

This is demonstrated by a cube with a passage through it: $V = 16$, $E = 32$, $F = 16$, $H = 0$, $P = 1$, and $B = 1$.

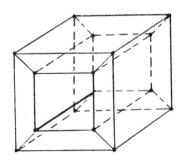

A cell is, itself, a closed polyhedron.

Here are the 18 faces of the example. The V_i correspond to the $\mathbf{p}_i$.

F_1: V_1, V_2, V_3, V_4
F_2: V_5, V_6, V_7, V_8
F_3: V_1, V_4, V_8, V_5
F_4: V_4, V_3, V_7, V_8
F_5: V_3, V_2, V_6, V_7
F_6: V_2, V_1, V_5, V_6
F_7: V_1, V_4, V_9
F_8: V_4, V_3, V_9
F_9: V_3, V_2, V_9
F_{10}: V_2, V_1, V_9
F_{11}: V_5, V_8, V_9
F_{12}: V_8, V_7, V_9
F_{13}: V_7, V_6, V_9
F_{14}: V_6, V_5, V_9
F_{15}: V_1, V_5, V_9
F_{16}: V_4, V_8, V_9
F_{17}: V_3, V_7, V_9
F_{18}: V_2, V_6, V_9

Alternatively: define a connectivity number n. For a sphere and all topologically equivalent shapes $n = 0$. For toruslike shapes $n = 2$. For figure-eightlike shapes $n = 4$, etc. Then

$$V - E + F = 2 - n$$

Convex Hull of a Polyhedron

The convex hull of a polyhedron is analogous to the convex hull of a polygon. The convex hull of a convex polyhedron is identical to the polyhedron itself. The convex hull of a concave polyhedron is formed by "wrapping" the concave polyhedron in a rubber sheet, producing an enveloping convex polyhedron. A convex hull is the minimum convex polyhedron that will enclose the concave polyhedron.

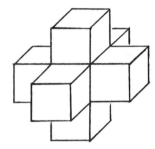 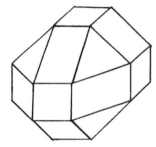

Kinds of Geometry

- Demonstrative, synthetic: Formal, classical geometry; from a set of axioms many theorems are deduced and proved.
- Plane geometry: Properties and relationships of 2-D figures.
- Solid geometry: Properties and relationships of 3-D figures.
- Trigonometry: Properties of triangles in a plane.
- Spherical trigonometry: Properties of triangles on a spherical surface.
- Analytic geometry: Employs a coordinate system, thus allowing the application of algebra and analysis to the study of geometry.
- Metric geometry: Studies the properties of figures that are unchanged when the figures are subjected to rigid motions.
- Differential geometry: Studies properties of figures that depend only on the neighborhood of one of its elements.
- Descriptive geometry: Studies projections, shadow, intersections, properties of surfaces; forms the basis for mechanical drawing.
- Topology: Studies the properties of geometric objects that are invariant under certain deforming transformations.
- Noneuclidean geometry: study of curved metric spaces; generalization of euclidean geometry by negating the parallel postulate.
- Projective geometry: Properties of figures invariant under a group of projective transformations.
- Others include abstract geometry, group theory, computational geometry.

Polyhedron Face Planarity Test

How valid are the data defining a polyhedron? One of the first questions to ask is: Do the vertices surrounding each face lie in a common plane? To test this, use any three of the set of vertex points surrounding the face to define a plane containing the face. Then all other vertex points surrounding the face must satisfy this equation.

Other tests verify connectivity and topology. See **Euler's Formula**.

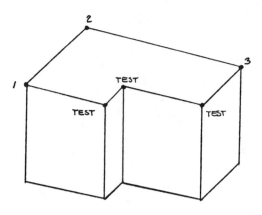

Connectivity Matrix

A two-dimensional list or table, called a **connectivity matrix**, is a useful way to describe how vertices are connected by edges to form a polyhedron. A connectivity matrix is square, with as many rows and columns as there are vertices. If element $a_{ij} = 1$, then vertices i and j are connected by an edge. If element $a_{ij} = 0$, then vertices i and j are not connected. A connectivity matrix is symmetric about the main diagonal, which is comprised of all zeros.

Example

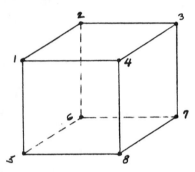

$$C = \begin{bmatrix} 0 & 1 & 0 & 1 & 1 & 0 & 0 & 0 \\ 1 & 0 & 1 & 0 & 0 & 1 & 0 & 0 \\ 0 & 1 & 0 & 1 & 0 & 0 & 1 & 0 \\ 1 & 0 & 1 & 0 & 0 & 0 & 0 & 1 \\ 1 & 0 & 0 & 0 & 0 & 1 & 0 & 1 \\ 0 & 1 & 0 & 0 & 1 & 0 & 1 & 0 \\ 0 & 0 & 1 & 0 & 0 & 1 & 0 & 1 \\ 0 & 0 & 0 & 1 & 1 & 0 & 1 & 0 \end{bmatrix}$$

Model Data Structure

Here is an example of one form of model data structure for a polyhedron. The polyhedron is a cube in this instance.

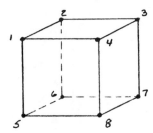

Vertex	Coordinates	Face	Face Plane Coefficients (A,B,C,D)	
v_1	$(1,1,2)$	f_1	$(-1,0,0,1)$	
v_2	$(1,2,2)$	f_2	$(1,0,0,-2)$	
v_3	$(2,2,2)$	f_3	$(0,-1,0,1)$	
v_4	$(2,1,2)$	f_4	$(0,1,0,-2)$	Geometry
v_5	$(1,1,1)$	f_5	$(0,0,-1,1)$	
v_6	$(1,2,1)$	f_6	$(0,0,1,-2)$	
v_7	$(2,2,1)$			
v_8	$(2,1,1)$			

Faces
(Vertices listed in ccw order as viewed from outside cube)

Edges

Face	Vertices	Edge		Edge		
f_1	(v_1,v_2,v_6,v_5)	e_1	(v_1,v_2)	e_7	(v_7,v_8)	
f_2	(v_3,v_4,v_8,v_9)	e_2	(v_2,v_3)	e_8	(v_8,v_5)	
f_3	(v_5,v_8,v_4,v_1)	e_3	(v_3,v_4)	e_9	(v_1,v_5)	
f_4	(v_2,v_3,v_7,v_6)	e_4	(v_4,v_1)	e_{10}	(v_2,v_6)	Connectivity (topology)
f_5	(v_5,v_6,v_7,v_8)	e_5	(v_5,v_6)	e_{11}	(v_3,v_7)	
f_6	(v_4,v_3,v_2,v_1)	e_6	(v_6,v_7)	e_{12}	(v_4,v_8)	

Polyhedra as Half-Spaces

A convex polyhedron with n faces can be defined by the intersection of n half-spaces. The plane of each face defines a half-space. The intersection of the set of all such half-spaces defines the polyhedron P.

$$P = \bigcap_{i=1}^{n} f_i(x,y,z)$$

$$\bigcap_{i=1}^{n} f_i = f_1 \cap f_2 \cap f_3 \cap \cdots \cap f_n$$

Example

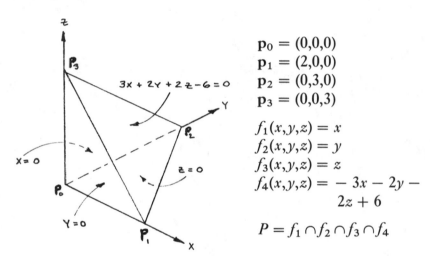

$$\mathbf{p}_0 = (0,0,0)$$
$$\mathbf{p}_1 = (2,0,0)$$
$$\mathbf{p}_2 = (0,3,0)$$
$$\mathbf{p}_3 = (0,0,3)$$

$$f_1(x,y,z) = x$$
$$f_2(x,y,z) = y$$
$$f_3(x,y,z) = z$$
$$f_4(x,y,z) = -3x - 2y - 2z + 6$$

$$P = f_1 \cap f_2 \cap f_3 \cap f_4$$

The sign of f_4 is adjusted so that $f_4 > 0$ is inside polyhedron.

Given a test point $\mathbf{p}_T = (\frac{1}{3},1,1)$ classify it with respect to the polyhedron:

$$f_1(\tfrac{1}{3},1,1) = \tfrac{1}{3} \qquad f_3(\tfrac{1}{3},1,1) = 1$$
$$f_2(\tfrac{1}{3},1,1) = 1 \qquad f_4(\tfrac{1}{3},1,1) = 1$$

Since the f_i evaluated at $\mathbf{p}_T$ are all positive, $\mathbf{p}_T$ is inside the polygon.

Parametric Equations

A parametric curve is one whose defining equations are given in terms of a simple, common, independent variable called the parametric variable. A curve segment is a point-bounded collection of points whose coordinates are given by continuous, one-parameter, single-valued functions of the form

$$x = x(u) \qquad y = y(u) \qquad z = z(u)$$

The parametric variable u is constrained to the interval $u \in [0,1]$. The positive sense on the curve is the direction in which u increases.

Treat the coordinates of any point on a parametric curve as the components of a vector $\mathbf{p}(u)$. Thus

$$\mathbf{p}(u) = [x(u) \ \ y(u) \ \ z(u)]$$

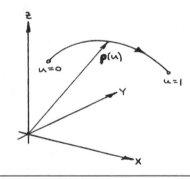

Advantages of the parametric form:

- Separation of variables
- Treat each variable alike
- More degrees of freedom/control
- Transform parametric equations directly
- Handles infinite slope without computational breakdown
- Easy to express as vectors
- Amenable to plotting and digitizing
- Easy dimensional extension or contraction
- Inherently bounded when parametric variable is constrained to a specified interval

For n dimensions:

$$\mathbf{p}(u) = [x_1(u) \ x_2(u) \ \cdots \ x_n(u)]$$

The positive sense on a curve defined by parametric equations is, by convention, the sense in which the parameter increases.

Examples

$$x = a + lu \qquad y = b + mu \qquad z = c + nu$$

$$x = u \qquad y = u^2 \qquad z = u^3$$

$$x = a \cos u \qquad y = a \sin u \qquad z = bu$$

A straight line: $\mathbf{p}(0) = [a \ \ b \ \ c]$, $\mathbf{p}(1) = [(a + l) \ \ (b + m) \ \ (c + n)]$.

Cubical parabola.

Circular helix.

"There is no branch of mathematics, however abstract, which may not some day be applied to phenomena of the real world."

Nicolai Ivanovitch Lobachevsky

Parametric Derivative

Differentiating $\mathbf{p}(u)$ yields the tangent vector $\mathbf{p}^u(u)$:

$$\mathbf{p}^u = \frac{d\mathbf{p}(u)}{au}$$

The vector components of $\mathbf{p}^u(u)$ are

$$x^u = \frac{dx(u)}{du} \qquad y^u = \frac{dy(u)}{du} \qquad z^u = \frac{dz(u)}{du}$$

These are parametric derivatives. They are related to the ordinary Cartesian derivatives as follows:

$$\frac{dy}{dx} = \frac{dy(u)}{du} \Bigg/ \frac{dx(u)}{du} = \frac{y^u}{x^u}$$

similarly for dy/dz and dz/dx.

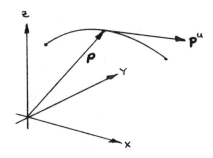

Examples

1. $\mathbf{p}(u) = [u \quad u^2 \quad u^3]$
    $\mathbf{p}^u(u) = [1 \quad 2u \quad 3u^2]$

2. $\mathbf{p}(u) = [a \cos u \quad a \sin u \quad bu]$
    $\mathbf{p}^u(u) = [-a \sin u \quad a \cos u \quad b]$

Parametric Cubic (PC) Curve: Algebraic Form

The algebraic form of a parametric cubic (PC) curve is given by three polynomials

$$
\begin{aligned}
x(u) &= a_x u^3 + b_x u^2 + c_x u + d_x \\
y(u) &= a_y u^3 + b_y u^2 + c_y u + d_y \\
z(u) &= a_z u^3 + b_z u^2 + c_z u + d_z
\end{aligned}
\qquad (7.1)
$$

or more compactly as a vector equation

$$
\mathbf{p}(u) = \mathbf{a}u^3 + \mathbf{b}u^2 + \mathbf{c}u + \mathbf{d} \qquad (7.2)
$$

$$
\mathbf{p}(u) = \sum_{i=0}^{3} \mathbf{a}_i u^i
$$

where $u \in [0,1]$.

Write Eq. (7.2) as the product of two matrices

$$
\mathbf{p} = [u^3 \ \ u^2 \ \ u \ \ 1][\mathbf{a} \ \ \mathbf{b} \ \ \mathbf{c} \ \ \mathbf{d}]^T
$$

and let $\mathbf{U} = [u^3 \ \ u^2 \ \ u \ \ 1]$ and $\mathbf{A} = [a \ \ b \ \ c \ \ d]^T$, then

$$
\mathbf{p} = \mathbf{UA} \qquad (7.3)
$$

For brevity drop the functional notation $\mathbf{p}(u)$ in favor of $\mathbf{p}$.

The set of 12 constant algebraic coefficients, the elements of the matrix $\mathbf{A}$, determines a unique PC curve—its size, shape, and position in space. Two curves of the same size and shape have different algebraic coefficients if they occupy different positions in space.

Example

$$
\begin{aligned}
x &= 2u^3 + 1 \\
y &= u^3 + u^2 \qquad u \in [0,1] \\
z &= 3u - 2
\end{aligned}
$$

$$
\begin{aligned}
\mathbf{p}(0) &= [1 \ \ 0 \ -2] \\
\mathbf{p}(0.5) &= [1.25 \ \ 0.375 \ -0.5] \\
\mathbf{p}(0.8) &= [2.024 \ \ 1.152 \ \ 0.4] \\
\mathbf{p}(1) &= [3 \ \ 2 \ \ 1]
\end{aligned}
$$

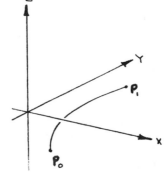

Let $\mathbf{p}(0) = \mathbf{p}_0$, $\mathbf{p}(1) = \mathbf{p}_1$.

Parametric Cubic (PC) Curve: Geometric Form

Algebraic coefficients are not always the most convenient way of controlling the shape of a curve, nor do they contribute much to an intuitive sense of a curve. The geometric form offers a practical alternative, defining a PC curve in terms of conditions at its end points, or boundaries. These boundary conditions are specified as four vectors: the end points themselves, $\mathbf{p}_0$ and $\mathbf{p}_1$, and the tangent vectors at these points, $\mathbf{p}_0^u$ and $\mathbf{p}_1^u$. Since each of these four vectors has three components, there are a total of 12 geometric coefficients. From (7.2),

$$\mathbf{p}_0 = \mathbf{d} \qquad \mathbf{p}_1 = \mathbf{a} + \mathbf{b} + \mathbf{c} + \mathbf{d}$$
$$\mathbf{p}_0^u = \mathbf{c} \qquad \mathbf{p}_1^u = 3\mathbf{a} + 2\mathbf{b} + \mathbf{c}$$

Solve this set of equations for $\mathbf{a}$, $\mathbf{b}$, $\mathbf{c}$, $\mathbf{d}$.

$$\mathbf{a} = 2\mathbf{p}_0 - 2\mathbf{p}_1 + \mathbf{p}_0^u + \mathbf{p}_1^u \qquad \mathbf{c} = \mathbf{p}_0^u$$
$$\mathbf{b} = -3\mathbf{p}_0 + 3\mathbf{p}_1 - 2\mathbf{p}_0^u - \mathbf{p}_1^u \qquad \mathbf{d} = \mathbf{p}_0$$

Substitute these expressions into (7.2) and rearrange, thus:

$$\mathbf{p} = (2u^3 - 3u^2 + 1)\mathbf{p}_0 + (-2u^3 + 3u^2)\mathbf{p}_1$$
$$+ (u^3 - 2u^2 + u)\mathbf{p}_0^u + (u^3 - u^2)\mathbf{p}_1^u$$

Let $\quad F_1 = (2u^3 - 3u^2 + 1)$, $F_2 = (-2u^3 + 3u^2)$,
$\quad F_3 = (u^3 - 2u^2 + u)$, $F_4 = (u^3 - u^2)$, then

$$\mathbf{p} = F_1\mathbf{p}_0 + F_2\mathbf{p}_1 + F_3\mathbf{p}_0^u + F_4\mathbf{p}_1^u$$

Let $\mathbf{F} = [F_1 \ F_2 \ F_3 \ F_4]$ and $\mathbf{B} = [\mathbf{p}_0 \ \mathbf{p}_1 \ \mathbf{p}_0^u \ \mathbf{p}_1^u]^T$, then

$$\mathbf{p} = \mathbf{FB} \qquad\qquad (7.4)$$

Curves defined by interpolating points and tangents at those points are often called Hermitian curves. Hermité was a 19th century French mathematician who did significant work in cubic and quintic polynomials.

$$\mathbf{p}^u = 3\mathbf{a}u^2 + 2\mathbf{b}u + \mathbf{c}$$

F_1, F_2, F_3, F_4 are called blending functions, or Hermité polynomial basis functions.

$\mathbf{B}$ is called the matrix of geometric coefficients.

$\mathbf{F}$ is the blending function matrix.

Implicit equations of a curve: $f(x,y) = 0$, 2-D space
$$f(x,y,z) = 0 \Big\} \text{ 3-D space, two}$$
$$g(x,y,z) = 0 \Big\} \text{ simultaneous equations}$$

Explicit equations of a curve: $y = f(x)$, 2-D space
$$y = f(x) \Big\} \text{ 3-D space, two}$$
$$z = g(x) \Big\} \text{ simultaneous equations}$$

Parametric Cubic (PC) Curves:
Universal Transformation Matrix ·

There is a convenient mathematical relationship between the algebraic and geometric forms of a PC curve. More precisely, there is a matrix transformation that allows **B** to be computed given **A**, and vice versa. The blending function matrix **F** can be written as the product of two matrices:

F = UM

U, F, and M are constant for all PC curves.

where

$$\mathbf{M} = \begin{bmatrix} 2 & -2 & 1 & 1 \\ -3 & 3 & -2 & -1 \\ 0 & 0 & 1 & 0 \\ 1 & 0 & 0 & 0 \end{bmatrix} \qquad (7.5)$$

M is called the universal transformation matrix.
   Rewrite (7.4) as

p = UMB   (7.6)

Since from (7.3) **p = UA**, obtain

A = MB

and conversely

B = M⁻¹A

where

$$\mathbf{M}^{-1} = \begin{bmatrix} 0 & 0 & 0 & 1 \\ 1 & 1 & 1 & 1 \\ 0 & 0 & 1 & 0 \\ 3 & 2 & 1 & 0 \end{bmatrix} \qquad (7.7)$$

Tangent Vectors

Specifying the end-points and slopes (or direction cosines) of a PC curve accounts for 10 of the 12 degrees of freedom associated with both the algebraic and geometric coefficients. Six are supplied by the two sets of end-point coordinates, and four by the slopes or direction cosines of the tangent vectors at each end. Remember, there are only two independent direction cosines associated with any tangent line; since $\cos^2 \alpha + \cos^2 \beta + \cos^2 \gamma = 1$, the third direction cosine is determined. The magnitudes of the tangent vectors supply the additional two degrees of freedom.

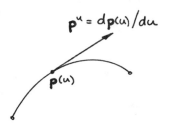

Define a unit tangent vector $\mathbf{t}$ by

$$\mathbf{t} = \mathbf{p}^u / |\mathbf{p}^u|$$

Then

$$|\mathbf{t}| = \sqrt{t_x^2 + t_y^2 + t_z^2} = 1$$

Clearly, t_x, t_y, t_z are the direction cosines. If $k = |\mathbf{p}^u|$, then

$$\mathbf{p}^u = k\mathbf{t}$$

or $\mathbf{p}_0^u = k_0 \mathbf{t}_0$ and $\mathbf{p}_1^u = k_1 \mathbf{t}_1$. $\mathbf{B}$ then is expressed as

$$\mathbf{B} = [\mathbf{p}_0 \quad \mathbf{p}_1 \quad k_0 \mathbf{t}_0 \quad k_1 \mathbf{t}_1]^T$$

Many different curves may be created, all of which have the same end points and slopes, yet have entirely different internal shapes, depending on the magnitudes of k_0 and k_1.

Blending Functions: Parametric Cubic (PC) Curves

For a parametric cubic curve, the blending functions "blend" the contributions of the end points and tangent vectors to produce the points that lie along the curve. Thus

$$\mathbf{p} = F_1\mathbf{p}_0 + F_2\mathbf{p}_1 + F_3\mathbf{p}_0^u + F_4\mathbf{p}_1^u \qquad (7.8)$$

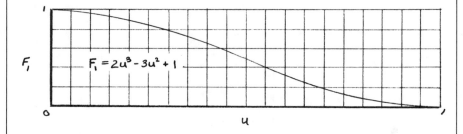

$$F_1 = 2u^3 - 3u^2 + 1$$

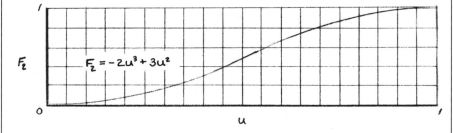

$$F_2 = -2u^3 + 3u^2$$

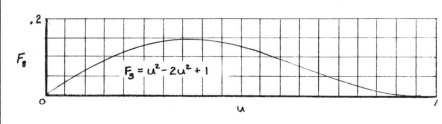

$$F_3 = u^2 - 2u^2 + 1$$

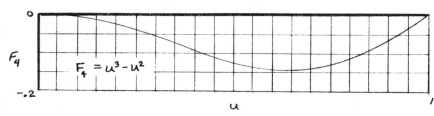

$$F_4 = u^3 - u^2$$

Blending functions are also called polynomial basis functions.

$$\mathbf{p} = \mathbf{FB}$$

Here is a useful observation:
$$\mathbf{p}(0.5) = (\mathbf{p}_0 + \mathbf{p}_1)/2 + (\mathbf{p}_0^u - \mathbf{p}_1^u)/8$$

Note the symmetry between pairs of these curves: F_1 and F_2, F_3 and F_4.

For a given polynomial degree, different blending function schemes are interchangeable through a matrix transformation. Let $\mathbf{B}_F$ represent a matrix of control points defining a curve $\mathbf{p}(u) = \mathbf{UM}_F\mathbf{B}_F$ using blending functions $\mathbf{F} = \mathbf{UM}_F$. Then for another system of blending functions $\mathbf{G} = \mathbf{UM}_G$, find a set of control points $\mathbf{B}_G$ that reproduces the same curve, $\mathbf{p}(u)$. This means that

$$\mathbf{UM}_G\mathbf{B}_G = \mathbf{UM}_F\mathbf{B}_F$$

and thus

$$\mathbf{B}_G = \mathbf{M}_G^{-1}\mathbf{M}_F\mathbf{B}_F$$

Similar blending functions are generated for other odd-degree Hermitian polynomials. Even-degree polynomial basis functions require special treatment, since they have an odd number of degrees of freedom prohibiting establishing symmetrical conditions at $u = 0$ and $u = 1$, and are seldom used.

Blending Functions: Tangent Vectors

There is a set of blending functions $\mathbf{F}^u = [F_1^u \; F_2^u \; F_3^u \; F_4^u]$ that produces the tangent vector $\mathbf{p}^u$ at any point $\mathbf{p}$ on a PC curve by blending the contributions of the end points and tangent vectors. Thus

$$\mathbf{p}^u = F_1^u \mathbf{p}_0 + F_2^u \mathbf{P}_1 + F_3^u \mathbf{p}_0^u + F_4^u \mathbf{p}_1^u \qquad (7.9)$$

$\mathbf{F}^u = d\mathbf{F}(u)/du$

$\mathbf{p}^u = \mathbf{F}^u \mathbf{B}$

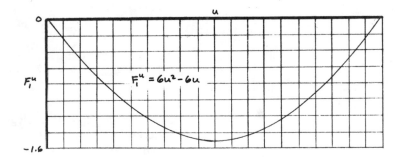

$F_1^u = 6u^2 - 6u$

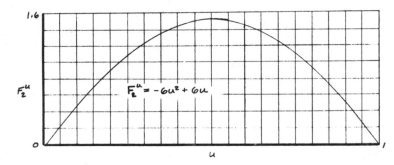

$F_2^u = -6u^2 + 6u$

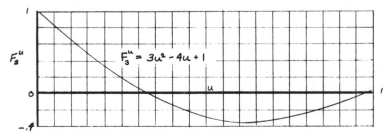

$F_3^u = 3u^2 - 4u + 1$

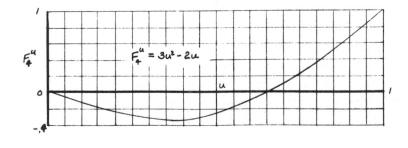

$F_4^u = 3u^2 - 2u$

Reparametrization of Parametric Cubic (PC) Curves

Reparametrization of a curve produces a change in the parametric interval so that neither the shape nor the position of the curve is changed. A function $v = f(u)$ describes the precise way this interval is changed.

For example, sometimes it is necessary to reverse the direction of parametrization (this is the simplest form of reparametrization); here $v = 1 - u$. Let $[\mathbf{q}_0 \quad \mathbf{q}_1 \quad \mathbf{q}_0^v \quad \mathbf{q}_1^v]$ define the geometric coefficients of the reparametrized curve, then

$$\mathbf{q}_0 = \mathbf{p}_1$$

$$\mathbf{q}_1 = \mathbf{p}_0$$

$$\mathbf{q}_0^v = -\mathbf{p}_1^u$$

$$\mathbf{q}_1^v = -\mathbf{p}_0^u$$

Reversing the direction of parametrization.

For a more general reparametrization use $v = au + b$, where $dv = a\,du$. Then, since $v_i = au_i + b$ and $v_j = au_j + b$, determine a and b and subsequently

$$\mathbf{q}^v = \frac{u_j - u_i}{v_j - v_i} \mathbf{p}^u \qquad (7.10)$$

A linear relationship is required to preserve the cubic form of the parametric equations.

Thus

$$\mathbf{q}_i = \mathbf{p}_i$$

$$\mathbf{q}_j = \mathbf{p}_j$$

$$\mathbf{q}_i^v = \frac{u_j - u_i}{v_j - v_i} \mathbf{p}_i^u$$

$$\mathbf{q}_j^v = \frac{u_j - u_i}{v_j - v_i} \mathbf{p}_j^u$$

If u_i and u_j are successive integers, then $u_j - u_i = 1$, and similarly for v_j and v_i. Then

$$\mathbf{q}^v = \mathbf{p}^u$$

Truncating a Parametric Cubic (PC) Curve

It is often necessary to investigate, or retain in a model, only a portion of a PC curve. This is expedited by transforming the parametric variable in such a way that the new parametric interval also runs from zero to one.

Given a PC curve to be truncated as shown below, determine the geometric coefficients $\mathbf{q}$ of the new segment assuming it spans the unit interval $v \in [0,1]$ on the new parametric variable v.

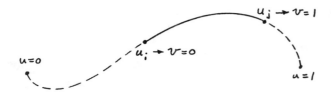

Let $v = au + b$, then

$$\mathbf{q}_0 = \mathbf{p}_i$$
$$\mathbf{q}_1 = \mathbf{p}_j$$
$$\mathbf{q}_0^v = (u_j - u_i)\mathbf{p}_i^u$$
$$\mathbf{q}_1^v = (u_j - u_i)\mathbf{p}_j^u$$

If a curve is divided into n segments corresponding to equal intervals on the parametric variable, then the matrix of geometric coefficients of the ith segment is

$$\mathbf{B}_i = [\mathbf{p}_{(i-1)/n} \ \ \mathbf{p}_{i/n} \ \ (1/n)\mathbf{p}_{(i-1)/n} \ \ (1/n)\mathbf{p}_{i/n}^u]^T \qquad (7.11)$$

General Parametric Transformation

There is a general parametric transformation that applies to any polynomial or rational polynomial parametric curve. A linear relationship between initial and transformed parametric variables is required to preserve the degree of the polynomial. Let $v = au + b$, then for $v_i = 0$ and $v_j = 1$

$$u = u_i + (u_j - u_i)v$$

or

$$u = u_i + \Delta u_i v$$

where

$$\Delta u_i = u_j - u_i$$

The transformations are

$$u^n = \sum_{k=0}^{n} {}^nC_k u_i^k (\Delta u_i v)^{n-k}$$

extract from this a transformation matrix $\mathbf{T}$ so that

$$\mathbf{U} = \mathbf{VT} \tag{7.12}$$

If $v_i \neq 0$ and/or $v_i \neq 1$, then

$$u = \left(\frac{u_i v_j - u_j v_i}{v_j - v_i} \right) + \left(\frac{u_j - u_i}{v_j - v_i} \right) v$$

Apply the binomial theorem to

$$u = u_i + \Delta u_i v$$

${}^nC_k$ is the binomial coefficient:

$${}^nC_k = \frac{n!}{k!(n-k)!}$$

Example

For a PC curve $\mathbf{p} = \mathbf{UMB}$, so that imposing a parametric transformation as defined above

$$\mathbf{p} = \mathbf{VTMB} = \mathbf{VMB^*}$$
$$\mathbf{TMB} = \mathbf{MB^*}$$
$$\mathbf{B^*} = \mathbf{M^{-1}TMB}$$

where

$$\mathbf{U} = [u^3 \ u^2 \ u \ 1]$$
$$\mathbf{V} = [v^3 \ v^2 \ v \ 1]$$

$$\mathbf{T} = \begin{bmatrix} \Delta u_i^3 & 0 & 0 & 0 \\ 3u_i \Delta u_i^2 & \Delta u_i^2 & 0 & 0 \\ 3u_i^2 \Delta u_i & 2u_i \Delta u_i & \Delta u_i & 0 \\ u_i^3 & u_i^2 & u_i & 1 \end{bmatrix}$$

$\mathbf{B^*}$ = matrix of transformed geometric coefficients.

For a PC curve:

$$\mathbf{M} = \begin{bmatrix} 2 & -2 & 1 & 1 \\ -3 & 3 & -2 & -1 \\ 0 & 0 & 1 & 0 \\ 1 & 0 & 0 & 0 \end{bmatrix}$$

Parametric Cubic (PC) Curve: Four-Point Form

An alternative to defining a PC curve by specifying the end points and tangent vectors is to specify four points through which the curve must pass. Usually these points are the two endpoints p_1 and p_4 and two intermediate points p_2 and p_3. If the points are about equally distributed along the curve segment, then $u_1 = 0$, $u_2 = 1/3$, $u_3 = 2/3$, and $u_4 = 1$.

Let $\mathbf{P} = [p_1 \ p_2 \ p_3 \ p_4]^T$ and $\mathbf{B} = \mathbf{KP}$. Then, since $p = \mathbf{UMB}$, obtain

$$p = \mathbf{UMKP} \qquad (7.13)$$

$$\mathbf{K} = \begin{bmatrix} 1 & 0 & 0 & 0 \\ 0 & 0 & 0 & 1 \\ -11/2 & 9 & -9/2 & 1 \\ -1 & 9/2 & -9 & 11/2 \end{bmatrix}$$

To simplify, let $\mathbf{N} = \mathbf{MK}$, then

$$p = \mathbf{UNP} \qquad (7.14)$$

$$\mathbf{N} = \begin{bmatrix} -9/2 & 27/2 & -27/2 & 9/2 \\ 9 & -45/2 & 18 & -9/2 \\ -11/2 & 9 & -9/2 & 1 \\ 1 & 0 & 0 & 0 \end{bmatrix}$$

If values of u other than 0, 1/3, 2/3, 1 are used, then a new $\mathbf{K}$ matrix must be derived.

Parameter Cubic (PC) Conic Approximation

A segment of a conic curve can be closely approximated by a PC curve. Three points p_0, p_1, p_2 and a scalar ρ are sufficient. The general equation is

$$\mathbf{p} = \mathbf{F}[\mathbf{p}_0 \quad \mathbf{p}_1 \quad 4\rho(\mathbf{p}_2 - \mathbf{p}_0) \quad 4\rho(\mathbf{p}_1 - \mathbf{p}_2)]^T \qquad (7.15)$$

where $\rho \in [0,1]$.

$\mathbf{F}$ is the blending function matrix.

Ellipse: $0 \le \rho < 0.5$
Parabola: $\rho = 0.5$
Hyperbola: $0.5 < \rho \le 1$

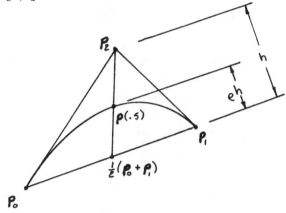

Observe that $\mathbf{p}_0^u = 4\rho(\mathbf{p}_2 - \mathbf{p}_0)$ and $\mathbf{p}_1^u = 4\rho(\mathbf{p}_1 - \mathbf{p}_2)$. Also $\mathbf{p}_0$, $\mathbf{p}_1$, $\mathbf{p}_2$ determine the plane of the conic. Note that the tangent vector at $\mathbf{p}(0.5)$ is parallel to $\mathbf{p}_1 - \mathbf{p}_0$, that is,

$$\mathbf{p}_{0.5}^u = (1.5 - \rho)(\mathbf{p}_1 - \mathbf{p}_0)$$

Parametric Cubic (PC) Parabola

A segment of a parabola can be represented exactly by a parametric cubic curve. Let $\rho = 0.5$, then from (7.15)

$$\mathbf{p} = \mathbf{F}[\mathbf{p}_0 \ \mathbf{p}_1 \ 2(\mathbf{p}_2 - \mathbf{p}_0) \ 2(\mathbf{p}_1 - \mathbf{p}_2)]^T \qquad (7.16)$$

This equation generates points along a parabola from $\mathbf{p}_0$ to $\mathbf{p}_1$.

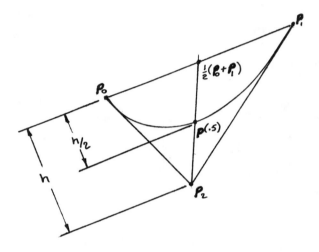

Here is a simplified version of (7.16):

$$\mathbf{p} = u^2(\mathbf{p}_0 + \mathbf{p}_1 - 2\mathbf{p}_2) + 2u(\mathbf{p}_2 - \mathbf{p}_0) + \mathbf{p}_0 \qquad (7.17)$$

Verify the tangent vectors thusly:

$$\frac{d\mathbf{p}}{du} = 2u(\mathbf{p}_0 + \mathbf{p}_1 - 2\mathbf{p}_2) + 2(\mathbf{p}_2 - \mathbf{p}_0)$$

$$\mathbf{p}_0^u = 2(\mathbf{p}_2 - \mathbf{p}_0), \quad \mathbf{p}_1^u = 2(\mathbf{p}_1 - \mathbf{p}_2) \qquad \text{QED}$$

Parametric Cubic (PC) Circle

A circular arc can be approximated by a PC curve. The match is not perfect; however, the smaller the angle subtended by the arc, the better the approximation. Using some simple geometric relationships, find

$$\mathbf{p} = F\left[\mathbf{p}_0 \ \mathbf{p}_1 \ \frac{4 \cos \theta}{1 + \cos \theta} (\mathbf{p}_2 - \mathbf{p}_0) \ \frac{4 \cos \theta}{1 + \cos \theta} (\mathbf{p}_1 - \mathbf{p}_2)\right]^T \quad (7.18)$$

For angles less than 45°,
$$\Delta R/R < 5 \times 10^{-6}$$

$$\mathbf{p}(0.5) = (\mathbf{p}_0 + \mathbf{p}_1)/2 + (\mathbf{p}_0^u - \mathbf{p}_1^u)/8$$

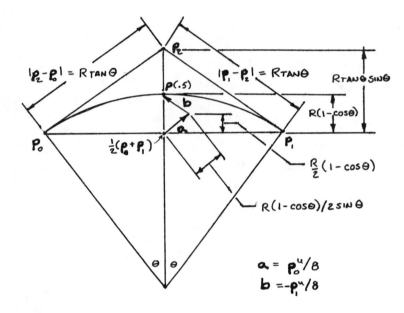

$$|\mathbf{p}_2 - \mathbf{p}_0| = R \tan \theta$$
$$|\mathbf{p}_1 - \mathbf{p}_2| = R \tan \theta$$
$$R \tan \theta \sin \theta$$
$$R(1 - \cos \theta)$$
$$\frac{R}{2}(1 - \cos \theta)$$
$$R(1 - \cos \theta)/2 \sin \theta$$
$$a = \mathbf{p}_0^u/8$$
$$b = -\mathbf{p}_1^u/8$$

Parametric Cubic (PC) Sine Wave

Compute the geometric coefficients of a PC curve that approximates a sine wave from $x = 0$ to $x = \pi/2$ for $y = \sin x$. This is one quarter of the full sine wave. The remaining quarter segments are simple transformations of these coefficients.

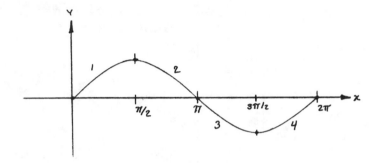

The sine curve has points of inflection at $x = 0$, $\pm \pi$, $\pm 2\pi$, ..., $\pm n\pi$; the slope at $\mathbf{p}_0$ is $dy/dx = 1$, and at $\mathbf{p}_1$ it is $dy/dx = 0$. One additional constraint is required: let $\mathbf{p}(0.5)$ lie exactly on the sine curve. Then, with some algebraic and geometric sleight-of-hand, find

$$
\mathbf{B}_1 = \begin{bmatrix} 0 & 0 & 0 \\ 1.571 & 1 & 0 \\ 1.520 & 1.520 & 0 \\ 1.712 & 0 & 0 \end{bmatrix}
$$

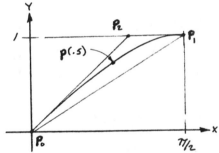

For zero curvature at $\mathbf{p}_0$

$$\mathbf{p}_0^u = k(\mathbf{p}_2 - \mathbf{p}_0)$$

$$\mathbf{p}_1^u = 3(\mathbf{p}_1 - \mathbf{p}_2)$$

The other three quarter-wave segments are:

$$
\mathbf{B}_2 = \begin{bmatrix} 1.571 & 1 & 0 \\ 3.142 & 0 & 0 \\ 1.712 & 0 & 0 \\ 1.520 & -1.520 & 0 \end{bmatrix}
\qquad
\mathbf{B}_3 = \begin{bmatrix} 3.142 & 0 & 0 \\ 4.712 & -1 & 0 \\ 1.520 & -1.520 & 0 \\ 1.712 & 0 & 0 \end{bmatrix}
$$

$$
\mathbf{B}_4 = \begin{bmatrix} 4.712 & -1 & 0 \\ 6.283 & 0 & 0 \\ 7.712 & 0 & 0 \\ 1.520 & 1.520 & 0 \end{bmatrix}
$$

Composite Parametric Cubic (PC) Curves

If two or more PC curve segments are joined together, they form a continuous composite curve. One way to illustrate this is to blend a new curve between two existing curves to form a composite curve consisting of three segments.

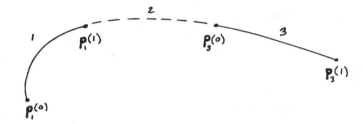

Given the geometric coefficients $\mathbf{B}_1$ and $\mathbf{B}_3$ of two disjoint curves, find the geometric coefficients $\mathbf{B}_2$ of a curve joining them so that the two curve segments meeting at each of the joints are tangent to the same line.

Let $\qquad \mathbf{B}_1 = [\mathbf{p}_1(0) \ \ \mathbf{p}_1(1) \ \ \mathbf{p}_1^u(0) \ \ \mathbf{p}_1^u(1)]^T$

and $\qquad \mathbf{B}_3 = [\mathbf{p}_3(0) \ \ \mathbf{p}_3(1) \ \ \mathbf{p}_3^u(0) \ \ \mathbf{p}_3^u(1)]^T$

The end points must coincide so that $\mathbf{p}_2(0) = \mathbf{p}_1(1)$ and $\mathbf{p}_2(1) = \mathbf{p}_3(0)$. Next, the unit tangent vectors at each joint must be equal, although their magnitudes may differ. Thus,

$$\mathbf{B}_2 = \left[\mathbf{p}_1(1) \ \ \mathbf{p}_3(0) \ \ a\frac{\mathbf{p}_1^u(1)}{|\mathbf{p}_1^u(1)|} \ \ b\frac{\mathbf{p}_3^u(0)}{|\mathbf{p}_3^u(0)|}\right]^T$$

For the more general case of a sequence of smoothly joined curve segments, find for the ith segment:

$$\mathbf{B}_i = \left[\mathbf{p}_{i-1}(1) \ \ \mathbf{p}_{i+1}(0) \ \ a_i\frac{\mathbf{p}_{i-1}^u(1)}{|\mathbf{p}_{i-1}^u(1)|} \ \ b_i\frac{\mathbf{p}_{i+1}^u(0)}{|\mathbf{p}_{i+1}^u(0)|}\right]^T$$

An infinite number of PC segments will satisfy these conditions.

"Bees . . . by virtue of a certain geometrical forethought . . . know that the hexagon is greater than the square and triangle, and will hold more honey for the same expenditure of material."

Pappus of Alexandria

Continuity

A curve, or a joined set of curve segments, is either continuous at all points or has one or more points of discontinuity. The simplest form of continuity ensures that there are no gaps between the beginning and ending points of a curve, or composite curve. This is called C^0 continuity. Two curves joined at a common end point have at least C^0 continuity.

If two curves are tangent to a common line through their joining point, then C^1 continuity prevails across the joint. This means that here their unit tangent vectors are equal.

C^2 continuity requires that the two curves possess equal curvature at their joint. This means that the following conditions must be met:

$$\mathbf{p}_{i+1}(0) = \mathbf{p}_i(1)$$

$$\mathbf{p}_{i+1}^{u}(0) = k_1 \mathbf{p}_i^{u}(1)$$

$$\mathbf{p}_{i+1}^{uu}(0) = k_2 \mathbf{p}^{uu}(1)$$

where k_1 and k_2 are some arbitrary scalar factors. This relationship between the parametric second derivatives ensures that $y_{i+1}^{xx} = y_i^{xx}$. One additional condition must be met for C^2 continuity: the osculating planes of the two curves must coincide (their binormals must be collinear).

A more sophisticated refinement of continuity control in parametric polynomial splines (such as B-splines), or in a string of Hermitian curve segments distinguishes between **parametric continuity and geometric continuity**. For example, B-splines of degree n exhibit $(n-1)$-order continuity of the parametric derivatives. However, the intrinsic differential properties of a curve (e.g., the unit tangent vector and curvature) are independent of parametrization. Geometric continuity of a curve is defined as the continuity of these intrinsic geometric properties. Parametric continuity turns out to absorb more degrees of freedom than geometric continuity. If the conditions producing parametric continuity are relaxed while maintaining geometric continuity, then additional degrees of freedom are available for controlling geometric shape. Barsky's β-spline curves provide extra shape control parameters by taking advantage of this distinction. Similar methods apply to surfaces.

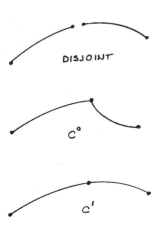

n disjoint PC curves have $12n$ degrees of freedom. n PC curves joined to form a composite curve with C^1 continuity have $7n + 5$ degrees of freedom.

Parametric Cubic (PC) Quick Subdivision

A PC curve may be recursively subdivided so that a set of points is generated on the curve at 2^n equal parametric intervals of length $1/2^n$. Proceed as follows:

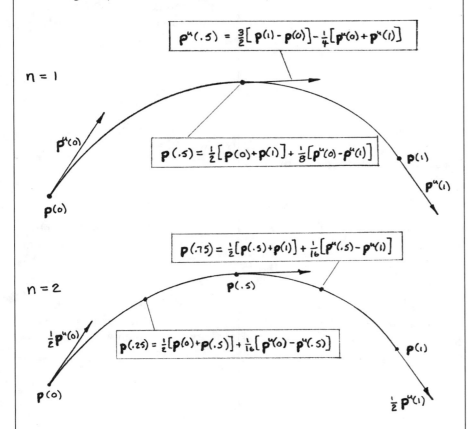

$F_1^u(0.5) = -1.5$
$F_2^u(0.5) = 1.5$
$F_3^u(0.5) = -0.25$
$F_4^u(0.5) = -0.25$

$F_1(0.5) = 0.5$
$F_2(0.5) = 0.5$
$F_3(0.5) = 0.125$
$F_4(0.5) = -0.125$

Renormalize the intervals [0,0.5] and [0.5,1] so that they are each unit intervals [0,1]. This reparametrization introduces the factor of 1/2 applied to the tangent vectors, so that $\mathbf{p}^u \leftarrow \frac{1}{2}\mathbf{p}^u$.

For $m = 1, n$ and $i = 1, n - 1$ (increment by 2), compute:

$$\mathbf{p}(i/2^m) = \frac{1}{2}\left[\mathbf{p}\left(\frac{i-1}{2^m}\right) + \mathbf{p}\left(\frac{i+1}{2^m}\right)\right] + \frac{1}{16}\left[\mathbf{p}^u\left(\frac{i-1}{2^m}\right) + \mathbf{p}^u\left(\frac{i+1}{2^m}\right)\right]$$

If $m \neq n$, then compute

$$\mathbf{p}^u(i/2^m) = \frac{3}{2}\left[\mathbf{p}\left(\frac{i+1}{2^m}\right) - \mathbf{p}\left(\frac{i-1}{2^m}\right)\right] - \frac{1}{4}\left[\mathbf{p}^u\left(\frac{i-1}{2^m}\right) + \mathbf{p}^u\left(\frac{i+1}{2^m}\right)\right]$$

Renormalize the interval(s) of length $i/2^{m+1}$, producing

$$\mathbf{p}^u(i/2^m) \leftarrow \frac{1}{2}\mathbf{p}^u(i/2^m)$$

Bézier Curves

A Bézier curve is defined by parametric functions of the form

$$\mathbf{p}(u) = \sum_{i=0}^{n} \mathbf{p}_i B_{i,n}(u) \qquad u \in [0,1] \qquad (7.19)$$

with blending functions:

$$B_{i,n}(u) = {}^n C_i u^i (1-u)^{n-i}$$

where ${}^n C_i$ is the binomial coefficient:

$${}^n C_i = \frac{n!}{i!(n-i)!}$$

The $\mathbf{p}_i$ are control points, and there are $n+1$ of them defining the vertices of a characteristic polygon.

The blending functions have these properties:

1. They interpolate the first and last vertex points. The curve starts on $\mathbf{p}_0$ and ends on $\mathbf{p}_n$.
2. The tangent vector at $\mathbf{p}_0$ is given by $k_0(\mathbf{p}_1 - \mathbf{p}_0)$ and at $\mathbf{p}_n$ by $k_n(\mathbf{p}_n - \mathbf{p}_{n-1})$.
3. Property 2 is generalized for higher derivatives at the curve's end points. Thus, the second derivative (and curvature) at $\mathbf{p}_0$ is controlled by $\mathbf{p}_0, \mathbf{p}_1,$ and $\mathbf{p}_2$. In general, the rth derivative at an end point is determined by its r neighboring vertices.
4. The functions $B_{i,n}(u)$ are symmetric with respect to u and $1-u$. Thus, reversing the sequence of control points does not change the shape of the curve.

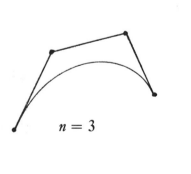

$n = 3$

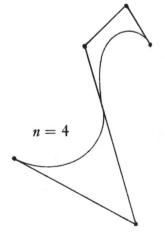

$n = 4$

$B_{i,n}(u)$ yields an nth degree polynomial. The functions are called Bernstein polynomials.

Let $u^i = 1$ when i and $u = 0$. Also, $0! = 1$.

A curve interpolates the control points if it passes through them.

This permits almost unlimited control of continuity at joints between segments of a composite Bézier curve.

A Bézier curve always lies within the convex hull of the characteristic polygon.

Bézier Curves: $n = 2$

For three points, $n = 2$ and

$$\mathbf{p}(u) = (u^2 - 2u + 1)\mathbf{p}_0$$
$$+ (- 2u^2 + 2u)\mathbf{p}_1 + u^2\mathbf{p}_2 \qquad (7.20)$$

where $u \in [0,1]$.

Let $\mathbf{P} = [\mathbf{p}_0 \ \mathbf{p}_1 \ \mathbf{p}_2]^T$ and $\mathbf{B} = [B_{0,2} \ B_{1,2} \ B_{2,2}]$, then in matrix form

$$\mathbf{p} = \mathbf{BP}$$

Let $\mathbf{B} = \mathbf{UM}$, then

$$\mathbf{p} = \mathbf{UMP}$$

where $\mathbf{u} = [u^2 \ u \ 1]$

$$\mathbf{M} = \begin{bmatrix} 1 & -2 & 1 \\ -2 & 2 & 0 \\ 1 & 0 & 0 \end{bmatrix}$$

The tangent vector is given by

$$\mathbf{p}^u = \mathbf{B}^u\mathbf{P}$$

$B_{0,2} = u^2 - 2u + 1$
$B_{1,2} = - 2u^2 + 2u$
$B_{2,2} = u^2$

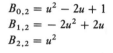

$B_{0,2}^u = 2u - 2$
$B_{1,2}^u = - 4u + 2$
$B_{2,2}^u = 2u$

Example

At $\mathbf{p}_0$, $u = 0$ and $\mathbf{p}_0^u = 2(\mathbf{p}_1 - \mathbf{p}_0)$
At $\mathbf{p}_2$, $u = 1$ and $\mathbf{p}_2^u = 2(\mathbf{p}_2 - \mathbf{p}_1)$

Bézier Curves: $n = 3$

For four points, $n = 3$ and

$$\mathbf{p}(u) = (1 - u)^3 \mathbf{p}_0 + 3u(1 - u)^2 \mathbf{p}_1 \\ + 3u^2(1 - u)\mathbf{p}_2 + u^3 \mathbf{p}_3 \qquad (7.21)$$

where $u \in [0,1]$.

Let $\mathbf{P} = [\mathbf{p}_0 \ \ \mathbf{p}_1 \ \ \mathbf{p}_2 \ \ \mathbf{p}_3]^T$

and $\mathbf{B} = [B_{0,3} \ \ B_{1,3} \ \ B_{2,3} \ \ B_{3,3}]$, then in matrix form

$$\mathbf{p} = \mathbf{BP}$$

Let $\mathbf{B} = \mathbf{UM}$, then

$$\mathbf{p} = \mathbf{UMP}$$

where

$$\mathbf{U} = [u^3 \ \ u^2 \ \ u \ \ 1]$$

$$\mathbf{M} = \begin{bmatrix} -1 & 3 & -3 & 1 \\ 3 & -6 & 3 & 0 \\ -3 & 3 & 0 & 0 \\ 1 & 0 & 0 & 0 \end{bmatrix}$$

The tangent vector is given by

$$\mathbf{p}^u = \mathbf{B}^u \mathbf{P}$$

$B_{0,3} = -u^3 + 3u^2 - 3u + 1$
$B_{1,3} = 3u^3 - 6u^2 + 3u$
$B_{2,3} = -3u^3 + 3u^2$
$B_{3,3} = u^3$

Compare $\mathbf{M}$ of Bézier curve ($n = 3$) to that of the PC curve.

$B_{0,3}^u = -3u^2 + 6u - 3$
$B_{1,3}^u = 9u^2 - 12u + 3$
$B_{2,3}^u = -9u^2 + 6u$
$B_{3,3}^u = 3u^2$

Example

At $\mathbf{p}_0$, $u = 0$ and $\mathbf{p}^u(0) = 3(\mathbf{p}_1 - \mathbf{p}_0)$
At $\mathbf{p}_3$, $u = 1$ and $\mathbf{p}^u(1) = 3(\mathbf{p}_3 - \mathbf{p}_2)$

Bézier Curves: $n = 4$

For five points, $n = 4$ and

$$p(u) = (1 - u)^4 p_0 + 4u(1 - u)^3 p_1$$
$$+ 6u^2(1 - u)^2 p_2$$
$$+ 4u^3(1 - u)p_3 + u^4 p_4 \qquad (7.22)$$

where $u \in [0,1]$.

Let $\mathbf{P} = [p_0 \ p_1 \ p_2 \ p_3 \ p_4]^T$
and $\mathbf{B} = [B_{0,4} \ B_{1,4} \ B_{2,4} \ B_{3,4} \ B_{4,4}]$, then in matrix form

$$\mathbf{p} = \mathbf{BP}$$

Let $\mathbf{B} = \mathbf{UM}$, then

$$\mathbf{p} = \mathbf{UMP}$$

where

$$\mathbf{U} = [u^4 \ u^3 \ u^2 \ u \ 1]$$

$B_{0,4} = u^4 - 4u^3 + 6u^2 - 4u + 1$
$B_{1,4} = -4u^4 + 12u^3 - 12u^2 + 4u$
$B_{2,4} = 6u^4 - 12u^3 + 6u^2$
$B_{3,4} = -4u^4 + 4u^3$
$B_{4,4} = u^4$

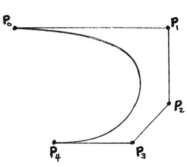

$$\mathbf{M} = \begin{bmatrix} 1 & -4 & 6 & -4 & 1 \\ -4 & 12 & -12 & 4 & 0 \\ 6 & -12 & 6 & 0 & 0 \\ -4 & 4 & 0 & 0 & 0 \\ 1 & 0 & 0 & 0 & 0 \end{bmatrix}$$

The tangent vector is given by

$$\mathbf{p}^u = \mathbf{B}^u \mathbf{P}$$

$B_{0,4}^u = 4u^3 - 12u^2 + 12u - 4$
$B_{1,4}^u = -16u^3 + 36u^2 - 24u + 4$
$B_{2,4}^u = 24u^3 - 36u^2 + 12u$
$B_{3,4}^u = -16u^3 + 12u^2$
$B_{4,4}^u = 4u^3$

Example

At p_0, $u = 0$ and $\mathbf{p}^u(0) = 4(p_1 - p_0)$
At p_4, $u = 1$ and $\mathbf{p}^u(1) = 4(p_4 - p_3)$

For a Bézier curve of degree n:

$\mathbf{p}^u(0) = n(p_1 - p_0)$
$\mathbf{p}^u(1) = n(p_n - p_{n-1})$

Bézier Curves: $n = 5$

For six points, $n = 5$ and

$$
\begin{aligned}
\mathbf{p}(u) = &(1 - u)^5 \mathbf{p}_0 + 5u(1 - u)^4 \mathbf{p}_1 \\
&+ 10u_2(1 - u)^3 \mathbf{p}_2 \\
&+ 10u^3(1 - u)^2 \mathbf{p}_3 \\
&+ 5u^4(1 - u)\mathbf{p}_4 + u^5 \mathbf{p}_5
\end{aligned}
\tag{7.23}
$$

where $u \in [0,1]$.

Let $\mathbf{P} = [\mathbf{p}_0 \ \mathbf{p}_1 \ \mathbf{p}_2 \ \mathbf{p}_3 \ \mathbf{p}_4 \ \mathbf{p}_5]^T$
and $\mathbf{B} = [\bar{B}_{0,5} \ \bar{B}_{1,5} \ B_{2,5} \ B_{3,5} \ B_{4,5} \ B_{5,5}]$, then in matrix form

$$\mathbf{p} = \mathbf{BP}$$

Let $\mathbf{B} = \mathbf{UM}$, then

$$\mathbf{p} = \mathbf{UMP}$$

where

$$U = [u^5 \ u^4 \ u^3 \ u^2 \ u \ 1]$$

$$
M = \begin{bmatrix}
-1 & 5 & -10 & 10 & -5 & 1 \\
5 & -20 & 30 & -20 & 5 & 0 \\
-10 & 30 & -30 & 10 & 0 & 0 \\
10 & -20 & 10 & 0 & 0 & 0 \\
-5 & 5 & 0 & 0 & 0 & 0 \\
1 & 0 & 0 & 0 & 0 & 0
\end{bmatrix}
$$

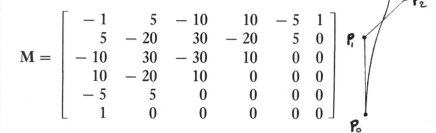

The tangent vector is given by

$$\mathbf{p}^u = \mathbf{B}^u \mathbf{P}$$

$$
\begin{aligned}
B_{0,5} &= -u^5 + 5u^4 - 10u^3 \\
&\quad + 10u^2 - 5u + 1 \\
B_{1,5} &= 5u^5 - 20u^4 + 30u^3 - 20u^2 + 5u \\
B_{2,5} &= -10u^5 + 30u^4 - 30u^3 + 10u^2 \\
B_{3,5} &= 10u^5 - 20u^4 + 10u^3 \\
B_{4,5} &= -5u^5 + 5u^4 \\
B_{5,5} &= u^5
\end{aligned}
$$

$$
\begin{aligned}
B_{0,5}^u &= -5u^4 + 20u^3 - 30u^3 + 20u - 5 \\
B_{1,5}^u &= 25u^4 - 80u^3 + 90u^2 - 40u + 5 \\
B_{2,5}^u &= -50u^4 + 120u^3 - 90u^2 + 20u \\
B_{3,5}^u &= 50u^4 - 80u^3 + 30u^2 \\
B_{4,5}^u &= -25u^4 + 20u^3 \\
B_{5,5}^u &= 5u^4
\end{aligned}
$$

Example:

At $\mathbf{p}_0$, $u = 0$ and $\mathbf{p}^u(0) = 5(\mathbf{p}_1 - \mathbf{p}_0)$
At $\mathbf{p}_5$, $u = 1$ and $\mathbf{p}^u(1) = 5(\mathbf{p}_5 - \mathbf{p}_4)$

Bézier Curves: Blending Functions $B_{i,2}$

For a Bézier curve with $n = 2$, the blending functions $B_{i,2}$ "blend" the contributions of the three control points to produce the points that lie along and define the curve. Thus

$$\mathbf{p} = B_{0,2}\mathbf{p}_0 + B_{1,2}\mathbf{p}_1 + B_{2,2}\mathbf{p}_2 \qquad (7.24)$$

where

$$B_{0,2} = u^2 - 2u + 1$$
$$B_{1,2} = -2u^2 + 2u$$
$$B_{2,2} = u^2$$

If curve and surface equations are to be independent of the coordinate system origin, then the blending functions must satisfy:

$$\sum_i B_i(u) = 1 \quad \text{curves}$$

$$\sum_{j,k} B_{jk}(u,w) = 1 \quad \text{surfaces}$$

A curve or surface lies in the convex hull of its control points if and only if

$$B_i(u) \geq 0 \quad \text{curves}$$
$$B_{jk}(u,w) \geq 0 \quad \text{surfaces}$$

for $u, w \in [0,1]$.

Note that $B_{0,2}$ and $B_{2,2}$ are mirror images.

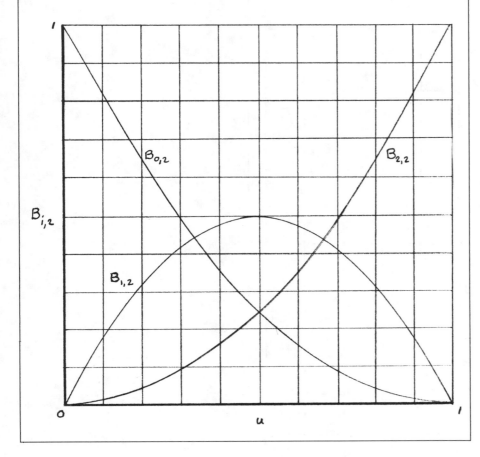

Bézier Curves: Blending Functions $B_{i,3}$

For a Bézier curve with $n = 3$, the blending functions $B_{i,3}$ "blend" the contributions of the four control points to produce the points that lie along and define the curve. Thus,

$$\mathbf{p} = B_{0,3}\mathbf{p}_0 + B_{1,3}\mathbf{p}_1 + B_{2,3}\mathbf{p}_2 + B_{3,3}\mathbf{p}_3 \qquad (7.25)$$

where

$$B_{0,3} = -u^3 + 3u^2 - 3u + 1$$
$$B_{1,3} = 3u^3 - 6u^2 + 3u$$
$$B_{2,3} = -3u^3 + 3u^2$$
$$B_{3,3} = u^3$$

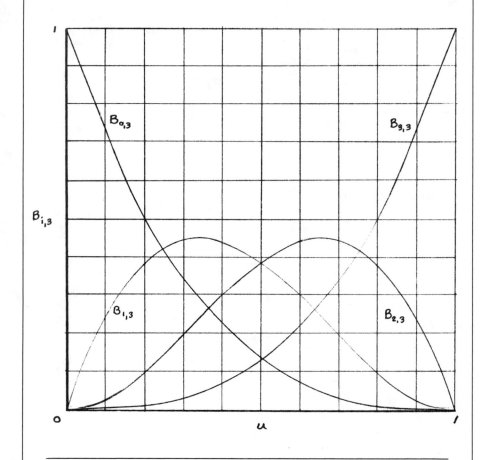

Bézier Curves: Blending Functions $B_{i,4}$

For a Bézier curve with $n = 4$, the blending functions $B_{i,4}$ "blend" the contributions of the five control points to produce the points that lie along and define the curve. Thus,

$$\mathbf{p} = B_{0,4}\mathbf{p}_0 + B_{1,4}\mathbf{p}_1 + B_{2,4}\mathbf{p}_2$$
$$+ B_{3,4}\mathbf{p}_3 + B_{4,4}\mathbf{p}_4 \tag{7.26}$$

where

$$B_{0,4} = u^4 - 4u^3 + 6u^2 - 4u + 1$$
$$B_{1,4} = -4u^4 + 12u^3 - 12u^2 + 4u$$
$$B_{2,4} = 6u^4 - 12u^3 + 6u^2$$
$$B_{3,4} = -4u^4 + 4u^3$$
$$B_{4,4} = u^4$$

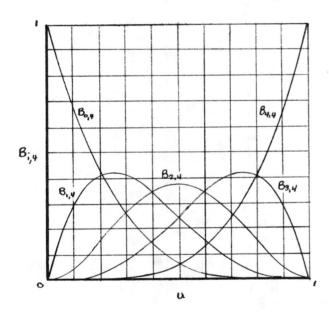

"The knowledge at which geometry aims is knowledge of the eternal, and not of aught perishing and transient."

Plato

Bézier Curves: Blending Functions $B_{i,5}$

For a Bézier curve with $n = 5$, the blending functions $B_{i,5}$ "blend" the contributions of the six control points to produce the points that lie along and define the curve. Thus,

$$\mathbf{p} = B_{0,5}\mathbf{p}_0 + B_{1,5}\mathbf{p}_1 + B_{2,5}\mathbf{p}_2$$
$$+ B_{3,5}\mathbf{p}_3 + B_{4,5}\mathbf{p}_4 + B_{5,5}\mathbf{p}_5 \qquad (7.27)$$

where

$$B_{0,5} = -u^5 + 5u^4 - 10u^3 + 10u^2 - 5u + 1$$
$$B_{1,5} = 5u^5 - 20u^4 + 30u^3 - 20u^2 + 5u$$
$$B_{2,5} = -10u^5 + 30u^4 - 30u^3 + 10u^2$$
$$B_{3,5} = 10u^5 - 20u^4 + 10u^3$$
$$B_{4,5} = -5u^5 + 5u^4$$
$$B_{5,5} = u^5$$

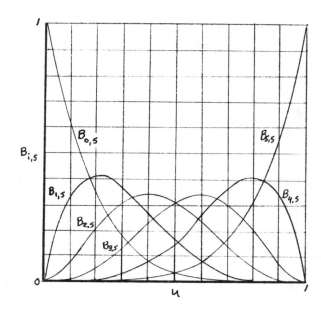

Bézier Curves: Blending Functions $B_{i,2}^u$

There is a set of blending functions $B_{i,2}^u$ that produces the tangent vector $\mathbf{p}^u$ at any point $\mathbf{p}$ on the Bézier curve, $n = 2$:

$$\mathbf{p}^u = B_{0,2}^u \mathbf{p}_0 + B_{1,2}^u \mathbf{p}_1 + B_{2,2}^u \mathbf{p}_2 \qquad (7.28)$$

where

$$B_{0,2}^u = 2u - 2$$

$$B_{1,2}^u = -4u + 2$$

$$B_{2,2}^u = 2u$$

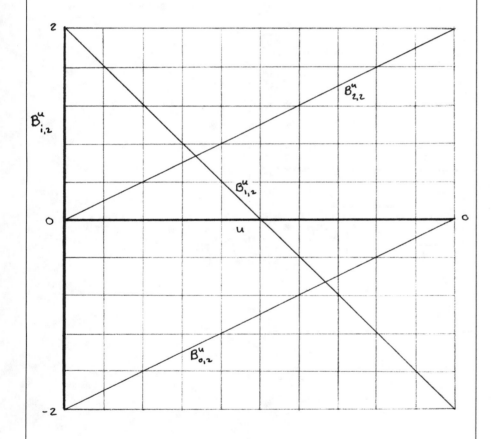

Bézier Curves: Blending Functions $B_{i,3}^u$

There is a set of blending functions $B_{i,3}^u$ that produces the tangent vector $\mathbf{p}^u$ at any point $\mathbf{p}$ on the Bézier curve, $n = 3$:

$$\mathbf{p}^u = B_{0,3}^u \mathbf{p}_0 + B_{1,3}^u \mathbf{p}_1 + B_{2,3}^u \mathbf{p}_2 + B_{3,3}^u \mathbf{p}_3 \qquad (7.29)$$

where

$$B_{0,3}^u = -3u^2 + 6u - 3$$

$$B_{1,3}^u = 9u^2 - 12u + 3$$

$$B_{2,3}^u = -9u^2 + 6u$$

$$B_{3,3}^u = 3u^2$$

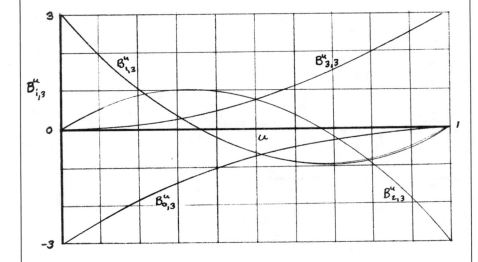

Bézier Curves: Blending Functions $B_{i,4}^u$

There is a set of blending functions $B_{i,4}^u$ that produces the tangent vector $\mathbf{p}^u$ at any point $\mathbf{p}$ on the Bézier curve, $n = 4$:

$$\mathbf{p}^u = B_{0,4}^u \mathbf{p}_0 + B_{1,4}^u \mathbf{p}_1 + B_{2,4}^u \mathbf{p}_2 \\ + B_{3,4}^u \mathbf{p}_3 + B_{4,4}^u \mathbf{p}_4 \tag{7.30}$$

where

$$B_{0,4}^u = 4u^3 - 12u^2 + 12u - 4 \qquad\qquad B_{3,4}^u = -16u^3 + 12u^2$$

$$B_{1,4}^u = -16u^3 + 36u^2 - 24u + 4 \qquad\qquad B_{4,4}^u = 4u^3$$

$$B_{2,4}^u = 24u^3 - 36u^2 + 12u$$

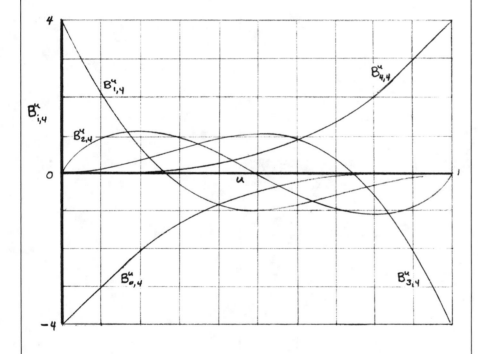

Bézier Curves: Blending Functions $B_{i,5}^u$

There is a set of blending functions $B_{i,5}^u$ that produces the tangent vector $\mathbf{p}^u$ at any point $\mathbf{p}$ on the Bézier curve, $n = 5$:

$$\mathbf{p}^u = B_{0,5}^u \mathbf{p}_0 + B_{1,5}^u \mathbf{p}_1 + B_{2,5}^u \mathbf{p}_2 + B_{3,5}^u \mathbf{p}_3 \\ + B_{4,5}^u \mathbf{p}_4 + B_{5,5}^u \mathbf{p}_5 \qquad (7.31)$$

where

$$B_{0,5}^u = -5u^4 + 20u^3 - 30u^2 + 20u - 5 \qquad B_{3,5}^u = 50u^4 - 80u^3 + 30u^2$$
$$B_{1,5}^u = 25u^4 - 80u^3 + 90u^2 - 40u + 5 \qquad B_{4,5}^u = -25u^4 + 20u^3$$
$$B_{2,5}^u = -50u^4 + 120u^3 - 90u^2 + 20u \qquad B_{5,5}^u = 5u^4$$

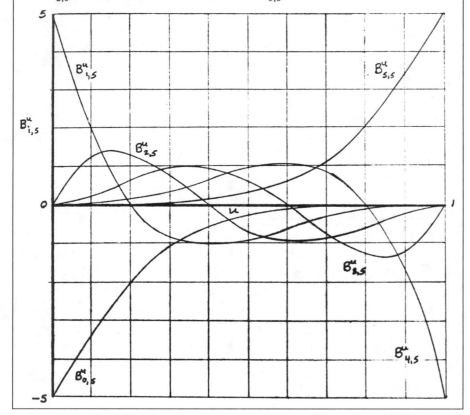

"We attempt to abstract from the complexity of phenomena some simple systems whose properties are susceptible of being described mathematically. This power of abstraction is responsible for the amazing mathematical description of nature."

Morris Kline

Bézier Curve: Curvature

A condition for C^2 continuity at a joint between two Bézier curves (or the two ends of a closed curve) is that the five vertices $\mathbf{p}_{n-2}$, $\mathbf{p}_{n-1}$, $\mathbf{p}_n = \mathbf{q}_0$, $\mathbf{q}_1$, $\mathbf{q}_2$ must be coplanar. The equations for the curvature at each end of an nth degree Bézier curve, $\kappa(0)$ and $\kappa(1)$, are

$$\kappa(0) = \frac{2\left|(\mathbf{p}_1 - \mathbf{p}_0) \times (\mathbf{p}_2 - \mathbf{p}_1)\right|}{3\left|\mathbf{p}_1 - \mathbf{p}_0\right|^3} \qquad (7.32)$$

$$\kappa(1) = \frac{2\left|(\mathbf{p}_{n-1} - \mathbf{P}_{n-2}) \times (\mathbf{p}_n - \mathbf{p}_{n-1})\right|}{3\left|\mathbf{p}_n - \mathbf{p}_{n-1}\right|} \qquad (7.33)$$

where curvature is a scalar quantity. Note: if $\mathbf{p}_0$, $\mathbf{p}_1$, $\mathbf{p}_2$ are collinear, then $\kappa(0) = 0$, since $(\mathbf{p}_1 - \mathbf{p}_0) \times (\mathbf{p}_2 - \mathbf{p}_1) = 0$.

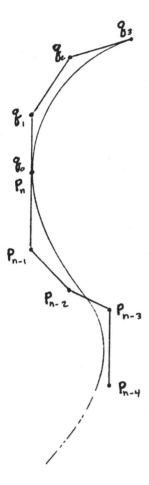

Closed Bézier Curve

If the first and last points (vertices) of the characteristic polygon coincide, then a closed curve is produced. The continuity across the join depends on the spatial arrangement of the adjacent control points.

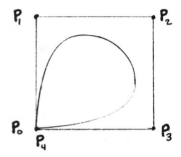

C^0 continuity
p_0, p_4 coincident

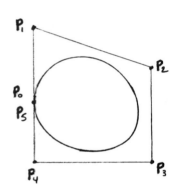

C^1 continuity

p_0, p_5 coincident
p_0, p_1, p_4, p_5 collinear

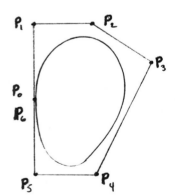

C^2 continuity

p_0, p_6 coincident
p_0, p_1, p_5, p_6 collinear
$\left.\begin{array}{l} p_0, p_1, p_2 \\ p_4, p_5, p_6 \end{array}\right\}$ coplanar

$\kappa(0) = \kappa(1)$

Modifying a Bézier Curve

Ease of modification is characteristic of the Bézier curve; it was, in fact, a paramount objective in its development. The two simplest and most obvious ways to change the shape of a Bézier curve are to move one or more of the control points or to add coincident points.

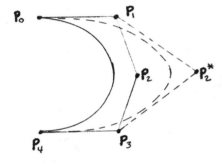

Shape change by moving a control point p_2.

All changes produce global effects.

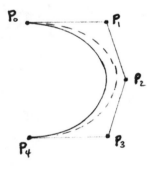

Shape change by adding coincident points at p_2. This increases the degree of the curve.

Composite Bézier Curves

Bézier curves of the same or different degree may be joined to form a single composite curve.

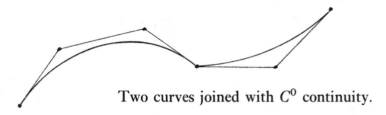

Two curves joined with C^0 continuity.

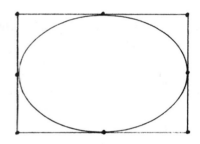

Four curves joined with C^1 continuity.

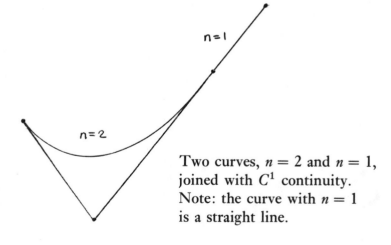

Two curves, $n = 2$ and $n = 1$, joined with C^1 continuity. Note: the curve with $n = 1$ is a straight line.

Cubic Bézier and Parametric Cubic (PC) (Hermitian) Curves

A PC curve has an equivalent Bézier representation. In its geometric form the PC curve is one form of Hermitian curve, defined by interpolation points and tangents, while the Bézier curve is defined by a set of points only proximal to the curve. The Hermitian definition of a curve is an interpolation scheme, that is, the curve interpolates or passes through all the defining points. The Bézier definition of a curve is an approximation scheme, that is, the curve does not necessarily pass through any of the points. (Bézier curves do pass through the first and last points.)

Let the geometric coefficients of a PC curve be $[\mathbf{p}_0 \ \mathbf{p}_3 \ k_0(\mathbf{p}_1 - \mathbf{p}_0) \ k_1(\mathbf{p}_3 - \mathbf{p}_2)]^T$. If $k_0 = k_1 = 3$, then the PC curve is identical to the cubic ($n = 3$) Bézier curve whose control points are $[\mathbf{p}_0 \ \mathbf{p}_1 \ \mathbf{p}_2 \ \mathbf{p}_3]$.

If a Bézier curve is given by the four control points $[\mathbf{p}_0 \ \mathbf{p}_1 \ \mathbf{p}_2 \ \mathbf{p}_3]$, the equivalent Hermitian curve's geometric coefficients are

$$[\mathbf{p}_0 \ \mathbf{p}_3 \ 3(\mathbf{p}_1 - \mathbf{p}_0) \ 3(\mathbf{p}_3 - \mathbf{p}_2)].$$

If a Hermitian curve is given by the geometric coefficients $[\mathbf{p}_0 \ \mathbf{p}_1 \ \mathbf{p}_0^u \ \mathbf{p}_1^u]$, the equivalent Bézier curve's four control points are

$$[\mathbf{p}_0 \ (\mathbf{p}_0 + \tfrac{1}{3}\mathbf{p}_0^u) \ (\mathbf{p} - \tfrac{1}{3}\mathbf{p}_1^u) \ \mathbf{p}_1].$$

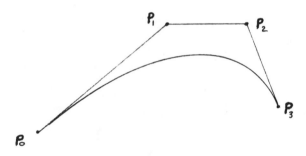

Proof:

For a Bézier curve ($n = 3$)

$$p(u) = (-3u^2 + 6u - 3)\mathbf{p}_0 + (9u^2 - 12u + 3)\mathbf{p}_1 \\ + (-9u^2 + 6u)\mathbf{p}_2 + 3u^2\mathbf{p}_3$$

At $u = 0$, $\ \mathbf{p}^u(0) = 3(\mathbf{p}_1 - \mathbf{p}_0)$

At $u = 1$, $\ \mathbf{p}^u(1) = 3(\mathbf{p}_3 - \mathbf{p}_2)$ QED

"Sesostris . . . made a division of the soil of Egypt among the inhabitants . . . If the river carried away any portion of a man's lot, . . . the King sent persons to examine, and determine by measurement the exact extent of the loss . . . From this practice, I think, geometry first came to be known in Egypt, whence it passed into Greece."

Herodotus

Bézier Curve Parametric Transformation: $n = 2$

The general parametric transformation for a Bézier curve ($n = 2$) is developed as follows: Given the three control points defining the curve, find the three new control points defining a segment of the curve in the parametric interval $u \in [u_i, u_j]$, where the interval is normalized to the new parameter, say v, such that $v \in [0,1]$.

See Eq. (7.12).

Given $\quad$ $\mathbf{p} = \mathbf{UMP}$

Let $\quad\quad$ $\mathbf{U} = \mathbf{VT}$

Then $\quad\quad$ $\mathbf{p} = \mathbf{VTMP} = \mathbf{VMP^*}$

so that $\quad$ $\mathbf{TMP} = \mathbf{MP^*}$

and $\quad\quad$ $\mathbf{P^*} = \mathbf{M^{-1}TMP}$

$$\mathbf{U} = [u^2 \ u \ 1]$$
$$\mathbf{V} = [v^2 \ v \ 1]$$
$$\mathbf{P} = [\mathbf{p}_0 \ \mathbf{p}_1 \ \mathbf{p}_2]^T$$

where $\quad$
$$\mathbf{T} = \begin{bmatrix} \Delta u_i^2 & 0 & 0 \\ 2u_i\Delta u_i & \Delta u_i & 0 \\ u_i^2 & u_i & 1 \end{bmatrix},$$

$$\mathbf{M} = \begin{bmatrix} 1 & -2 & 1 \\ -2 & 2 & 0 \\ 1 & 0 & 0 \end{bmatrix},$$

$$\mathbf{M}^{-1} = \begin{bmatrix} 0 & 0 & 1 \\ 0 & 1/2 & 1 \\ 1 & 1 & 1 \end{bmatrix}$$

$\mathbf{P^*} = [\mathbf{p}_0^* \ \mathbf{p}_1^* \ \mathbf{p}_2^*]^T$

$\mathbf{P}_0^* = (1 - u_i)^2\mathbf{p}_0 + 2u_i(1 - u_i)\mathbf{p}_1 + u_i^2\mathbf{p}_2$

$\mathbf{P}_1^* = (1 - u_i)(1 - u_j)\mathbf{p}_0 + (-2u_iu_j + u_j + u_i)\mathbf{p}_1 + u_iu_j\mathbf{p}_2$

$\mathbf{P}_2^* = (1 - u_j)^2\mathbf{p}_0 + 2u_j(1 - u_j)\mathbf{p}_1 + u_j^2\mathbf{p}_2$

"Neglect of mathematics works injury to all knowledge, since he who is ignorant of it cannot know the other sciences or things of this world."

Roger Bacon

Béezier Curve Parametric Transformation: $n = 3$

The general parametric transformation for a Bézier curve ($n = 3$) is developed as follows: Given the four control points defining the curve, find the four new control points defining a segment of the curve in the parametric interval $u \in [u_i, u_j]$, where the interval is normalized to the new parameter, say v, such that $v \in [0,1]$.

See Eq. (7.12)

Given $\quad$ $\mathbf{p} = \mathbf{UMP}$

Let $\quad$ $\mathbf{U} = \mathbf{VT}$

Then $\quad$ $\mathbf{p} = \mathbf{VTMP} = \mathbf{VMP^*}$

so that $\quad$ $\mathbf{TMP} = \mathbf{MP^*}$

and $\quad$ $\mathbf{P^*} = \mathbf{M}^{-1}\mathbf{TMP}$

$\mathbf{U} = [u^3 \ u^2 \ u \ 1]$
$\mathbf{V} = [v^3 \ v^2 \ v \ 1]$
$\mathbf{P} = [\mathbf{p}_0 \ \mathbf{p}_1 \ \mathbf{p}_2 \ \mathbf{p}_3]^T$

where $\quad$ $\mathbf{T} = \begin{bmatrix} \Delta u_i^3 & 0 & 0 & 0 \\ 3u_i \Delta u_i^2 & \Delta u_i^2 & 0 & 0 \\ 3u_i^2 \Delta u_i & 2u_i \Delta u_i & \Delta u_i & 0 \\ u_i^3 & u_i^2 & u_i & 1 \end{bmatrix}$

$\mathbf{M} = \begin{bmatrix} -1 & 3 & -3 & 1 \\ 3 & -6 & 3 & 0 \\ -3 & 3 & 0 & 0 \\ 1 & 6 & 0 & 0 \end{bmatrix}$

$\mathbf{P^*} = [\mathbf{p}_0^* \ \mathbf{p}_1^* \ \mathbf{p}_2^* \ \mathbf{p}_3^*]^T$

$\mathbf{P}_0^* = (1 - u_i)^3 \mathbf{p}_0 + 3u_i(1 - u_i)^2 \mathbf{p}_1 + 3u_i^2(1 - u_i)\mathbf{p}_2 + u_i^3 \mathbf{p}_2$

$\mathbf{P}_1^* = (1 - u_i)^2(1 - u_j)\mathbf{p}_0 + (1 - u_i)(2u_i + u_j - 3u_i u_j)\mathbf{p}_1$
$\qquad + u_i(2u_j + u_i - 3u_i u_j)\mathbf{p}_2 + u_i^2 u_j \mathbf{p}_3$

$\mathbf{P}_2^* = (1 - u_i)(1 - u_j)^2 \mathbf{p}_0 + (1 - u_j)(2u_j + u_i - 3u_i u_j)\mathbf{p}_i$
$\qquad + u_j(2u_i + u_j - 3u_i u_j)\mathbf{p}_2 + u_i u_j^2 \mathbf{p}_3$

$\mathbf{P}_3^* = (1 - u_j)^3 \mathbf{p}_0 + 3u_j(1 - u_j)^2 \mathbf{p}_1 + 3u_j^2(1 - u_j)\mathbf{p}_2 + u_j^3 \mathbf{p}_3$

Subdividing a Bézier Curve: $n = 3$

A Bézier curve recursively subdivided s times produces a set of points on the curve at 2^s intervals, whose parametric length is approximately $1/2^s$. Continue to subdivide until the segments are small enough to plot as straight line segments or display as a single pixel. Proceed by finding $p(0.5)$ on the initial curve. This divides the initial curve into two smaller curves. Use the general parametric transformation to find the full set of control points for each of these two smaller curves. Repeat the subdivision process as far as necessary.

Step 1: Compute $p(0.5) = p_0/8 + 3p_1/8 + 3p_2/8 + p_3/8$

Step 2: Use the general parametric transformation for segment $u \in [0,0.5]$ [from Eq. (7.12)] to compute P_a^*.

$$P^* = M^{-1}TMP \quad T = \begin{bmatrix} 0.125 & 0 & 0 & 0 \\ 0 & 0.25 & 0 & 0 \\ 0 & 0 & 0.5 & 0 \\ 0 & 0 & 0 & 1 \end{bmatrix}$$

$$P_a^* = [p_0 \; 0.5(p_0 + p_1) \; 0.25(p_0 + 2p_1 + p_2) \\ 0.125(p_0 + 3p_1 + 3p_2 + p_3)]^T$$

Step 3: Use the general parametric transformation again, this time for segment $u \in [0.5,1]$, to compute its P_b^*.

$$T = \begin{bmatrix} 0.125 & 0 & 0 & 0 \\ 0.375 & 0.25 & 0 & 0 \\ 0.375 & 0.50 & 0.5 & 0 \\ 0.125 & 0.25 & 0.5 & 1 \end{bmatrix}$$

$$P_b^* = [0.125(p_0 + 3p_1 + 3p_2 + p_3) \\ 0.25(p_1 + 2p_2 + p_3) \; 0.5(p_2 + p_3) \; p_3]^T$$

Now the midpoints of each of these two curve segments can be found and the above process repeated.

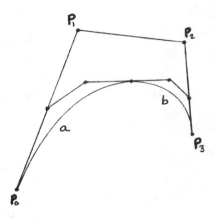

$$p = UMP$$

$$U = [u^3 \; u^2 \; u \; 1]$$

$$M = \begin{bmatrix} -1 & 3 & -3 & 1 \\ 3 & -6 & 3 & 0 \\ -3 & 3 & 0 & 0 \\ 1 & 6 & 0 & 0 \end{bmatrix}$$

Subdividing a Bézier Curve:
Geometric Construction

Bézier offers a geometric construction to find a point on a Bézier curve corresponding to the parametric value u. Here is how it goes:

Find the point on each edge of the control polygon that subdivides it fractionally according to the value of u. Connect these points to form a set of line segments. Subdivide each of these new line segments fractionally according to u. Repeat the process of subdivision and line segment construction until only one line segment can be constructed. The point that subdivides this line is the point on the curve corresponding to u. The example at the right finds the point at $u = 0.25$.

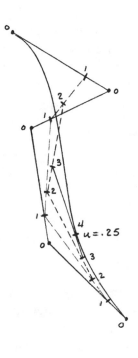

Points labeled 0 are the initial control points. Those labeled 1, 2, 3, 4 are subsequent sequential subdivisions.

This construction can be described quite nicely by some vector algebra and a simple recursion algorithm. Try it! The first cycle of recursion operates on the initial control points, like this:

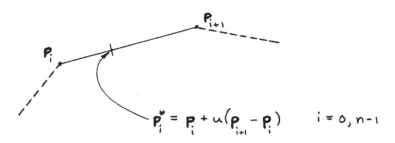

$$P_i^* = P_i + u(P_{i+1} - P_i) \qquad i = 0, n-1$$

In general, there are n cycles of subdivision. The number of line segments decreases by one each cycle.

Here is the construction of $u = 0.5$ for a cubic Bézier curve.

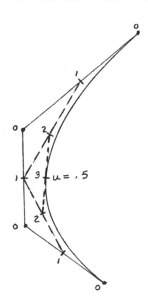

Rational Bézier Curves

A rational Bézier curve is defined by parametric functions of the form

$$\mathbf{p}(u) = \frac{\sum_{i=0}^{n} h_i \mathbf{p}_i B_{i,n}(u)}{\sum_{i=0}^{n} h_i B_{i,n}(u)} \qquad u \in [0,1]$$

The homogeneous components h_i, also called weights, provide extra degrees of freedom to modify the curve shape without changing the control polygon. This means that for each point two polynomials are evaluated and then a division is executed. Here is the expression for a rational cubic Bézier curve:

$$\mathbf{p}(u) = \frac{(1-u)^3 \mathbf{p}_0 h_0 + 3u(1-u)^2 \mathbf{p}_1 h_1 + 3u^2(1-u)\mathbf{p}_2 h_2 + u^3 \mathbf{p}_3 h_3}{(1-u)^3 h_0 + 3u(1-u)^2 h_1 + 3u^2(1-u)h_2 + u^3 h_3}$$

It is possible to construct a rational Bézier curve that is identically a conic curve. This is not possible using the nonrational form. Three control points are sufficient to produce the necessary rational quadratic polynomials. A circular arc is a good example.

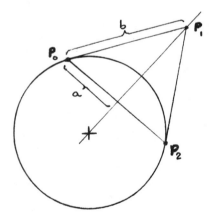

The points $\mathbf{p}_0$ and $\mathbf{p}_2$ lie on the circle and define the end points of the arc. $\mathbf{p}_1$ lies on the perpendicular bisector of the chord joining $\mathbf{p}_0$ and $\mathbf{p}_2$ so that $\mathbf{p}_1 - \mathbf{p}_0$ and $\mathbf{p}_2 - \mathbf{p}_1$ are tangent to the circle. Choose for weights $h_0 = h_2 = 1$ and $h_1 = a/b$. The expression looks like this:

$$\mathbf{p}(u) = \frac{(u^2 - 2u + 1)\mathbf{p}_0 + (a/b)(-2u^2 + 2u)\mathbf{p}_1 + u^2 \mathbf{p}_2}{(u^2 - 2u + 1) + (a/b)(-2u^2 + 2u) + u^2}$$

or, rearranging,

$$\mathbf{p}(u) = \frac{\mathbf{p}_0 + u\{-2[\mathbf{p}_0 - (a/b)\mathbf{p}_1] + u[\mathbf{p}_0 - 2(a/b)\mathbf{p}_1 + \mathbf{p}_2]\}}{1 - 2u(1 - a/b)(u - 1)}$$

Other basis functions also have analogous rational forms.

The numerator and denominator polynomials are usually evaluated using forward differencing techniques. To do this it becomes necessary to expand the polynomial and rearrange terms.

Different values of h_1 produce other conic curves. Setting $h_1 = -a/b$ provides another arc, outside the control polygon, such that the two arcs together form the complete circle.

B-Spline Curves

A *B*-spline curve is defined by parametric functions of the form

$$\mathbf{p}(u) = \sum_{i=0}^{n} \mathbf{p}_i N_{i,k}(u) \qquad u \in [0,(n-k+2)] \qquad (7.34)$$

generating what is known as a piecewise polynomial. There are $n+1$ control points $\mathbf{p}_i$. The $N_{i,k}(u)$ blending functions are defined recursively as

$$N_{i,1}(u) = 1 \qquad \text{if } t_i \leq u < t_{i+1}$$

$$= 0 \qquad \text{otherwise}$$

and

$$N_{i,k}(u) = \frac{(u - t_i)N_{i,k-1}(u)}{t_{i+k-1} - t_i} + \frac{(t_{i+k} - u)N_{i+1,k-1}(u)}{t_{i+k} - t_{i+1}}$$

The resulting parametric polynomials are of degree $(k-1)$. The t_i are called knot values. For an open curve they are

$$\left. \begin{array}{ll} t_i = 0 & \text{if } i < k \\ t_i = i - k + 1 & \text{if } k \leq i \leq n \\ t_i = n - k + 2 & \text{if } i > n \end{array} \right\} \; i \in [0, n+k]$$

A rational *B*-spline curve is expressed as

$$\mathbf{p}(u) = \frac{\sum_{i=0}^{n} \mathbf{p}_i h_i N_{i,k}(u)}{\sum_{i=0}^{n} h_i N_{i,k}(u)}$$

where the h_i are weights.

The $N_{i,1}$ functions act as switches turning on and off the blending functions inside and outside the appropriate parametric interval.

These blending functions confine the effects of a control point movement to the immediate locale. Thus, curve shape change is local, not global as it is for Bézier curves.

Since the denominators of the $N_{i,k}(u)$ blending functions can be zero, use the convention: $0/0 = 0$.

There are two kinds of *B*-spline curve: the periodic and the nonperiodic. The nonperiodic curve blending functions influenced by the end points and those very near them differ from the interior blending functions, while for the periodic curve, all blending functions are identical.

Nonperiodic curves interpolate the first and last control points and are tangent to the characteristic polygon at those points.

B-Spline Curves: $n = 5$, $k = 2$

For the *B*-spline curve with $n = 5$, $k = 2$, there are six control points $(n + 1)$ and the parametric polynomials are linear $(k - 1)$. For the parametric variable u, find $u \in [0,5]$. For the knot value computation $i \in [0,7]$ and

$$t_0 = 0 \qquad t_3 = 2 \qquad t_6 = 5$$
$$t_1 = 0 \qquad t_4 = 3 \qquad t_7 = 5$$
$$t_2 = 1 \qquad t_5 = 4$$

Compute the $N_{i,k}(u)$ for $i \in [0,5]$

$$N_{0,2}(u) = (1 - u)N_{1,1}(u)$$
$$N_{1,2}(u) = uN_{1,1}(u) + (2 - u)N_{2,1}(u)$$
$$N_{2,2}(u) = (u - 1)N_{2,1}(u) + (3 - u)N_{3,1}(u)$$
$$N_{3,2}(u) = (u - 2)N_{3,1}(u) + (4 - u)N_{4,1}(u)$$
$$N_{4,2}(u) = (u - 3)N_{4,1}(u) + (5 - u)N_{5,1}(u)$$
$$N_{5,2}(u) = (u - 4)N_{5,1}(u)$$

$N_{0,1}(u) = 1$ for $u = 0$
$\qquad = 0$ otherwise
$N_{1,1}(u) = 1$ for $u \in [0,1]$
$\qquad = 0$ otherwise
$N_{2,1}(u) = 1$ for $u \in [1,2]$
$\qquad = 0$ otherwise
$N_{3,1}(u) = 1$ for $u \in [2,3]$
$\qquad = 0$ otherwise
$N_{4,1}(u) = 1$ for $u \in [3,4]$
$\qquad = 0$ otherwise
$N_{5,1}(u) = 1$ for $u \in [4,5]$
$\qquad = 0$ otherwise

Applying these blending functions to the six control points using Eq. (7.34) generates five distinct equations, one for each curve segment defined in successive unit parametric intervals. The $N_{i,1}$ functions act as switches:

$$\mathbf{p}_1(u) = (1 - u)\mathbf{p}_0 + u\mathbf{p}_1 \qquad u \in [0,1]$$
$$\mathbf{p}_2(u) = (2 - u)\mathbf{p}_1 + (u - 1)\mathbf{p}_2 \qquad u \in [1,2]$$
$$\mathbf{p}_3(u) = (3 - u)\mathbf{p}_2 + (u - 2)\mathbf{p}_3 \qquad u \in [2,3]$$
$$\mathbf{p}_4(u) = (4 - u)\mathbf{p}_3 + (u - 3)\mathbf{p}_4 \qquad u \in [3,4]$$
$$\mathbf{p}_5(u) = (5 - u)\mathbf{p}_4 + (u - 4)\mathbf{p}_5 \qquad u \in [4,5]$$

The resulting "curve" is a sequence of straight lines connecting the control points. This, of course, is true only for $k = 2$ curves. [Do not confuse the function $\mathbf{p}_i(u)$ with control point $\mathbf{p}_i$.]

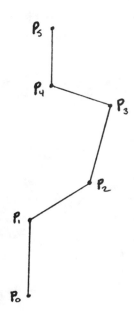

B-Spline Curves: $n = 5$, $k = 3$

For the *B*-spline curve with $n = 5$, $k = 3$, there are six control points $(n + 1)$, and the parametric polynomials are second degree $(k - 1)$. For the parametric variable u, find $u \in [0,4]$. For the knot value computation $i \in [0,8]$ and

$$
\begin{array}{lll}
t_0 = 0 & t_3 = 1 & t_6 = 4 \\
t_1 = 0 & t_4 = 2 & t_7 = 4 \\
t_2 = 0 & t_5 = 3 & t_8 = 4
\end{array}
$$

Compute the $N_{i,k}(u)$ for $i \in [0,5]$:

$N_{0,3}(u) = (1 - u)^2 N_{2,1}(u)$

$N_{1,3}(u) = \frac{1}{2}u(4 - 3u)N_{2,1}(u) + \frac{1}{2}(2 - u)^2 N_{3,1}(u)$

$N_{2,3}(u) = \frac{1}{2}u^2 N_{2,1}(u) + \frac{1}{2}(-2u^2 + 6u - 3)N_{3,1}(u) + \frac{1}{2}(3 - u)^2 N_{4,1}(u)$

$N_{3,3}(u) = \frac{1}{2}(u - 1)^2 N_{3,1}(u) + \frac{1}{2}(-2u^2 + 10u - 11)N_{4,1}(u)$
$\qquad\qquad + \frac{1}{2}(4 - u)^2 N_{5,1}(u)$

$N_{4,3}(u) = \frac{1}{2}(u - 2)^2 N_{4,1}(u) + \frac{1}{2}(-3u^2 + 20u - 32)N_{5,1}(u)$

$N_{5,3}(u) = (u - 3)^2 N_{5,1}(u)$

Points $\mathbf{p}(u)$ defining the curve are given by a different equation for each unit interval in u through the action of the $N_{i,1}$ "switches," generating the nonperiodic curve

$$
\begin{array}{ll}
\mathbf{p}_1(u) = (1 - u)^2 \mathbf{p}_0 + \frac{1}{2}u(4 - 3u)\mathbf{p}_1 + \frac{1}{2}u^2 \mathbf{p}_2 & u \in [0,1] \\
\mathbf{p}_2(u) = \frac{1}{2}(2 - u)^2 \mathbf{p}_1 + \frac{1}{2}(-2u^2 + 6u - 3)\mathbf{p}_2 + \frac{1}{2}(u - 1)^2 \mathbf{p}_3 & u \in [1,2] \\
\mathbf{p}_3(u) = \frac{1}{2}(3 - u)^2 \mathbf{p}_2 + \frac{1}{2}(-2u^2 + 10u - 11)\mathbf{p}_3 + \frac{1}{2}(u - 2)^2 \mathbf{p}_4 & u \in [2,3] \\
\mathbf{p}_4(u) = \frac{1}{2}(4 - u)^2 \mathbf{p}_3 + \frac{1}{2}(-3u^2 + 20u - 32)\mathbf{p}_4 + (u - 3)^2 \mathbf{p}_5 & u \in [3,4]
\end{array}
$$

The complete curve is a composite of these four curve segments connected with C^1 continuity. Note that the curve passes through the first and last points $\mathbf{p}_0$ and $\mathbf{p}_5$ and is tangent to $\mathbf{p}_1 - \mathbf{p}_0$ and $\mathbf{p}_5 - \mathbf{p}_4$. A second-degree *B*-spline curve (such as this is) is also tangent to each successive side of the characteristic polygon. [Do not confuse the function $\mathbf{p}_i(u)$ with the control point $\mathbf{p}_i$.]

$N_{0,1}(u) = 1$ for $u = 0$
$\qquad\quad = 0$ otherwise
$N_{1,1}(u) = 1$ for $u = 0$
$\qquad\quad = 0$ otherwise
$N_{2,1}(u) = 1$ $u \in [0,1]$
$\qquad\quad = 0$ otherwise
$N_{3,1}(u) = 1$ $u \in [1,2]$
$\qquad\quad = 0$ otherwise
$N_{4,1}(u) = 1$ $u \in [2,3]$
$\qquad\quad = 0$ otherwise
$N_{5,1}(u) = 1$ $u \in [3,4]$
$\qquad\quad = 0$ otherwise

($N_{i,2}$ functions not shown)

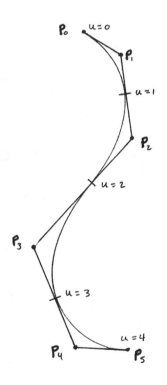

B-Spline Blending Functions:
$n = 5$, $k = 3$ (Nonperiodic)

For a nonperiodic *B*-spline curve with $n = 5$, $k = 2$, the blending functions $N_{i,k}(u)$ blend the contribution of the control points to produce the points that lie along the curve. Thus,

$$\mathbf{p}(u) = \mathbf{p}_0 N_{0,2}(u) + \mathbf{p}_1 N_{1,2}(u) + \mathbf{p}_2 N_{2,2}(u)$$
$$+ \mathbf{p}_3 N_{3,2}(u) + \mathbf{p}_4 N_{4,2}(u) + \mathbf{p}_5 N_{5,2}(u)$$

where

$$N_{0,2} = (1 - u)N_{1,1}$$
$$N_{1,2} = uN_{1,1} + (2 - u)N_{2,1}$$
$$N_{2,2} = (u - 1)N_{2,1} + (3 - u)N_{3,1}$$
$$N_{3,2} = (u - 2)N_{3,1} + (4 - u)N_{4,1}$$
$$N_{4,2} = (u - 3)N_{4,1} + (5 - u)N_{5,1}$$
$$N_{5,2} = (u - 4)N_{5,1}$$

The functional notation is dropped for conciseness.

The terms in these blending functions are activated by the $N_{i,1}$ switches:

$$N_{1,1} = 1 \quad \text{for } u \in [0,1]$$
$$N_{2,1} = 1 \quad \text{for } u \in [1,2]$$
$$N_{3,1} = 1 \quad \text{for } u \in [2,3]$$
$$N_{4,1} = 1 \quad \text{for } u \in [3,4]$$
$$N_{5,1} = 1 \quad \text{for } u \in [4,5]$$

Outside the indicated intervals the $N_{i,1} = 0$.

The addition of more control points does not change these blending functions. The extra blending functions will be of the same form as $N_{1,2}$ through $N_{4,2}$.

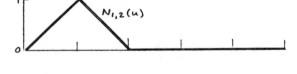

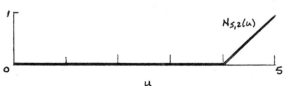

B-Spline Blending Functions:
$n = 5$, $k = 2$ (Nonperiodic)

For a nonperiodic *B*-spline curve with $n = 5$, $k = 3$, the blending functions blend the contribution of the control points as follows:

$$\mathbf{p}(u) = \mathbf{p}_0 N_{0,3}(u) + \mathbf{p}_1 N_{1,3}(u) + \mathbf{p}_2 N_{2,3}(u)$$
$$+ \mathbf{p}_3 N_{3,3}(u) + \mathbf{p}_4 N_{4,3}(u) + \mathbf{p}_5 N_{5,3}(u)$$

where

$N_{0,3} = (1 - u)^2 N_{2,1}$

$N_{1,3} = \frac{1}{2}u(4 - 3u)N_{2,1} + \frac{1}{2}(2 - u)^2 N_{3,1}$

$N_{2,3} = \frac{1}{2}u^2 N_{2,1} + \frac{1}{2}(-2u^2 + 6u - 3)N_{3,1} + \frac{1}{2}(3 - u)^2 N_{4,1}$

$N_{3,3} = \frac{1}{2}(u - 1)^2 N_{3,1} + \frac{1}{2}(-2u^2 + 10u - 11)N_{4,1} + \frac{1}{2}(4 - u)^2 N_{5,1}$

$N_{4,3} = \frac{1}{2}(u - 2)^2 N_{4,1} + \frac{1}{2}(-3u^2 + 20u - 32)N_{5,1}$

$N_{5,3} = (u - 3)^2 N_{5,1}$

$N_{2,1} = 1 \quad u \in [0,1]$
$N_{3,1} = 1 \quad u \in [1,2]$
$N_{4,1} = 1 \quad u \in [2,3]$
$N_{5,1} = 1 \quad u \in [3,4]$

Outside the indicated intervals the $N_{i,1} = 0$.

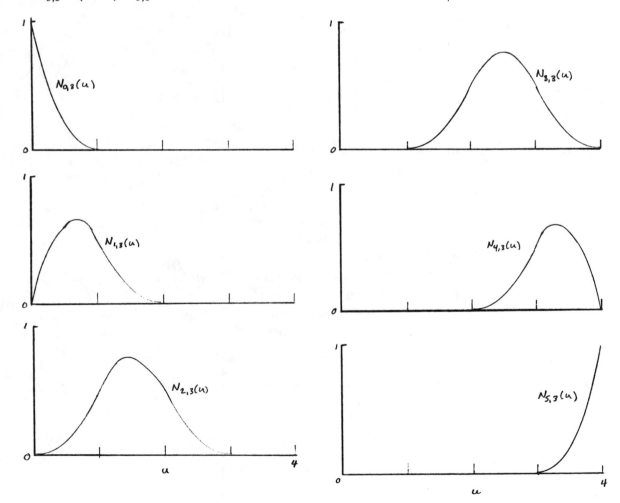

Periodic B-Spline Curves: Open

For an open* periodic B-spline curve with $k = 3$,

$$\mathbf{p}_i(u) = \tfrac{1}{2}[u^2 \ u \ 1] \begin{bmatrix} 1 & -2 & 1 \\ -2 & 2 & 0 \\ 1 & 1 & 0 \end{bmatrix} \begin{bmatrix} \mathbf{p}_{i-1} \\ \mathbf{p}_i \\ \mathbf{p}_{i+1} \end{bmatrix} \quad \begin{array}{l} i \in [1:n-1] \\ u \in [0,1] \end{array}$$

For $k = 4$ (again, an open curve),

$$\mathbf{p}_i(u) = \tfrac{1}{6}[u^3 \ u^2 \ u \ 1] \begin{bmatrix} -1 & 3 & -3 & 1 \\ 3 & -6 & 3 & 0 \\ -3 & 0 & 3 & 0 \\ 1 & 4 & 1 & 0 \end{bmatrix} \begin{bmatrix} \mathbf{p}_{i-1} \\ \mathbf{p}_i \\ \mathbf{p}_{i+1} \\ \mathbf{p}_{i+2} \end{bmatrix} \quad \begin{array}{l} i \in [1:n-2] \\ u \in [0,1] \end{array}$$

The general formulation for an open B-spline curve is

$$\mathbf{p}_i(u) = \mathbf{U}_k \mathbf{M}_k \mathbf{P}_k \qquad i \in [1:n+2-k] \qquad (7.35)$$

where

$$\mathbf{U}_k = [u^{k-1} \ u^{k-2} \ \cdots \ u \ 1]$$

and

$$\mathbf{p}_k = [\mathbf{p}_j] \qquad j \in [i-1:i+k-2]$$

---

*A closed periodic B-spline curve has a slightly different formulation.

To compute the $N_{i,k}$ for an open periodic B-spline curve choose an interval in i so that $i \in [k:n]$. This simplifies the calculation of the t_i knot values, so that $t_i = i - k + 1$. Use the recursive formulas supporting Eq. (7.34). Find an expression for $p(u)$ over an arbitrary segment, say for the interval $u \in [i, i+1]$. Reparametrize the interval so that $u \in [0,1]$. The resulting algebraic expression can then be easily recomposed into a matrix formulation as above.

Periodic because the blending function repeats itself identically over successive intervals.

i denotes both the curve segment number $\mathbf{p}_i(u)$ and the control point $\mathbf{p}_i$.

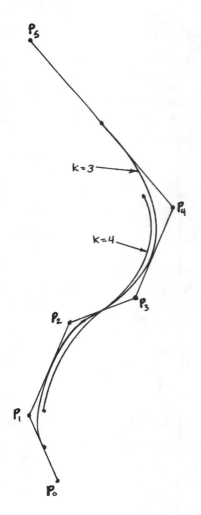

Periodic Blending Functions: $k = 2, 3, 4$

From Eq. (7.35) for $\mathbf{p}_3(u)$ and $\mathbf{p}_4(u)$ let

$$\mathbf{F}_3 = \mathbf{U}_3 \mathbf{M}_3 \quad \text{and} \quad \mathbf{F}_4 = \mathbf{U}_4 \mathbf{M}_4$$

$$\mathbf{M}_3 = \begin{bmatrix} 1 & -2 & 1 \\ -2 & 2 & 0 \\ 1 & 1 & 0 \end{bmatrix}$$

where $\mathbf{F}_3$ and $\mathbf{F}_4$ are blending function matrices. Thus,

$$\mathbf{F}_3 = [F_{1,3}(u) \ \ F_{2,3}(u) \ \ F_{3,3}(u)]$$

$$\mathbf{M}_4 = \begin{bmatrix} -1 & 3 & -3 & 1 \\ 3 & -6 & 3 & 0 \\ -3 & 0 & 3 & 0 \\ 1 & 4 & 1 & 0 \end{bmatrix}$$

$$F_{1,3}(u) = \tfrac{1}{2}(u^2 - 2u + 1)$$
$$F_{2,3}(u) = \tfrac{1}{2}(-2u^2 + 2u + 1)$$
$$F_{3,3}(u) = \tfrac{1}{2}u^2$$

and

$$\mathbf{F}_4 = [F_{1,4}(u) \ \ F_{2,4}(u) \ \ F_{3,4}(u) \ \ F_{4,4}(u)]$$

$$F_{1,4}(u) = \tfrac{1}{6}(-u^3 + 3u^2 - 3u + 1)$$
$$F_{2,4}(u) = \tfrac{1}{6}(3u^3 - 6u^2 + 4)$$
$$F_{3,4}(u) = \tfrac{1}{6}(-3u^3 + 3u^2 + 3u + 1)$$
$$F_{4,4}(u) = \tfrac{1}{6}u^3$$

$$F_{1,4}^u(u) = \tfrac{1}{2}(-u^2 + 2u - 1)$$
$$F_{2,4}^u(u) = \tfrac{1}{2}(3u^2 - 4u)$$
$$F_{3,4}^u(u) = \tfrac{1}{2}(-3u^2 + 2u + 1)$$
$$F_{4,4}^u(u) = \tfrac{1}{2}u^2$$

It is instructive to interpret the $\mathbf{F}_i$ as $N_{i,k}$ distributed over n intervals.

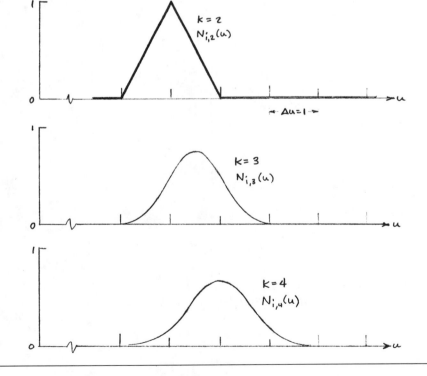

$$\left. \begin{aligned} F_{1,3} &= N_{i+1,3} \\ F_{2,3} &= N_{i,3} \\ F_{3,3} &= N_{i-1,3} \end{aligned} \right\} u \in [i-1, i+1]$$

$$\left. \begin{aligned} F_{1,4} &= N_{i+2,4} \\ F_{2,4} &= N_{i+1,4} \\ F_{3,4} &= N_{i,4} \\ F_{4,4} &= N_{i-1,4} \end{aligned} \right\} u \in [i-1, i+2]$$

Periodic *B*-Spline Curves: Closed

The periodic *B*-spline curves are well suited to produce closed curves. Equation (7.35) is adapted to this end by simple modification of the segment number range and the subscripts on the control points.

For $k = 3$:

$$\mathbf{p}_i(u) = \mathbf{U}_3\mathbf{M}_3 \begin{bmatrix} \mathbf{P}_{(i-1)\bmod(n+1)} \\ \mathbf{P}_{i\bmod(n+1)} \\ \mathbf{P}_{(i+1)\bmod(n+1)} \end{bmatrix} \quad i\in[1:n+1]$$

For $k = 4$:

$$\mathbf{p}_i(u) = \mathbf{U}_4\mathbf{M}_4 \begin{bmatrix} \mathbf{P}_{(i-1)\bmod(n+1)} \\ \mathbf{P}_{i\bmod(n+1)} \\ \mathbf{P}_{(i+1)\bmod(n+1)} \\ \mathbf{P}_{(i+2)\bmod(n+1)} \end{bmatrix} \quad i\in[i:n+1]$$

Multi-coincident control points produce local changes in a curve that bring it closer to the characteristic polygon.

Where "mod" is the remaindering operator (i.e., 3 mod 7 = 3, 9 mod 7 = 2, 7 mod 7 = 0, etc.).

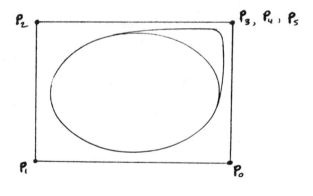

"All that transcend geometry, transcends our comprehension."
Blaise Pascal

Vector Equation of a Surface

A surface is a collection of points whose coordinates are given by continuous, two-parameter, single-valued mathematical functions of the form

$$x = x(u,w) \qquad y = y(u,w) \qquad z = z(u,w)$$

If the parametric variables u and w are constrained to a finite interval, then a finite, curve-bounded piece of a surface is produced, sometimes called a **patch**.

Surfaces are effectively represented by a vector equation, in two parameters, of the form

$$\mathbf{p}(u,w) = [x(u,w) \; y(u,w) \; z(u,w)] \qquad u,w \in [0,1]$$

Here a patch is defined over **the unit square** in parametric space.

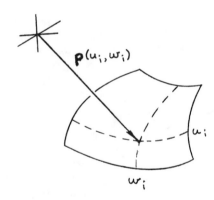

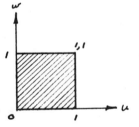

The parametric representation covers a surface with two families of curves: $u = $ constant curves and $w = $ constant curves.

Example

The parametric equations of a sphere of radius r and centered at (x_0, y_0, z_0) are

$$\begin{aligned}
x &= x_0 + r \cos u \cos w \qquad & u \in [-\pi/2, \pi/2] \\
y &= y_0 + r \cos u \sin w \qquad & w \in [0, 2\pi] \\
z &= z_0 + r \sin u
\end{aligned}$$

General Characteristics of a Parametric Patch

A parametrically defined patch $\mathbf{p} = \mathbf{p}(u,w)$, with $u,w \in [0,1]$, has several well-defined characteristics. These include boundary conditions and interior properties.

The four boundary curves correspond to $u = 0$, $u = 1$, $w = 0$, and $w = 1$: $\mathbf{p} = \mathbf{p}(0,w)$, $\mathbf{p} = \mathbf{p}(1,w)$, $\mathbf{p} = \mathbf{p}(u,0)$, and $\mathbf{p} = \mathbf{p}(u,1)$. The four corner points are $\mathbf{p}_{00} = \mathbf{p}(0,0)$, $\mathbf{p}_{10} = \mathbf{p}(1,0)$, $\mathbf{p}_{01} = \mathbf{p}(0,1)$, and $\mathbf{p}_{11} = \mathbf{p}(1,1)$.

At any point on a patch there are two tangent vectors and a normal vector: $\mathbf{p}^u(u,w)$, $\mathbf{p}^w(u,w)$, and $\mathbf{n}(u,w)$. Later sections describe their computation.

Finally, the parametric net of two one-parameter families of curves on the patch are formed by holding constant first one and then the other parametric variable: $\mathbf{p} = \mathbf{p}(u_i,w)$ and $\mathbf{p} = \mathbf{p}(u,w_j)$, where u_i and w_j are constants.

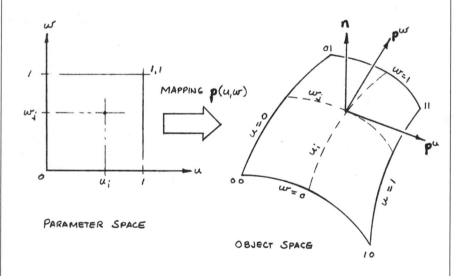

PARAMETER SPACE

OBJECT SPACE

The parametric equations map points from the u,w parameter space into the x,y,z object space.

A net of curves on a patch is two one-parameter families of curves having the properties that through each point on the patch there passes just one curve of each family, and the two tangents are distinct.

An orthogonal net of curves on a patch is a net such that at each point on the patch the two curves of the net intersect at right angles. A necessary and sufficient condition that the parametric net is orthogonal is

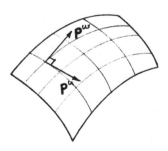

$$\mathbf{p}^u \cdot \mathbf{p}^w = 0$$

Tensor Product Polynomials

Single parametric variable polynomials describe curves (one-dimensional geometric objects). Polynomials in two parametric variables describe surfaces or surface patches (two-dimensional geometric objects). To describe objects of higher dimension requires a system for generating polynomial functions of many parametric variables.

Let $(u_1, u_2, \ldots)$ be a set of independent parametric variables and $B_i(u_1)$, $B_j(u_2)$, $\ldots$, be a set of basis polynomials in these parameters. The simplest way to produce a polynomial function of these parameters requires forming the **tensor product** of the basis functions,

$$\sum_i \sum_j \cdots a_{ij\ldots} B_i(u_1) B_j(u_2) \cdots$$

The coefficients $a_{ij\ldots}$ are treated as a multidimensional matrix or tensor. There is a subscript index on $a_{ij\ldots}$ for each parametric variable. The summation of the products of each coefficient with its corresponding basis functions is called a **contraction** of $a_{ij\ldots}$ on those basis functions. Each index is contracted on the basis in its corresponding parametric variable.

This is very basic, very general stuff. The point of presenting it here is that it forms the foundation for many surface modeling schemes: Hermité, Bézier, B-spline, and others. Also, by starting at this level you can "invent" your own basis functions, albeit with considerable care and attention to a lot of nasty little details.

Bicubic Patch: Algebraic Form

The algebraic form of a bicubic patch is given by

$$\mathbf{p}(u,w) = \sum_{i=0}^{3} \sum_{j=0}^{3} \mathbf{a}_{ij} u^i w^j \qquad u,w \in [0,1] \qquad (8.1)$$

where $\mathbf{p}(u,w)$ is a point on the patch, u and w are the parametric variables, and the vectors $\mathbf{a}_{ij}$ are called the algebraic coefficients. When expanded, the equation provides a 16-term polynomial in u and w:

$$\begin{aligned}
\mathbf{p}(u,w) = \; & \mathbf{a}_{33}u^3w^3 + \mathbf{a}_{32}u^3w^2 + \mathbf{a}_{31}u^3w + \mathbf{a}_{30}u^3 \\
& + \mathbf{a}_{23}u^2w^3 + \mathbf{a}_{22}u^2w^2 + \mathbf{a}_{21}u^2w + \mathbf{a}_{20}u^2 \\
& + \mathbf{a}_{13}uw^3 + \mathbf{a}_{12}uw^2 + \mathbf{a}_{11}uw + \mathbf{a}_{10}u \\
& + \mathbf{a}_{03}w^3 + \mathbf{a}_{02}w^2 + \mathbf{a}_{01}w + \mathbf{a}_{00}
\end{aligned}$$

Using matrix notation, the algebraic form is

$$\mathbf{p} = \mathbf{A}\mathbf{U}\mathbf{W}^T \qquad (8.2)$$

where $\mathbf{u} = [u^3 \; u^2 \; u \; 1]$, $\mathbf{W} = [w^3 \; w^2 \; w \; 1]$, and

$$\mathbf{A} = \begin{bmatrix} \mathbf{a}_{33} & \mathbf{a}_{32} & \mathbf{a}_{31} & \mathbf{a}_{30} \\ \mathbf{a}_{23} & \mathbf{a}_{22} & \mathbf{a}_{21} & \mathbf{a}_{20} \\ \mathbf{a}_{13} & \mathbf{a}_{12} & \mathbf{a}_{11} & \mathbf{a}_{10} \\ \mathbf{a}_{03} & \mathbf{a}_{02} & \mathbf{a}_{01} & \mathbf{a}_{00} \end{bmatrix}$$

The four corner points are

$$\begin{aligned}
\mathbf{p}_{00} &= \mathbf{a}_{00} \\
\mathbf{p}_{01} &= \mathbf{a}_{03} + \mathbf{a}_{02} + \mathbf{a}_{01} + \mathbf{a}_{00} \\
\mathbf{p}_{10} &= \mathbf{a}_{30} + \mathbf{a}_{20} + \mathbf{a}_{10} + \mathbf{a}_{00} \\
\mathbf{p}_{11} &= \mathbf{a}_{33} + \mathbf{a}_{32} + \mathbf{a}_{31} + \cdots + \mathbf{a}_{01} + \mathbf{a}_{00}
\end{aligned}$$

The four boundary curves are

$$\begin{aligned}
\mathbf{p}_{u0} &= \mathbf{a}_{30}u^3 + \mathbf{a}_{20}u^2 + \mathbf{a}_{10}u + \mathbf{a}_{00} \\
\mathbf{p}_{u1} &= (\mathbf{a}_{33} + \mathbf{a}_{32} + \mathbf{a}_{31} + \mathbf{a}_{30})u^3 \\
& \quad + \cdots + (\mathbf{a}_{03} + \mathbf{a}_{02} + \mathbf{a}_{01} + \mathbf{a}_{00}) \\
\mathbf{p}_{0w} &= \mathbf{a}_{03}w^3 + \mathbf{a}_{02}w^2 + \mathbf{a}_{01}w + \mathbf{a}_{00} \\
\mathbf{p}_{1w} &= (\mathbf{a}_{33} + \mathbf{a}_{23} + \mathbf{a}_{13} + \mathbf{a}_{03})w^2 \\
& \quad + \cdots + (\mathbf{a}_{30} + \mathbf{a}_{20} + \mathbf{a}_{10} + \mathbf{a}_{00})
\end{aligned}$$

The bicubic patch is the two-dimensional analog of the parametric cubic curve.

Each u,w pair produces a point $\mathbf{p}(u,w)$.

Since each $\mathbf{a}_{ij}$ vector coefficient has three independent components, there is a total of 48 algebraic coefficients, or 48 degrees of freedom.

Note: here the subscripts on $\mathbf{a}$ do not happen to correspond to normal matrix element notation.

To evaluate the polynomial, an efficient arrangement that readily adapts to forward differencing is

$$\begin{aligned}
\mathbf{p}(u,w) = \; & \\
\mathbf{a}_{00} + & w(\mathbf{a}_{01} + w(\mathbf{a}_{02} + \mathbf{a}_{03}w)) \\
+ u\{ & \mathbf{a}_{10} + w(\mathbf{a}_{11} + w(\mathbf{a}_{12} + \mathbf{a}_{13}w)) \\
+ u\{ & \mathbf{a}_{20} + w(\mathbf{a}_{21} + w(\mathbf{a}_{22} + \mathbf{a}_{23}w)) \\
+ u\{ & \mathbf{a}_{30} + w(\mathbf{a}_{31} + w(\mathbf{a}_{32} + \mathbf{a}_{33}w))\}\}\}
\end{aligned}$$

Bicubic Patch: Geometric Form

The geometric form is based on certain patch boundary conditions. These, in turn, yield geometric coefficients. There must be 48 of them, or 16 if in vector form. The boundary conditions are: the four corner points, eight tangent vectors (two at each corner, one in the u direction and one in the w direction), and four twist vectors* (one at each corner).

Twist vectors:

$$\mathbf{p}_{00}^{uw} \quad \mathbf{p}_{10}^{uw}$$
$$\mathbf{p}_{01}^{uw} \quad \mathbf{p}_{11}^{uw}$$

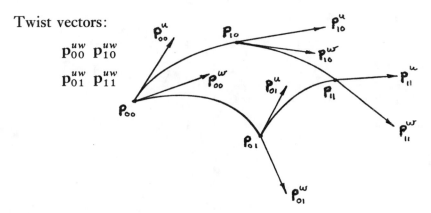

$$\mathbf{p}^u = \frac{\partial \mathbf{p}(u,w)}{\partial u}$$

$$\mathbf{p}^w = \frac{\partial \mathbf{p}(u,w)}{\partial w}$$

$$\mathbf{p}^{uw} = \frac{\partial \mathbf{p}(u,w)}{\partial u \partial w}$$

In matrix form:

$$\mathbf{p}(u,w) = \mathbf{UMBM}^T\mathbf{W}^T \tag{8.3}$$

where

$$\mathbf{B} = \begin{bmatrix} \mathbf{p}_{00} & \mathbf{p}_{01} & \mathbf{p}_{00}^w & \mathbf{p}_{01}^w \\ \mathbf{p}_{10} & \mathbf{p}_{11} & \mathbf{p}_{10}^w & \mathbf{p}_{11}^w \\ \mathbf{p}_{00}^u & \mathbf{p}_{01}^u & \mathbf{p}_{00}^{uw} & \mathbf{p}_{01}^{uw} \\ \mathbf{p}_{10}^u & \mathbf{p}_{11}^u & \mathbf{p}_{10}^{uw} & \mathbf{p}_{11}^{uw} \end{bmatrix}$$

Alternatively:

$$\mathbf{p}(u,w) = \mathbf{F}(u)\mathbf{BF}(w)^T$$

---

*Less intuitively, but more formally known as the mixed partial derivative vectors.

"This science [mathematics] does not have for its unique objective to eternally contemplate its own navel; it touches nature and some day it will make contact with it."

Henri Poincaré

Bicubic Patch: Geometric Coefficients

The 16 vectors comprising the geometric coefficients are easily expressed in terms of the algebraic coefficients.

$\mathbf{p}_{00} = \mathbf{a}_{00}$

$\mathbf{p}_{01} = \mathbf{a}_{03} + \mathbf{a}_{02} + \mathbf{a}_{01} + \mathbf{a}_{00}$

$\mathbf{p}_{10} = \mathbf{a}_{30} + \mathbf{a}_{20} + \mathbf{a}_{10} + \mathbf{a}_{00}$

$\begin{aligned} \mathbf{p}_{11} = {}& \mathbf{a}_{33} + \mathbf{a}_{32} + \mathbf{a}_{31} + \mathbf{a}_{30} \\ & + \mathbf{a}_{23} + \mathbf{a}_{22} + \mathbf{a}_{21} + \mathbf{a}_{20} \\ & + \mathbf{a}_{13} + \mathbf{a}_{12} + \mathbf{a}_{11} + \mathbf{a}_{10} \\ & + \mathbf{a}_{03} + \mathbf{a}_{02} + \mathbf{a}_{01} + \mathbf{a}_{00} \end{aligned}$

$\mathbf{p}_{00}^{u} = \mathbf{a}_{10}$

$\mathbf{p}_{01}^{u} = \mathbf{a}_{13} + \mathbf{a}_{12} + \mathbf{a}_{11} + \mathbf{a}_{10}$

$\mathbf{p}_{10}^{u} = 3\mathbf{a}_{30} + 2\mathbf{a}_{20} + \mathbf{a}_{10}$

$\begin{aligned} \mathbf{p}_{11}^{u} = {}& 3\mathbf{a}_{33} + 3\mathbf{a}_{32} + 3\mathbf{a}_{31} + 3\mathbf{a}_{30} \\ & + 2\mathbf{a}_{23} + 2\mathbf{a}_{22} + 2\mathbf{a}_{21} + 2\mathbf{a}_{20} \\ & + \mathbf{a}_{13} + \mathbf{a}_{12} + \mathbf{a}_{11} + \mathbf{a}_{10} \end{aligned}$

$\mathbf{p}^{u} = \dfrac{\partial \mathbf{p}(u,w)}{\partial u}$

$\mathbf{p}_{00}^{w} = \mathbf{a}_{01}$

$\mathbf{p}_{01}^{w} = 3\mathbf{a}_{03} + 2\mathbf{a}_{02} + \mathbf{a}_{01}$

$\mathbf{p}_{01}^{w} = \mathbf{a}_{31} + \mathbf{a}_{21} + \mathbf{a}_{11} + \mathbf{a}_{01}$

$\begin{aligned} \mathbf{p}_{11}^{w} = {}& 3\mathbf{a}_{33} + 2\mathbf{a}_{32} + \mathbf{a}_{31} \\ & + 3\mathbf{a}_{23} + 2\mathbf{a}_{22} + \mathbf{a}_{21} \\ & + 3\mathbf{a}_{13} + 2\mathbf{a}_{12} + \mathbf{a}_{11} \\ & + 3\mathbf{a}_{03} + 2\mathbf{a}_{02} + \mathbf{a}_{01} \end{aligned}$

$\mathbf{p}^{w} = \dfrac{\partial \mathbf{p}(u,w)}{\partial w}$

$\mathbf{p}_{00}^{uw} = \mathbf{a}_{11}$

$\mathbf{p}_{01}^{uw} = 3\mathbf{a}_{13} + 2\mathbf{a}_{12} + \mathbf{a}_{11}$

$\mathbf{p}_{10}^{uw} = 3\mathbf{a}_{31} + 2\mathbf{a}_{21} + \mathbf{a}_{11}$

$\begin{aligned} \mathbf{p}_{11}^{uw} = {}& 9\mathbf{a}_{33} + 6\mathbf{a}_{32} + 3\mathbf{a}_{31} \\ & + 6\mathbf{a}_{23} + 4\mathbf{a}_{22} + 2\mathbf{a}_{21} \\ & + 3\mathbf{a}_{13} + 2\mathbf{a}_{12} + \mathbf{a}_{11} \end{aligned}$

$\mathbf{p}^{uw} = \dfrac{\partial \mathbf{p}(u,w)}{\partial u \partial w}$

The algebraic and geometric coefficients are interrelated:

$\mathbf{A} = \mathbf{MBM}^{T}$

$\mathbf{B} = \mathbf{M}^{-1}\mathbf{AM}^{T-1}$

Bicubic Patch: 16–Point Form

A 4×4 grid of points is sufficient to define a bicubic patch. Assume the u,w values are at the third points:

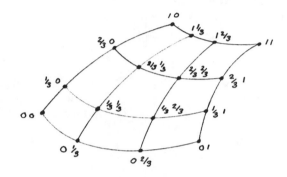

$$\mathbf{p}(u,w) = \mathbf{UNPN}^T\mathbf{W}^T \tag{8.4}$$

This expression is derived in Mortenson's *Geometric Modeling*.

where

$$\mathbf{P} = \begin{bmatrix} \mathbf{p}(0,0) & \mathbf{p}(0,1/3) & \mathbf{p}(0,2/3) & \mathbf{p}(0,1) \\ \mathbf{p}(1/3,0) & \mathbf{p}(1/3,1/3) & \mathbf{p}(1/3,2/3) & \mathbf{p}(1/3,1) \\ \mathbf{p}(2/3,0) & \mathbf{p}(2/3,1/3) & \mathbf{p}(2/3,2/3) & \mathbf{p}(2/3,1) \\ \mathbf{p}(1,0) & \mathbf{p}(1,1/3) & \mathbf{p}(1,2/3) & \mathbf{p}(1,1) \end{bmatrix}$$

and

$$\mathbf{N} = \begin{bmatrix} -9/2 & 27/2 & -27/2 & 9/2 \\ 9 & -45/2 & 18 & -9/2 \\ -11/2 & 9 & -9/2 & 1 \\ 1 & 0 & 0 & 0 \end{bmatrix}$$

Since

$$\mathbf{P} = \mathbf{UMBM}^T\mathbf{W}^T = \mathbf{UNPN}^T\mathbf{W}^T,$$

then

$$\mathbf{B} = \mathbf{LPL}^T$$

where

$$\mathbf{L} = \mathbf{M}^{-1}\mathbf{N} = \begin{bmatrix} 1 & 0 & 0 & 0 \\ 0 & 0 & 0 & 1 \\ -11/2 & 9 & -9/2 & 1 \\ -1 & 9/2 & -9 & 11/2 \end{bmatrix}$$

Bicubic Patch: Cylindrical Surface

A cylindrical surface is generated by a straight line as it moves parallel to itself along a director curve. If the direction and length of the straight line are defined by the vector $\mathbf{a}$, and if the director curve is given by a parametric cubic curve, then a cylindrical bicubic patch is produced by these geometric coefficients:

$$\mathbf{B} = \begin{bmatrix} \mathbf{p}_0 & \mathbf{p}_0 + \mathbf{a} & \mathbf{a} & \mathbf{a} \\ \mathbf{p}_1 & \mathbf{p}_1 + \mathbf{a} & \mathbf{a} & \mathbf{a} \\ \mathbf{p}_0^u & \mathbf{p}_0^u & 0 & 0 \\ \mathbf{p}_1^u & \mathbf{p}_1^u & 0 & 0 \end{bmatrix}$$

Note: here the director curve corresponds to the $w = 0$ boundary curve of the patch.

A more general form of cylindrical surface is

$$\mathbf{p}(u,w) = \mathbf{q}(u) + w\mathbf{r}$$

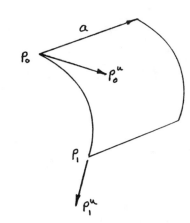

"Let us grant that the pursuit of mathematics is a divine madness of the human spirit."

Alfred North Whitehead

Composite Bicubic Patches

Many bicubic patches can be assembled in a rectangular grid to represent a surface too complex for a single patch.

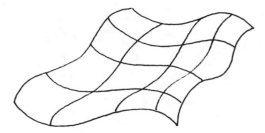

To preserve C^1 continuity certain relationships must hold at the boundaries between patches. Here is an example of conditions prevailing at the point common to four patches.

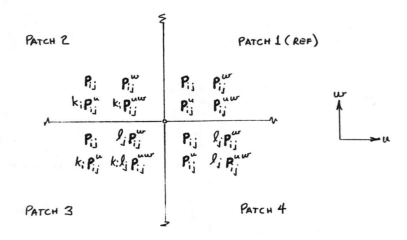

k_i and l_j are scalars.

Bézier Surface

The equation defining points on a Bézier surface patch is analogous to that defining points on a Bézier curve:

$$\mathbf{p}(u,w) = \sum_{i=0}^{m} \sum_{j=0}^{n} \mathbf{p}_{ij} B_{i,m}(u) B_{j,n}(w) \qquad (8.5)$$

where $u,w \in [0,1]$. The $\mathbf{p}_{ij}$ form a $(m+1) \times (n+1)$ rectangular array of control points and are the vertices of the so-called characteristic polyhedron. $B_{i,m}(u)$ and $B_{j,n}(w)$ are the Bézier basis functions (or blending functions), defined exactly as for Bézier curves.

A 4×4 array of points defines a bicubic Bézier patch:

$$\mathbf{p}(u,w) = [(1-u)^3 \ \ 3u(1-u)^2 \ \ 3u^2(1-u) \ \ u^3]\mathbf{P} \begin{bmatrix} (1-w)^3 \\ 3w(1-w)^2 \\ 3w^2(1-w) \\ w^3 \end{bmatrix} \qquad (8.6)$$

where $\mathbf{P} = \begin{bmatrix} \mathbf{p}_{11} & \mathbf{p}_{12} & \mathbf{p}_{13} & \mathbf{p}_{14} \\ \mathbf{p}_{21} & \mathbf{p}_{22} & \mathbf{p}_{23} & \mathbf{p}_{24} \\ \mathbf{p}_{31} & \mathbf{p}_{32} & \mathbf{p}_{33} & \mathbf{p}_{34} \\ \mathbf{p}_{41} & \mathbf{p}_{42} & \mathbf{p}_{43} & \mathbf{p}_{44} \end{bmatrix}$

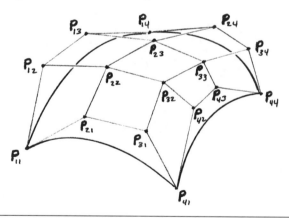

A rational Bézier surface is expressed as

$$\mathbf{p}(u,w) = \frac{\sum_{i=0}^{m} \sum_{j=0}^{n} \mathbf{p}_{ij} h_{ij} B_{i,m}(u) B_{j,n}(w)}{\sum_{i=0}^{m} \sum_{j=0}^{n} h_{ij} B_{i,m}(u) B_{j,n}(w)}$$

where the h_{ij} are weights.

Any tensor product surface can be converted into the Bézier form.

"Form ever follows function."

Louis Henri Sullivan

Bézier and Hermité Bicubic Patches

It is possible to convert from the bicubic Bézier to bicubic Hermitian basis, and vice versa.

First, from Eq. (8.6), the matrix of terms containing the parametric variable u decomposes as follows:

$$[(1 - u)^3 \quad 3u(1 - u)^2 \quad 3u^2(1 - u) \quad u^3]$$

$$= [u^3 \quad u^2 \quad u \quad 1] \begin{bmatrix} -1 & 3 & -3 & 1 \\ 3 & -6 & 3 & 0 \\ -3 & 3 & 0 & 0 \\ 1 & 0 & 0 & 0 \end{bmatrix} = \mathbf{UM}_z$$

Here the subscript z denotes a Bézier basis matrix and distinguishes it from the Hermité bicubic form. The matrix of w terms decomposes in an analogous way. Equation (8.5) can be written now as

$$\mathbf{p}(u,w) = \mathbf{UM}_z \mathbf{PM}_z^T \mathbf{W}^T$$

Equating this to the Hermitian form yields

$$\mathbf{UMBM}^T \mathbf{W}^T = \mathbf{UM}_z \mathbf{PM}_z^T \mathbf{W}^T$$

or

$$\mathbf{MBM}^T = \mathbf{M}_z \mathbf{PM}_z^T$$

so that

$$\mathbf{B} = \begin{bmatrix} p_{11} & p_{14} & 3(p_{12} - p_{11}) & 3(p_{14} - p_{13}) \\ p_{41} & p_{44} & 3(p_{42} - p_{41}) & 3(p_{44} - p_{43}) \\ 3(p_{21} - p_{11}) & 3(p_{24} - p_{14}) & 9(p_{11} - p_{21} - p_{12} + p_{22}) & 9(p_{13} - p_{23} - p_{14} + p_{24}) \\ 3(p_{41} - p_{31}) & 3(p_{44} - p_{24}) & 9(p_{31} - p_{41} - p_{32} + p_{42}) & 9(p_{33} - p_{43} - p_{34} + p_{44}) \end{bmatrix}$$

Composite Bézier Patches

Observe how some very simple geometric properties and their subsequent application allow several Bézier patches to be assembled with C^1 continuity along their common boundaries. Consider the two bicubic Bézier patches below (the control points are shown idealized in a rectangular grid for clarity). Their common boundary curve is defined by p_{14}, p_{24}, p_{34}, and p_{44}. To ensure slope (C^1) continuity across this boundary, all four sets of $\{p_{i,3}, p_{i,4}, p_{i,5}\}$, $i \in [1:4]$ must be collinear. This is easily generalized to other combinations of Bézier patches.

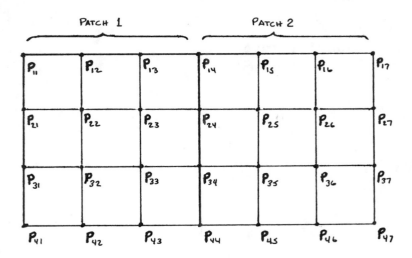

Eight-Patch Bézier Sphere

Here is an assembly of eight Bézier bicubic patches defining a sphere with unit radius and centered at the origin. It is an approximation, since these patches cannot be constructed to exactly represent a sphere. The coordinates of the complete set of control points are on the following page.

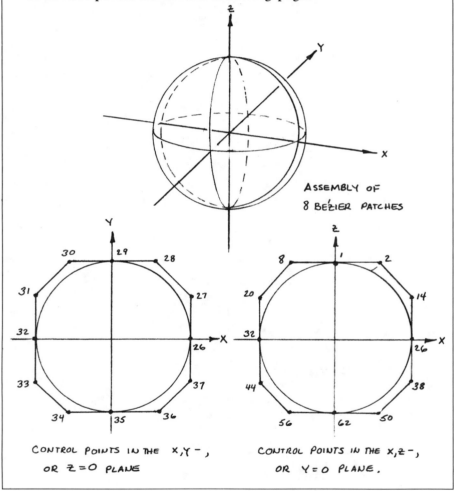

ASSEMBLY OF 8 BÉZIER PATCHES

CONTROL POINTS IN THE X,Y -, OR Z = 0 PLANE

CONTROL POINTS IN THE X,Z -, OR Y = 0 PLANE.

"The study of mathematics is apt to commence in disappointment . . . . We are told that by its aid the stars are weighed and the billions of molecules in a drop of water are counted. Yet, like the ghost of Hamlet's father, this great science eludes the efforts of our mental weapons to grasp it."

Alfred North Whitehead

Eight–Patch Bézier Sphere Data

Patch Number	Control Point Number															
1	1	1	1	1	2	3	4	5	14	15	16	17	26	27	28	29
2	1	1	1	1	5	6	7	8	17	18	19	20	29	30	31	32
3	1	1	1	1	8	9	10	11	20	21	22	23	32	33	34	35
4	1	1	1	1	11	12	13	2	23	24	25	14	35	36	37	26
5	26	27	28	29	38	39	40	41	50	51	52	53	62	62	62	62
6	29	30	31	32	41	42	43	44	53	54	55	56	62	62	62	62
7	32	33	34	35	44	45	46	47	56	57	58	59	62	62	62	62
8	35	36	37	26	47	48	49	38	59	60	61	50	62	62	62	62

Control Point	x	y	z	Control Point	x	y	z
1	0	0	1.0	32	−1.0	0	0
2	0.5523	0	1.0	33	−1.0	−0.5523	0
3	0.5523	0.3050	1.0	34	−0.5523	−1.0	0
4	0.3050	0.5523	1.0	35	0	−1.0	0
5	0	0.5523	1.0	36	0.5523	−1.0	0
6	−0.3050	0.5523	1.0	37	1.0	−0.5523	0
7	−0.5523	0.3050	1.0	38	1.0	0	−0.5523
8	−0.5523	0	1.0	39	1.0	0.5523	−0.5523
9	−0.5523	−0.3050	1.0	40	0.5523	1.0	−0.5523
10	−0.3050	−0.5523	1.0	41	0	1.0	−0.5523
11	0	−0.5523	1.0	42	−0.5523	1.0	−0.5523
12	0.3050	−0.5523	1.0	43	−1.0	0.5523	−0.5523
13	0.5523	−0.3050	1.0	44	−1.0	0	−0.5523
14	1.0	0	0.5523	45	−1.0	−0.5523	−0.5523
15	1.0	0.5523	0.5523	46	−0.5523	−1.0	−0.5523
16	0.5523	1.0	0.5523	47	0	−1.0	−0.5523
17	0	1.0	0.5523	48	0.5523	−1.0	−0.5523
18	−0.5523	1.0	0.5523	49	1.0	−0.5523	−0.5523
19	−1.0	0.5523	0.5523	50	0.5523	0	−1.0
20	−1.0	0	0.5523	51	0.5523	0.3050	−1.0
21	−1.0	−0.5523	0.5523	52	0.3050	0.5523	−1.0
22	−0.5523	−1.0	0.5523	53	0	0.5523	−1.0
23	0	−1.0	0.5523	54	−0.3050	0.5523	−1.0
24	0.5523	−1.0	0.5523	55	−0.5523	0.3050	−1.0
25	1.0	−0.5523	0.5523	56	−0.5523	0	−1.0
26	1.0	0	0	57	−0.5523	−0.3050	−1.0
27	1.0	0.5523	0	58	−0.3050	−0.5523	−1.0
28	0.5523	1.0	0	59	0	−0.5523	−1.0
29	0	1.0	0	60	0.3050	−0.5523	−1.0
30	−0.5523	1.0	0	61	0.5523	−0.3050	−1.0
31	−1.0	0.5523	0	62	0	0	−1.0

16-Patch Bézier Torus

Here is an assembly of four Bézier bicubic patches defining one quadrant of a 16-patch torus. The torus is centered at the origin, and its axis of symmetry corresponds to the z axis. The coordinates of the control points defining the four patches are on the following page. Those of the remaining three quadrants of the torus are easily computed by applying symmetry transformations.

The toroidal surface is generated by rotating a circle lying in the x,y plane around the z axis.

Control points in the $x = 0$ plane are located in like manner.

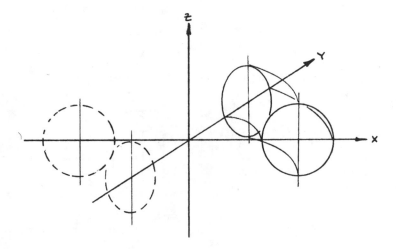

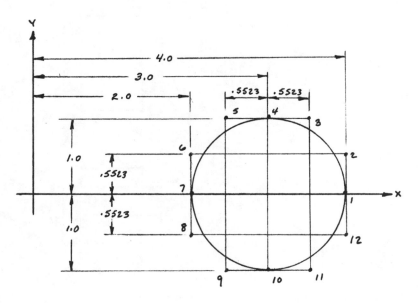

CONTROL POINTS IN THE X,Z, OR Y=0 PLANE

"It may be true that people who are 'merely' mathematicians have certain specific shortcomings; however, that is not the fault of mathematics, but is true of every exclusive occupation."
Carl Friedrich Gauss

16–Patch Bézier Torus Data

Patch Number	Control Point Number															
1	1	2	3	4	13	14	15	16	25	26	27	28	37	38	39	40
2	4	5	6	7	16	17	18	19	28	29	30	31	40	41	42	43
3	7	8	9	10	19	20	21	22	31	32	33	34	43	44	45	46
4	10	11	12	1	22	23	24	13	34	35	36	25	46	47	48	37

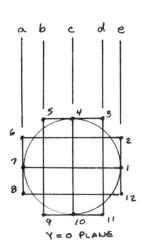

Y = 0 PLANE

Control Point	x	y	z	Control Point	x	y	z
1	4.0	0	0	25	2.2092	4.0	0
2	4.0	0	0.5523	26	2.2092	4.0	0.5523
3	3.5523	0	1.0	27	1.9619	3.5523	1.0
4	3.0	0	1.0	28	1.6569	3.0	1.0
5	2.4477	0	1.0	29	1.3519	2.4477	1.0
6	2.0	0	0.5523	30	1.0476	2.0	0.5523
7	2.0	0	0	31	1.0476	2.0	0
8	2.0	0	−0.5523	32	1.0476	2.0	−0.5523
9	2.4477	0	−1.0	33	1.3519	2.4477	−1.0
10	3.0	0	−1.0	34	1.6569	3.0	−1.0
11	3.5523	0	−1.0	35	1.9619	3.5523	−1.0
12	4.0	0	−0.5523	36	2.2092	4.0	−0.5523
13	4.0	2.2092	0	37	0	4.0	0
14	4.0	2.2092	0.5523	38	0	4.0	0.5523
15	3.5523	1.9619	1.0	39	0	3.5523	1.0
16	3.0	1.6569	1.0	40	0	3.0	1.0
17	2.4477	1.3519	1.0	41	0	2.4477	1.0
18	2.0	1.0476	0.5523	42	0	2.0	0.5523
19	2.0	1.0476	0	43	0	2.0	0
20	2.0	1.0476	−0.5523	44	0	2.0	−0.5523
21	2.4477	1.3519	−1.0	45	0	2.4477	−1.0
22	3.0	1.6569	−1.0	46	0	3.0	−1.0
23	3.5523	1.9619	−1.0	47	0	3.5523	−1.0
24	4.0	2.2092	−0.5523	48	0	4.0	−0.5523

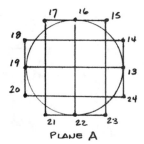

PLANE A

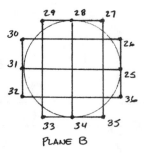

PLANE B

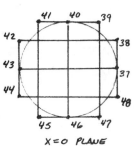

X = 0 PLANE

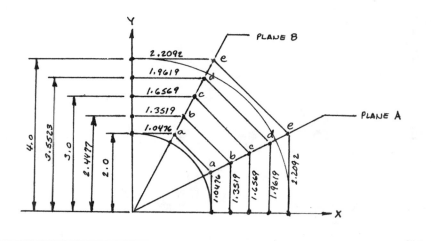

B-Spline Surface

The equation defining points on a *B*-spline surface is analogous to the equation for a *B*-spline curve:

$$\mathbf{p}(u,w) = \sum_{i=0}^{m} \sum_{j=0}^{n} \mathbf{p}_{ij} N_{ik}(u) N_{jl}(w) \tag{8.7}$$

where $u,w \in [0,1]$. The $\mathbf{p}_{ij}$ form an $(m+1) \times (n+1)$ rectangular array of control points, $N_{ik}(u)$ and $N_{jl}(w)$ are the *B*-spline basis functions, defined exactly as for *B*-spline curves.

The general matrix form of an open, periodic *B*-spline surface defined by an $(m+1) \times (n+1)$ array of points is

$$\mathbf{p}(u,w) = \mathbf{U}_k \mathbf{M}_k \mathbf{P}_{kl} \mathbf{M}_l^T \mathbf{W}_l^T \qquad \begin{array}{l} s \in [1 : m + 2 - k] \\ t \in [1 : n + 2 - l] \\ u,w \in [0,1] \end{array}$$

where k and l control the continuity of the surface and the degree of the blending function polynomials. s and t denote a particular patch of the surface. The range on s and t is a function of k and l and the dimensions of the array of control points.

$$\mathbf{U}_k = [u^{k-1} \quad u^{k-2} \quad \cdots \quad u^2 \quad u \quad 1]$$
$$\mathbf{W}_l = [w^{l-1} \quad w^{l-2} \quad \cdots \quad w^2 \quad w \quad 1]$$

Elements of the $k \times l$ matrix of control points $\mathbf{p}_{kl}$ depend on the particular patch to be evaluated. If $\mathbf{p}_{ij}$ denotes these matrix elements, then

$$\mathbf{p}_{kl} = \mathbf{p}_{ij} \qquad \begin{array}{l} i \in [s - 1 : s + k - 2] \\ j \in [t - 1 : t + l - 2] \end{array}$$

$\mathbf{M}_k$ and $\mathbf{M}_l$ are analogous to the $\mathbf{M}$ transformation matrix of the *B*-spline curve.

A rational *B*-spline surface is expressed as

$$\mathbf{p}(u,w) =$$
$$\frac{\sum_{i=0}^{m} \sum_{j=0}^{n} \mathbf{p}_{ij} h_{ij} N_{ik}(u) N_{jl}(w)}{\sum_{i=0}^{m} \sum_{j=0}^{n} h_{ij} N_{ik}(u) N_{jl}(w)}$$

where the h_{ij} are weights.

Curves on Surfaces

The parametric net of a surface patch presents a two-dimensional space able to support the analytic representation of curves. These curves, parametric themselves, can be used to define the irregular boundary of trimmed patches (often resulting from patch intersections, or Boolean combinations). Such curves are defined in terms of a new parameter, t, so that $u = u(t)$, $w = w(t)$.

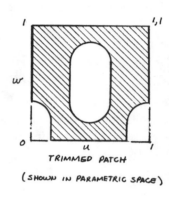

TRIMMED PATCH

(SHOWN IN PARAMETRIC SPACE)

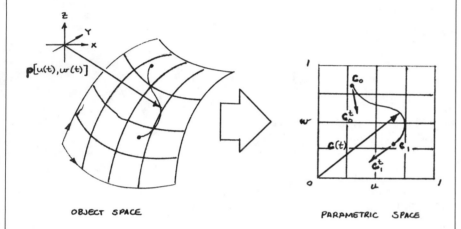

OBJECT SPACE   PARAMETRIC SPACE

In the u,w parametric space of the patch this curve is

$$\mathbf{c}(t) = \mathbf{u}(t) + \mathbf{w}(t)$$

so that, for a PC curve

$$\mathbf{c}(t) = \mathbf{TMB}_c$$

where

$$\mathbf{T} = [t^3 \ t^2 \ t \ 1]$$
$$\mathbf{B}_c = [\mathbf{c}_0 \ \mathbf{c}_1 \ \mathbf{c}_0^t \ \mathbf{c}_1^t]$$

The curve is mapped onto the patch in object space via

$$\mathbf{p}[u(t),w(t)] = \text{points on the curve, on the patch.}$$

The object space tangent vector $\mathbf{p}_t^t$ at any point t on the curve

$$\mathbf{p}_t^t = k_u \frac{\mathbf{p}^u}{|\mathbf{p}^u|} + k_w \frac{\mathbf{p}^w}{|\mathbf{p}^w|}$$

where k_u, k_w are the direction cosines of c_t^t (with respect to the u,w system).

Cartesian Surface Fitting

Here is a relatively simple, nonparametric, surface-fitting procedure:

$$z(x,y) = \sum_{i=0}^{m} \sum_{j=0}^{n} a_{ij} x^i y^j$$

where the a_{ij} coefficients are determined from specified data points. For a bicubic (that is, $m = n = 3$), 16 points must be given. Caution is advised here, for if m and n are large, then it becomes increasingly possible to generate surfaces with undesirable oscillations.

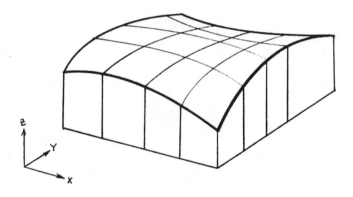

"Einstein, above his work and writing, held a long-term vision: There is nothing in the world except curved empty space. Geometry bent one way here describes gravitation. Rippled another way somewhere else it manifests all the qualities of an electromagnetic wave. Excited at still another place, the magic material that is space shows itself as a particle. There is nothing that is foreign and 'physical' immersed in space."

John Archibald Wheeler

Quadric Surfaces

The **algebraic form** of a quadric surface is given by the general quadratic equation:

$$Ax^2 + By^2 + Cz^2 + 2Dxy + 2Eyz + 2Fxz + 2Gx + 2Hy + 2Jz + K = 0$$

or in matrix form:

$$\mathbf{PQP}^T = 0$$

where

$$\mathbf{P} = [x \ y \ z \ 1],$$

and

$$\mathbf{Q} = \begin{bmatrix} A & D & F & G \\ D & B & E & H \\ F & E & C & J \\ G & H & J & K \end{bmatrix}$$

If $A = B = C = -K = 1$, and $D = E = F = G = H = J = 0$, then the equation produces a unit sphere at the origin.

A rigid-body motion is produced by pre- and postmultiplication by a 4×4 transformation matrix:

$$\mathbf{Q}^* = \mathbf{T}^{-1}\mathbf{Q}\mathbf{T}^{-T}$$

Where $\mathbf{T}^{-T} = [\mathbf{T}^{-1}]^T$

The 10 coefficients of **Q** have no direct geometric or physical meaning. Therefore, a **geometric form** of representation is often more practical. Conversion to the arithmetic form is done only when computationally necessary.

WARNING! Computational problems may arise when using the algebraic form. Their source is the very nature of floating point data representation and computation: imperfect accuracy and lack of robustness of intrinsic surface characteristics subjected to repeated transformations, which slowly degrade the data. Small changes in the coefficients may cause a change in computed surface type.

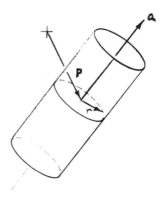

Every quadric surface can be represented by a data set consisting of vectors, scalars, and a type identifier. For example, two vectors and a scalar represent a right circular cylinder (one vector defines an arbitrary point on its axis, another vector defines the direction of the axis, and a scalar gives the radius).

Classification of Quadric Surfaces

Certain properties of the matrix of quadratic equation coefficients, $\mathbf{Q}$, are invariant under rigid-body transformations, including the determinants $|\mathbf{Q}|$ and $|\mathbf{Q}_u|$. This allows computation of surface type, center, vertex, and axes. [**WARNING!** The tests determining surface type are critically dependent on computing whether certain invariants are positive, negative, or zero. This is often computationally impractical or unrealizable with floating point arithmetic.]

$$\mathbf{Q} = \begin{bmatrix} A & D & F & G \\ D & B & E & H \\ F & E & C & J \\ G & H & J & K \end{bmatrix}$$

$$\mathbf{Q}_u = \begin{bmatrix} A & D & F \\ D & B & E \\ F & E & C \end{bmatrix}$$

$r_1 = \text{rank } \mathbf{Q}$

$r_2 = \text{rank } \mathbf{Q}_u$

$s = \text{signature } \mathbf{Q}_u$

$\tau_1 = A + B + C$

$\tau_2 = AB + AC + BC - D^2 - E^2 - F^2$

$\delta_1 = \tau_2 + \tau_1 K - G^2 - H^2 - J^2$

$\delta_2 = ABC + ACK + ABK + BCK$
$\quad + 2(DEF + FCJ + DGH + EHJ)$
$\quad - D^2(C + K) - E^2(A + K)$
$\quad - F^2(B + K) - G^2(B + C)$
$\quad - H^2(A + C) - J^2(A + B)$

$\alpha: \tau_2 > 0; \; |\mathbf{Q}_u| \tau_1 \leq 0, \text{ or } \tau_2 \leq 0$

$\beta: \tau_2 > 0; \; |\mathbf{Q}_u| \tau_1 > 0.$

r_1	r_2	s	Other Conditions	Surface Type
1	0	0		Invalid
1	1	1		Coincident planes
2	0	0		Single plane
2	1	1	$\delta_1 > 0$	Invalid
2	1	1	$\delta_1 < 0$	Two parallel planes
2	2	0	$\tau_2 < 0$	Two intersecting planes
2	2	2	$\tau_2 > 0$	Line
3	1	1		Parabolic cylinder
3	2	0	$\tau_2 < 0$	Hyperbolic cylinder
3	2	2	$\tau_2 > 0; \tau_1 \delta_2 < 0$	Elliptic cylinder
3	2	2	$\tau_2 > 0; \tau_1 \delta_2 > 0$	Invalid
3	3	1	α	Cone
3	3	3	β	Point

$|\mathbf{Q}_u|$	$|\mathbf{Q}|$	s	Other Conditions	Surface Type
0	+	0	$\tau_2 < 0$	Hyperbolic paraboloid
0	−	2	$\tau_2 > 0$	Elliptic paraboloid
±	+	1	α	Hyperboloid of one sheet
±	−	1	α	Hyperboloid of two sheets
±	+	3	β	Invalid
±	−	3	β	Ellipsoid

Note: the signature s of a quadratic form is defined as the difference between the number of positive and negative characteristic roots.

Quadric Surface of Revolution

A quadric surface of revolution is produced by rotating a conic curve about its axis. A general quadric surface is given by

$$PQP^T = 0$$

The surface is in its canonical position if and only if its center or vertex is at the origin and its axes coincide with the coordinate axes. In this position there are no cross terms in the quadratic equation. Thus, $D = E = F = 0$, so that

$$Ax^2 + By^2 + Cz^2 + 2Gx + 2Hy + 2Jz + K = 0$$

where $AG = BH = CJ = 0$, since there is only one term in each variable if the center or vertex is at the origin.

An additional condition is defined: the axis of rotation must be along the z axis. This means that the intersection of the xy-plane ($z = 0$) and a quadric surface of revolution in canonical position is a circle whose center is at the origin:

$$Ax^2 + By^2 + 2Gx + 2Hy + K = 0$$

Since for a circle $A = B \neq 0$ and $G = H = 0$, apply these conditions to the general quadratic equation, divide by A and obtain the canonical equation of a quadric surface of revolution:

$$x^2 + y^2 + Lz^2 + Mz + N = 0$$

where $LM = 0$. Here are eight families in this general class:

Surface	Canonical Equation
Sphere	$x^2 + y^2 + z^2 - N = 0$
Cylinder	$x^2 + y^2 - N = 0$
Cone	$x^2 + y^2 - Lz^2 = 0$
Paraboloid	$x^2 + y^2 + Mz = 0$
Prolate ellipsoid	$x^2 + y^2 + Lz^2 - N = 0, \; L < 1$
Oblate ellipsoid	$x^2 + y^2 + Lz^2 - N = 0 \; L > 1$
Hyperboloid of one sheet	$x^2 + y^2 - Lz^2 - N = 0$
Hyperboloid of two sheets	$x^2 + y^2 - Lz^2 + N = 0$

$$\mathbf{Q} = \begin{bmatrix} A & D & F & G \\ D & B & E & H \\ F & E & C & J \\ G & H & J & K \end{bmatrix}$$

$$\mathbf{P} = [x \; y \; z \; 1]$$

9. Solids

Hyperpatch: Algebraic Form

Most analytical forms used to represent solid objects are flawed because they do not define the interior of the object. This is generally true of schemes that define solids by their boundary surfaces. This limitation is overcome with the hyperpatch. This form of representation is particularly useful when the internal physical behavior of the object is subject to analysis (as for mechanical stresses or thermal gradients).

The hyperpatch is sometimes called the "tricubic solid."

A hyperpatch is a patch-bounded collection of points whose coordinates are given by continuous, three-parameter, single-valued mathematical functions of the form $x = x(u,v,w)$, $y = y(u,v,w)$, and $z = z(u,v,w)$. The algebraic form of a tricubic solid is

$$\mathbf{p}(u,v,w) = \sum_{i=0}^{3} \sum_{j=0}^{3} \sum_{k=0}^{3} \mathbf{a}_{ijk} u^i v^j w^k \quad u,v,w \in [0,1] \tag{9.1}$$

The vectors $\mathbf{a}_{ijk}$ are the algebraic coefficients, and there are 64 of them.

Partially expanded, this equation looks like

$$\mathbf{p}(u,v,w) = \mathbf{a}_{333} u^3 v^3 w^3 + \mathbf{a}_{332} u^3 v^3 w^2 + \cdots + \mathbf{a}_{000}$$

The terms are rearranged, and do not reflect the presumed order of summation.

Here is another way to index Eq. (9.1):

$$\mathbf{p}(u,v,w) = \sum_{i=1}^{4} \sum_{j=1}^{4} \sum_{k=1}^{4} \mathbf{a}_{ijk} u^{4-i} v^{4-j} w^{4-k}$$

Although this is somewhat messier than Eq. (9.1), it is a more acceptable form of tensor notation and it is compatible with the geometric form used for the hyperpatch. A further simplification yields

$$\mathbf{p} = \mathbf{a}_{ijk} u^{4-i} v^{4-j} w^{4-k} \tag{9.2}$$

Drop the summation signs and the functional notation.

with the following convention: for tricubics the range of the indices is from 1 to 4, and a repeated index implies summation over that index.

In matrix form

$$\mathbf{p} = \mathbf{U} \mathbf{A}_{uv} \mathbf{V}^T \mathbf{A}_w \mathbf{W}^T \tag{9.3}$$

where $\mathbf{U} \mathbf{A}_{uv} \mathbf{V}^T$ is the product of the first and second polynomials in u and v, and $\mathbf{A}_w \mathbf{W}^T$ represents the third polynomial, given in terms of w.

With three independent parametric variables, the matrix form is more cumbersome than for curves and surfaces.

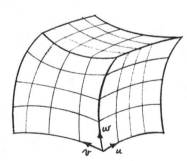

The edges are parametric cubic curves, and the faces are bicubic patches. There are 8 corner points, 24 tangent vectors, 24 twist vectors, and 8 vectors of triple mixed partial derivatives.

Geometric characteristics.

Hyperpatch: Geometric Form

The geometric form of a tricubic hyperpatch is

$$\mathbf{p} = F_i(u)F_j(v)F_k(w)\mathbf{b}_{ijk} \tag{9.4}$$

where $u,v,w \in [0,1]$, $i,j,k \in [1:4]$, the F terms are the familiar Hermité cubic blending functions [see Eq. (7.8)], and $\mathbf{b}_{ijk}$ is the array of boundary conditions or blending functions.

Each corner of the tricubic solid supports eight boundary condition vectors; at corner $\mathbf{p}_{011}$, for example

$\mathbf{p}_{011}$ corner point

$\left.\begin{matrix} \mathbf{p}_{011}^{u} \\ \\ \mathbf{p}_{011}^{v} \\ \\ \mathbf{p}_{011}^{w} \end{matrix}\right\} \dfrac{\partial}{\partial u}\mathbf{p}, \dfrac{\partial}{\partial v}\mathbf{p}, \dfrac{\partial}{\partial w}\mathbf{p}$

$\left.\begin{matrix} \mathbf{p}_{011} \\ \\ \mathbf{p}_{011} \\ \\ \mathbf{p}_{011} \end{matrix}\right\} \dfrac{\partial^2}{\partial u \partial v}\mathbf{p}, \dfrac{\partial^2}{\partial u \partial w}\mathbf{p}, \dfrac{\partial^2}{\partial v \partial w}\mathbf{p}$

$\mathbf{p}_{011} \quad \dfrac{\partial^3}{\partial u \partial v \partial w}\mathbf{p}$

The $\mathbf{b}_{ijk}$ are (after contraction on the index k):

$$\mathbf{b}_{ij1} = \begin{bmatrix} \mathbf{p}_{000} & \mathbf{p}_{010} & \mathbf{p}_{000}^{v} & \mathbf{p}_{010}^{v} \\ \mathbf{p}_{100} & \mathbf{p}_{110} & \mathbf{p}_{100}^{v} & \mathbf{p}_{110}^{v} \\ \mathbf{p}_{000}^{u} & \mathbf{p}_{010}^{u} & \mathbf{p}_{000}^{uv} & \mathbf{p}_{010}^{uv} \\ \mathbf{p}_{100}^{u} & \mathbf{p}_{110}^{u} & \mathbf{p}_{100}^{uv} & \mathbf{p}_{110}^{uv} \end{bmatrix}$$

$$\mathbf{b}_{ij2} = \begin{bmatrix} \mathbf{p}_{001} & \mathbf{p}_{011} & \mathbf{p}_{001}^{v} & \mathbf{p}_{011}^{v} \\ \mathbf{p}_{101} & \mathbf{p}_{111} & \mathbf{p}_{101}^{v} & \mathbf{p}_{111}^{v} \\ \mathbf{p}_{001}^{u} & \mathbf{p}_{011}^{u} & \mathbf{p}_{001}^{uv} & \mathbf{p}_{011}^{uv} \\ \mathbf{p}_{101}^{u} & \mathbf{p}_{111}^{u} & \mathbf{p}_{101}^{uv} & \mathbf{p}_{111}^{uv} \end{bmatrix}$$

$$\mathbf{b}_{ij3} = \begin{bmatrix} \mathbf{p}_{000}^{w} & \mathbf{p}_{010}^{w} & \mathbf{p}_{000}^{vw} & \mathbf{p}_{010}^{vw} \\ \mathbf{p}_{100}^{w} & \mathbf{p}_{110}^{w} & \mathbf{p}_{100}^{vw} & \mathbf{p}_{110}^{vw} \\ \mathbf{p}_{000}^{uw} & \mathbf{p}_{010}^{uw} & \mathbf{p}_{000}^{uvw} & \mathbf{p}_{010}^{uvw} \\ \mathbf{p}_{100}^{uw} & \mathbf{p}_{110}^{uw} & \mathbf{p}_{100}^{uvw} & \mathbf{p}_{110}^{uvw} \end{bmatrix}$$

$$\mathbf{b}_{ij4} = \begin{bmatrix} \mathbf{p}_{001}^{w} & \mathbf{p}_{011}^{w} & \mathbf{p}_{001}^{vw} & \mathbf{p}_{011}^{vw} \\ \mathbf{p}_{101}^{w} & \mathbf{p}_{111}^{w} & \mathbf{p}_{101}^{vw} & \mathbf{p}_{111}^{vw} \\ \mathbf{p}_{001}^{uw} & \mathbf{p}_{011}^{uw} & \mathbf{p}_{001}^{uvw} & \mathbf{p}_{011}^{uvw} \\ \mathbf{p}_{101}^{uw} & \mathbf{p}_{111}^{uw} & \mathbf{p}_{101}^{uvw} & \mathbf{p}_{111}^{uvw} \end{bmatrix}$$

Remember, repeated indices imply summation. Here a triple summation is indicated.

There are $4 \times 4 \times 4 = 64$ vectors in the $\mathbf{b}_{ijk}$ array.

$F_1(u) = 2u^3 - 3u^2 + 1$
$F_2(u) = -2u^3 + 3u^2$
$F_3(u) = u^3 - 2u^2 + u$
$F_4(u) = u^3 - u^2$

The transformation from geometric to algebraic coefficients is given by

$$\mathbf{a}_{ijk} = \sum_{l=1}^{4} \sum_{m=1}^{4} \sum_{n=1}^{4} \mathbf{M}_{il}\mathbf{M}_{jm}\mathbf{M}_{kn}\mathbf{b}_{lmn}$$

or more compactly as

$$\mathbf{a}_{ijk} = \mathbf{M}_{il}\mathbf{M}_{jm}\mathbf{M}_{kn}\mathbf{b}_{lmn}$$

"Before long, every physics and chemistry laboratory may bear over its entrance the Platonic caveat, 'let no man enter here who is not a geometer.' "

Gaston Bachelard

Hyperpatch: Defined by 64 Points

A tricubic hyperpatch can be defined by a three-dimensional $4 \times 4 \times 4$ array of 64 points. The values of the parametric variables are taken as those at the third points of the unit cube in u, v, w parametric space. Points in the hyperpatch are given by the triple summation

$$\mathbf{p}(u, v, w) = F_i^p(u) F_j^p(v) F_k^p(w) \mathbf{p}_{ijk} \qquad (9.5)$$

where

$$\left.\begin{aligned}
F_1^p(u) &= -4.5u^3 + 9u^2 - 5.5u + 1 \\
F_2^p(u) &= 13.5u^3 - 22.5u^2 + 9u \\
F_3^p(u) &= -13.5u^3 + 18u^2 - 4.5u \\
F_4^p(u) &= 4.5u^3 - 4.5u^2 + u
\end{aligned}\right\} \quad \begin{aligned} &\text{similarly for } F_j^p(v) \\ &\text{and } F_k^p(w) \end{aligned}$$

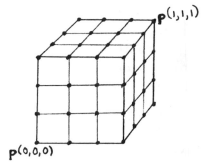

Contract the array $\mathbf{p}_{ijk}$ on the index k to yield

$$\mathbf{p}_{ij1} = \begin{bmatrix}
\mathbf{p}(0,0,0) & \mathbf{p}(0,\frac{1}{3},0) & \mathbf{p}(0,\frac{2}{3},0) & \mathbf{p}(0,1,0) \\
\mathbf{p}(\frac{1}{3},0,0) & \mathbf{p}(\frac{1}{3},\frac{1}{3},0) & \mathbf{p}(\frac{1}{3},\frac{2}{3},0) & \mathbf{p}(\frac{1}{3},1,0) \\
\mathbf{p}(\frac{2}{3},0,0) & \mathbf{p}(\frac{2}{3},\frac{1}{3},0) & \mathbf{p}(\frac{2}{3},\frac{2}{3},0) & \mathbf{p}(\frac{2}{3},1,0) \\
\mathbf{p}(1,0,0) & \mathbf{p}(1,\frac{1}{3},0) & \mathbf{p}(1,\frac{2}{3},0) & \mathbf{p}(1,1,0)
\end{bmatrix}$$

$$\mathbf{p}_{ij2} = \begin{bmatrix}
\mathbf{p}(0,0,\frac{1}{3}) & \mathbf{p}(0,\frac{1}{3},\frac{1}{3}) & \mathbf{p}(0,\frac{2}{3},\frac{1}{3}) & \mathbf{p}(0,1,\frac{1}{3}) \\
\mathbf{p}(\frac{1}{3},0,\frac{1}{3}) & \mathbf{p}(\frac{1}{3},\frac{1}{3},\frac{1}{3}) & \mathbf{p}(\frac{1}{3},\frac{2}{3},\frac{1}{3}) & \mathbf{p}(\frac{1}{3},1,\frac{1}{3}) \\
\mathbf{p}(\frac{2}{3},0,\frac{1}{3}) & \mathbf{p}(\frac{2}{3},\frac{1}{3},\frac{1}{3}) & \mathbf{p}(\frac{2}{3},\frac{2}{3},\frac{1}{3}) & \mathbf{p}(\frac{2}{3},1,\frac{1}{3}) \\
\mathbf{p}(1,0,\frac{1}{3}) & \mathbf{p}(1,\frac{1}{3},\frac{1}{3}) & \mathbf{p}(1,\frac{2}{3},\frac{1}{3}) & \mathbf{p}(1,1,\frac{1}{3})
\end{bmatrix}$$

$$\mathbf{p}_{ij3} = \begin{bmatrix}
\mathbf{p}(0,0,\frac{2}{3}) & \mathbf{p}(0,\frac{1}{3},\frac{2}{3}) & \mathbf{p}(0,\frac{2}{3},\frac{2}{3}) & \mathbf{p}(0,1,\frac{2}{3}) \\
\mathbf{p}(\frac{1}{3},0,\frac{2}{3}) & \mathbf{p}(\frac{1}{3},\frac{1}{3},\frac{2}{3}) & \mathbf{p}(\frac{1}{3},\frac{2}{3},\frac{2}{3}) & \mathbf{p}(\frac{1}{3},1,\frac{2}{3}) \\
\mathbf{p}(\frac{2}{3},0,\frac{2}{3}) & \mathbf{p}(\frac{2}{3},\frac{1}{3},\frac{2}{3}) & \mathbf{p}(\frac{2}{3},\frac{2}{3},\frac{2}{3}) & \mathbf{p}(\frac{2}{3},1,\frac{2}{3}) \\
\mathbf{p}(1,0,\frac{2}{3}) & \mathbf{p}(1,\frac{1}{3},\frac{2}{3}) & \mathbf{p}(1,\frac{2}{3},\frac{2}{3}) & \mathbf{p}(1,1,\frac{2}{3})
\end{bmatrix}$$

$$\mathbf{p}_{ij4} = \begin{bmatrix}
\mathbf{p}(0,0,1) & \mathbf{p}(0,\frac{1}{3},1) & \mathbf{p}(0,\frac{2}{3},1) & \mathbf{p}(0,1,1) \\
\mathbf{p}(\frac{1}{3},0,1) & \mathbf{p}(\frac{1}{3},\frac{1}{3},1) & \mathbf{p}(\frac{1}{3},\frac{2}{3},1) & \mathbf{p}(\frac{1}{3},1,1) \\
\mathbf{p}(\frac{2}{3},0,1) & \mathbf{p}(\frac{2}{3},\frac{1}{3},1) & \mathbf{p}(\frac{2}{3},\frac{2}{3},1) & \mathbf{p}(\frac{2}{3},1,1) \\
\mathbf{p}(1,0,1) & \mathbf{p}(1,\frac{1}{3},1) & \mathbf{p}(1,\frac{2}{3},1) & \mathbf{p}(1,1,1)
\end{bmatrix}$$

Hypersolids: Objects with Dimension > 3

The analytic representation of the patch and hyperpatch is easily extended to geometric forms of higher dimension. The polycubic form is presented here, but it can be modified to apply to any odd-ordered polynomial form. Compact notation is used, and the repeated index implies summation. The algebraic form is

$$p_i(u_1, u_2, \ldots, u_n) = a_{ij_1 j_2 \cdots j_n} u_1^{4-j_1} u_2^{4-j_2} \cdots u_n^{4-j_n} \tag{9.6}$$

where p_i is the ith component of a dependent variable vector of m components, each defined by this n-cubic parametric polynomial. The geometric object is of the nth order, and the equation of each component is of $3n$th degree and has $4n$ terms. There are m dependent variables and n independent variables. Generally $m \geq n$.

The range on the index j is 1 to 4, and $i \in [1:m]$.

The geometric form is

$$p_i(u_1, u_2, \ldots, u_n) = F_{j_1}(u_1) F_{j_2}(u_2) \cdots F_{j_n}(u_n) b_{ij_1 j_2 \cdots j_n} \tag{9.7}$$

The F-terms are matrices of the blending functions. For the rth F-term matrix, F_{j_r}:

$$
\begin{aligned}
j_r &= 1 & F_1(u_r) &= 2u_r^3 - 3u_r^2 + 1 \\
j_r &= 2 & F_2(u_r) &= -2u_r^3 + 3u_r^2 \\
j_r &= 3 & F_3(u_r) &= u_r^3 - 2u_r^2 + u_r \\
j_r &= 4 & F_4(u_r) &= u_r^3 - u_r^2
\end{aligned}
$$

The array of geometric coefficients $b_{ij_1 j_2 \cdots j_n}$ is interpretted using this table of conventions. Here the set of j subscripts conveys two kinds of information. First, it identifies the specific boundary on which the product of blending functions is to operate. Second, it identifies a sequence of n operators applied to p_i, evaluated at the previously determined boundary.

Here is an example: for $n = 2$ the object is a bicubic patch. The geometric coefficients are

$$b_{i14} = \{1\} \left\{ \frac{\partial}{\partial u_2} \right\} p_i(0,1) = \frac{\partial p_i(0,1)}{\partial u_2},$$

or

$$b_{i34} = \left\{ \frac{\partial}{\partial u_1} \right\} \left\{ \frac{\partial}{\partial u_2} \right\} p_i(0,1) = \frac{\partial^2 p_i(0,1)}{\partial u_1 \partial u_2}$$

If $i \leftarrow x$, and $u_1 \leftarrow u$, $u_2 \leftarrow w$, then $b_{i14} = x_{01}^w$ (a tangent vector), and $b_{i34} = x_{01}^{uw}$ (a twist vector).

j_r	Boundary	Operator
$j_r = 1$	$u_r = 0$	1
$j_r = 2$	$u_r = 1$	1
$j_r = 3$	$u_r = 0$	$\dfrac{\partial}{\partial u_r}$
$j_r = 4$	$u_r = 1$	$\dfrac{\partial}{\partial u_r}$

Translation: Point

Describe the translation of a point by stating the relative changes in its coordinates, denoting these changes as $\Delta x, \Delta y, \Delta z$, and relating them to the initial position x, y, z as follows:

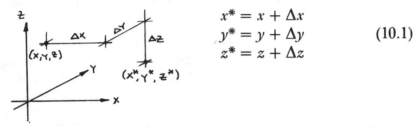

$$x^* = x + \Delta x$$
$$y^* = y + \Delta y \qquad (10.1)$$
$$z^* = z + \Delta z$$

A transformation implies changing position, orientation, or shape.

The simplest transformations are the so-called rigid-body transformations, such as translation and rotation.

An asterisk is used to indicate a transformed coordinate.

where x^*, y^*, z^* are the coordinates of the new location of the transformed point.

In vector notation this is expressed as

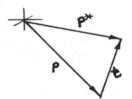

$$\mathbf{p}^* = \mathbf{p} + \mathbf{t} \qquad (10.2)$$

where
$$t_x = \Delta x, t_y = \Delta y, t_z = \Delta z.$$

Note: here it is the point that is translated, and not the vector $\mathbf{p}$, per se. Translation transformations do not apply to free vectors.

Using matrix algebra to express this transformation produces a notation and form very similar to vector notation:

$$\mathbf{P}^* = \mathbf{P} + \mathbf{T} \qquad (10.3)$$

where $\mathbf{P} = [x \ y \ z]$, $\mathbf{T} = [\Delta x \ \Delta y \ \Delta z]$, and
$\mathbf{P}^* = [x^* \ y^* \ z^*] = [(x + \Delta x) \ (y + \Delta y) \ (z + \Delta z)]$

A group is any set of elements G and a binary operator, say &, that satisfy the following properties:

Closure: If $a, b \in G$, then $a \& b$ is a unique element of G.

Associativity: If $a, b, c \in G$, then $a \& (b \& c) = (a \& b) \& c$.

Identity: There is an element e such that if $a \in G$, then $a \& e = e \& a = a$.

Inverse: If $a \in G$, then there is an $a' \in G$, such that $a \& a' = a' \& a = e$. a' is called the inverse of a.

An Abelian group has these four properties plus that of commutativity:

If $a, b \in G$, then $a \& b = b \& a$.

The notion of a group and the study of group theory is important in geometry. Rigid-body displacements form a group.

Translation: Line Segment

Consider a line segment as a "rigid body." Then its length and orientation must be unaffected by any translation transformation. Execute a translation by simply translating the end points defining the segment:

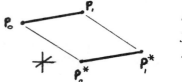

$$x_0^* = x_0 + \Delta x \qquad x_1^* = x_1 + \Delta x$$
$$y_0^* = y_0 + \Delta y \qquad y_1^* = y_1 + \Delta y$$
$$z_0^* = z_0 + \Delta z \qquad z_1^* = z_1 + \Delta z$$
$$(10.4)$$

The essence of a translation transformation is one of spatial displacement or relocation of a geometric object without a change in its orientation (i.e., no rotation occurs).

Since $x_1 - x_0 = x_1^* - x_0^*$, and similarly for y and z, the length and orientation of the line segment is unchanged under a translation transformation.

If a line segment is defined by the vector equation $\mathbf{p} = \mathbf{r}_0 + u\mathbf{r}_1$, where $\mathbf{r}_0$ is the initial end point of the line segment, $\mathbf{r}_1$ defines the direction, and u is some parametric variable, then

$$\mathbf{p}^* = (\mathbf{r}_0 + \mathbf{t}) + u\mathbf{r}_1 \qquad (10.5)$$

where $\mathbf{t}$ is the vector defining the translation.

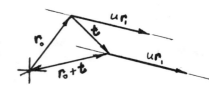

Note that the original and transformed line segments are parallel. This is because the free vector $\mathbf{r}_1$ is unaffected by the translation.

All points on the line need not be transformed. Only the defining equation is transformed. This is convenient since the number of points on a line segment is infinite. This important principle applies to all geometric transforms.

Translation: Curves and Surfaces

Translate a curve or surface simply by translating each of the control points. For the Bézier curve this is expressed as

$$p^* = \sum_{i=0}^{n} (p_i + t)B_{i,n} \tag{10.6}$$

and for the Bézier patch

$$p^* = \sum_{i=0}^{m} \sum_{j=0}^{n} (p_{ij} + t)B_{i,m}B_{j,n} \tag{10.7}$$

Similar equations apply to the B-spline curve and surface, as well as to the four-point Hermité curve and 16-point Hermité bicubic patch.

The geometric form of the Hermité parametric cubic curve and bicubic patch require a slightly different formulation, because these types are defined in terms of both end and corner points as well as tangent and twist vectors. Therefore, transform the matrices of geometric coefficients as follows:

$$B^* = B + T \tag{10.8}$$

for curves

$$T = [t \ \ t \ \ 0 \ \ 0]^T$$

and for patches

$$T = \begin{bmatrix} t & t & 0 & 0 \\ t & t & 0 & 0 \\ 0 & 0 & 0 & 0 \\ 0 & 0 & 0 & 0 \end{bmatrix}$$

The functional notation $p(u)$ and $B_{i,n}(u)$ are omitted for clarity.

Rotation: Point and Vector

The simplest rotation is that about the origin and in the x,y plane.

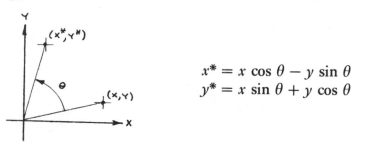

$$x^* = x \cos \theta - y \sin \theta \quad (10.9)$$
$$y^* = x \sin \theta + y \cos \theta$$

This is equivalent to a rotation about the z axis in a 3-D coordinate system.

Distance of the point from the origin is constant (invariant), since it is easy to show that
$$(x^*)^2 + (y^*)^2 = x^2 + y^2$$

For rotation in three dimensions use matrix algebra. Here rotation is defined by three components (θ,β,γ) about the z, y, and x axes, in that order. First, rotate about the z axis if $\theta \neq 0$. Next, rotate about the y axis if $\beta \neq 0$. Finally, rotate about the x axis if $\gamma \neq 0$. Using matrices this is expressed as

$$\mathbf{p}^* = \mathbf{p}\mathbf{R}_\theta \mathbf{R}_\beta \mathbf{R}_\gamma = \mathbf{p}\mathbf{R} \quad (10.10)$$

where $\mathbf{p}$ and $\mathbf{p}^*$ are 1×3 matrices and

This transformation applies to both points and (free) vectors. The magnitude of the vector is invariant (see above).

$$\mathbf{R}_\theta = \begin{bmatrix} \cos \theta & \sin \theta & 0 \\ -\sin \theta & \cos \theta & 0 \\ 0 & 0 & 1 \end{bmatrix},$$

$$\mathbf{R}_\beta = \begin{bmatrix} \cos \beta & 0 & -\sin \beta \\ 0 & 1 & 0 \\ \sin \beta & 0 & \cos \beta \end{bmatrix},$$

$$\mathbf{R}_\gamma = \begin{bmatrix} 1 & 0 & 0 \\ 0 & \cos \gamma & \sin \gamma \\ 0 & -\sin \gamma & \cos \gamma \end{bmatrix}$$

$$\mathbf{R} = \begin{bmatrix} \cos \theta \cos \beta & \sin \theta \cos \gamma + \cos \theta \sin \beta \sin \gamma & \sin \theta \sin \gamma - \cos \theta \sin \beta \cos \gamma \\ -\sin \theta \cos \beta & \cos \theta \cos \gamma - \sin \theta \sin \beta \sin \gamma & \cos \theta \sin \gamma + \sin \theta \sin \beta \cos \gamma \\ \sin \beta & -\cos \beta \sin \gamma & \cos \beta \cos \gamma \end{bmatrix}$$

This rotation matrix is applicable to any combination of component rotations $\mathbf{R}_\theta, \mathbf{R}_\beta, \mathbf{R}_\gamma$ so long as they are taken in that order.

A rotation convention consistent with the right-hand coordinate system.

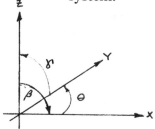

If a point is to be both translated and rotated, then, in general, the order is important. Thus,

$$\mathbf{p}^* = [\mathbf{p} + \mathbf{t}]\mathbf{R} \neq \mathbf{p}\mathbf{R} + \mathbf{t}.$$

Rotation: Line Segment

To rotate a line segment in the x,y plane about the origin, rotate the end points of the line segment. Thus,

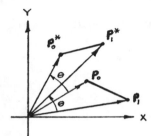

$$x_0^* = x_0 \cos \theta - y_0 \sin \theta$$
$$y_0^* = x_0 \sin \theta + y_0 \cos \theta$$
$$x_1^* = x_1 \cos \theta - y_1 \sin \theta \qquad (10.11)$$
$$y_1^* = x_1 \sin \theta + y_1 \cos \theta$$

To generalize this to three dimensions, apply Eq. (10.10) to each end point.

If the line segment is defined by the vector equation $\mathbf{p} = \mathbf{r}_0 + u\mathbf{r}_1$, then for a rotation $\mathbf{R}$

$$\mathbf{p}^* = \mathbf{r}_0\mathbf{R} + u\mathbf{r}_1\mathbf{R}$$

where $\mathbf{R}$ is the appropriate rotation matrix.

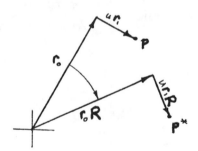

For any rotation $\mathbf{R}$, $|\mathbf{R}| = 1$; for example

$$\mathbf{R}_\theta = \begin{bmatrix} \cos \theta & \sin \theta & 0 \\ -\sin \theta & \cos \theta & 0 \\ 0 & 0 & 1 \end{bmatrix}$$

$$|\mathbf{R}_\theta| = \sin^2 \theta + \cos^2 \theta = 1$$

To return a rotated object to its initial position, use $\mathbf{R}^{-1}$, since $\mathbf{R}\mathbf{R}^{-1} = 1$. This, of course, is the same as using $-\theta, -\beta, -\gamma$, thus reversing the initial rotation θ, β, γ. (Note: $\mathbf{R}^{-1} = \mathbf{R}$, since $\mathbf{R}$ is orthogonal. Therefore, the inverse rotation is given by $\mathbf{R}^{-1}$ or $\mathbf{R}^T$.)

Rotation: Curves and Surfaces

Rotate a curve or surface by rotating each of the control points. For the Bézier curve this is expressed as

$$\mathbf{p}^* = \sum_{i=0}^{n} \mathbf{p}_i \mathbf{R} B_{i,n} \qquad (10.12)$$

and for the Bézier patch

$$\mathbf{p}^* = \sum_{i=0}^{m} \sum_{j=0}^{n} \mathbf{p}_{ij} \mathbf{R} B_{i,m} B_{j,n} \qquad (10.13)$$

Similar equations apply to the B-spline curve and surface, as well as the four-point Hermité curve and the 16-point Hermité bicubic patch.

The rotation of the Hermité curve and patch are expressed and interpreted as follows:

$$\mathbf{B}^* = \mathbf{B}\mathbf{R} \qquad (10.14)$$

For curves, $\mathbf{B}$ is a 4×1 matrix of vectors, so that it is actually a $4 \times 1 \times 3$ matrix of vector components. In carrying out the matrix multiplication of Eq. (10.14), each 1×3 vector in the $\mathbf{B}$ matrix is transformed by $\mathbf{R}$, itself a 3×3 array. The algebraic forms are transformed similarly; thus,

$$\mathbf{A}^* = \mathbf{A}\mathbf{R}$$

for both curves and surfaces.

$\mathbf{R}$ is the 3×3 rotation matrix.

Or, more fully expressed:

for curves

$$\mathbf{p}^* = \mathbf{UMBR}$$

for patches

$$\mathbf{p}^* = \mathbf{UMBRM}^T \mathbf{W}^T$$

"Mathematics takes us still further from what is human, into the region of absolute necessity, to which not only the actual world, but every possible world, must conform."

Bertrand Russell

Translation and Rotation of Coordinate Systems

The location of the origin and the orientation of the principal axes in a particular application are often quite arbitrary, and during the course of a problem definition or solution it may be advantageous to change this framework. First, consider transformations between two coordinate systems whose corresponding principal axes remain parallel. This is a translation transformation, and it is described as follows:

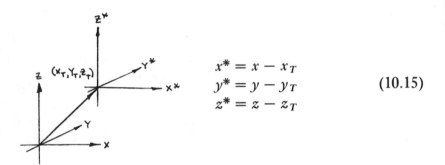

$$x^* = x - x_T$$
$$y^* = y - y_T \qquad (10.15)$$
$$z^* = z - z_T$$

The scalar product of two vectors is invariant under a coordinate system transformation.

where (x_T, y_T, z_T) are the coordinates of the origin of the transformed system in terms of the initial system, and (x^*, y^*, z^*) are the coordinates of an arbitrary point in terms of the transformed system. So, given a point (x, y, z) in one system you can easily compute its coordinates (x^*, y^*, z^*) in a second system translated with respect to the first.

Free vectors are unaffected by translation transformations.

Finally, consider the transformation between two coordinate systems whose origins coincide, but whose corresponding axes are rotated with respect to each other. Assertion: any orthogonal rotation matrix is equivalent to the product of not more than three plane orthogonal rotation matrices (no proof is given here). Therefore, apply successive plane rotations described by θ, β, γ as defined for Eq. (10.10), with the following exception: use $-\theta, -\beta,$ and $-\gamma$ (i.e., the net affect of a coordinate system rotation transformation is the reverse of the point or vector transformation). Thus,

For all proper rotations:

$$\mathbf{R}\mathbf{R}^T = \mathbf{I}$$

Furthermore, if $|\mathbf{R}| = -1$, then $\mathbf{R}$ produces a simultaneous rotation about an axis and a reflection in the plane perpendicular to that axis.

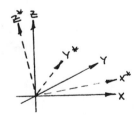

$$\mathbf{R}_\theta = \begin{bmatrix} \cos(-\theta) & \sin(-\theta) & 0 \\ -\sin(-\theta) & \cos(-\theta) & 0 \\ 0 & 0 & 1 \end{bmatrix}$$

with similar modification of $\mathbf{R}_\beta$ and $\mathbf{R}_\gamma$.

Find the orientation of the transformed coordinate system with respect to the initial system by applying the rotation matrices to the points (1,0,0), (0,1,0), and (0,0,1), using θ, β, γ.

Rotation about an Arbitrary Axis

Find the transformation matrices and operations that rotate a point **p** through an angle ϕ around an arbitrary line in space that passes through the points $\mathbf{r}_1$ and $\mathbf{r}_2$. Here is an algorithm for doing this:

Step 1. Translate the point and line so that $\mathbf{r}_1$ is at the origin. Thus, $\mathbf{p}^* = \mathbf{p} - \mathbf{r}_1$.

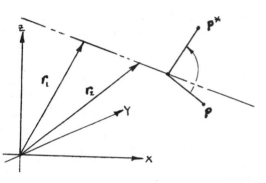

Step 2. Rotate the point and line so that the line is collinear with the x axis. Do this by rotating $-\theta$ degrees about the z axis and then $-\beta$ about the y axis, where

$$\theta = \tan^{-1}\left(\frac{y_2 - y_1}{x_2 - x_1}\right) \quad \text{and} \quad \beta = \sin^{-1}\left(\frac{z_2 - z_1}{|r_2 - r_1|}\right)$$

$\mathbf{p}^*$ now becomes: $\mathbf{p}^* = [\mathbf{p} - \mathbf{r}_1]\mathbf{R}_{\theta\beta}$.

Step 3. Rotate the point about the x axis. After the preceding two steps, $\gamma = \phi$, to yield

$$\mathbf{p}^* = [\mathbf{p} - \mathbf{r}_1]\mathbf{R}_{\theta\beta}\mathbf{R}_\gamma$$

Step 4. Reverse Step 2. Note the sign change in the rotations:

$$\mathbf{p}^* = [\mathbf{p} - \mathbf{r}_1]\mathbf{R}_{\theta\beta}\mathbf{R}_\gamma\mathbf{R}_{-(\theta\beta)}$$

Step 5. Reverse Step 1 to obtain the final transformation:

$$\mathbf{p}^* = [\mathbf{p} - \mathbf{r}_1]\mathbf{R}_{\theta\beta}\mathbf{R}_\gamma\mathbf{R}_{-(\theta\beta)} + \mathbf{r}_1$$

A 90° rotation about a vertical axis, followed by a 90° rotation about a horizontal axis, gives a net change in orientation that can be produced by a single rotation of 120° about an axis containing vertices 4 and 6.

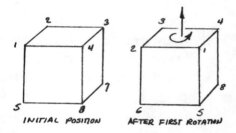

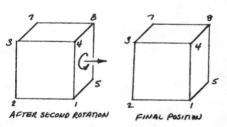

INITIAL POSITION   AFTER FIRST ROTATION

AFTER SECOND ROTATION   FINAL POSITION

"Art is the imposing of a pattern on experience, and our aesthetic enjoyment is recognition of the pattern."

Alfred North Whitehead

Trackball Rotation

Trackball rotation offers an unusually natural approach to executing rotation transformations. The concept presented here can be implemented through either real or virtual trackball devices.

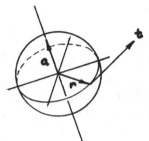

Here is the mathematical analog or geometric model of the trackball transformation. If the trackball is at the origin of the coordinate system, then let **r** denote the point of contact and **t** denote the tangential "force" inducing rotation. The axis of rotation is simply

$$\mathbf{a} = \mathbf{r} \times \mathbf{t}$$

A trackball operates by touching its spherical surface and applying a tangential force causing the ball to rotate. A similar effect can be simulated with mouse or cursor.

The angle of rotation is inferred from $|\mathbf{t}|$ (multiplied by an appropriate scale factor). In a virtual environment it is simply inferred from the distance the cursor moves.

If the trackball can be arbitrarily located, then proceed as with rotation about an arbitrary axis.

Virtual Trackball: Here, the axis of rotation **a** and tangent "force" **t** are computed from projections of the controlling elements.

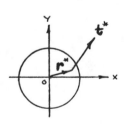

Let **r*** and **t*** denote the x,y projections of **r** and **t**, respectively. Assume a unit sphere centered at the origin, and projected onto the x,y plane (also assumed to be the screen plane). From the cursor position and motion we know **r*** and **t***.

Compute **r** from

$$\theta = \cos^{-1}|\mathbf{r^*}|, \; r_z = \sin\theta$$

The tangent plane at **r** is

$$r_x x + r_y y + r_z z + 1 = 0$$

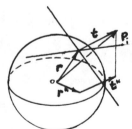

Compute the point of intersection $\mathbf{p}_i$ of the tangent plane with a line parallel to the z axis and through **r*** + **t***. Thus, **t** is readily found from $\mathbf{t} = \mathbf{p}_i - \mathbf{r}$, and the axis of rotation from $\mathbf{a} = \mathbf{r} \times \mathbf{t}$.

Uniform and Differential Scaling

The size of a curve or surface may be increased or decreased by multiplying its defining points or geometric coefficients by a scale factor s. If the same scale factor is applied to each coordinate component, then the curve or surface changes in size, but not in shape. If a different scale factor is applied to each component, then both size and shape change. The former transformation is called uniform scaling; the latter is called differential scaling.

Here is an example of the uniform scaling of a Bézier curve:

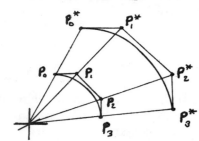

$$p^* = \sum_{i=0}^{n} s\mathbf{p}_i B_{i,n} \qquad (10.16)$$

where $s\mathbf{p}_i = [sx_i \ sy_i \ sz_i]$. The scale factor s is always positive. If it is negative, then a reflection transformation is produced.

Here is an example of the differential scaling of a Bézier curve:

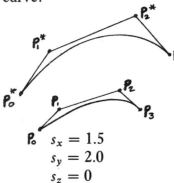

$s_x = 1.5$
$s_y = 2.0$
$s_z = 0$

$$p^* = \sum_{i=0}^{n} \mathbf{p}_i S B_{i,n} \qquad (10.17)$$

where

$$S = \begin{bmatrix} s_x & 0 & 0 \\ 0 & s_y & 0 \\ 0 & 0 & s_z \end{bmatrix}$$

and

$$\mathbf{p}_i S = [s_x x_i \ s_y y_i \ s_z z_i]$$

A scaling transformation necessarily changes the position of the object.

Note that for uniform scaling the tangent directions at the ends do not change.

To produce a uniform scaling transformation of a parametric cubic curve, multiply its geometric coefficients by the scale factor s.

$$B^* = sB = \begin{bmatrix} s\mathbf{p}_0 \\ s\mathbf{p}_1 \\ s\mathbf{p}_0^u \\ s\mathbf{p}_1^u \end{bmatrix}$$

Differential scaling changes the direction of tangents.

To produce uniform or differential scaling with respect to an arbitrary point r, apply this expression:

$$\mathbf{p}_i^* = (\mathbf{p}_i - \mathbf{r})S + \mathbf{r} \qquad (10.18)$$

i.e.,

$$\mathbf{p}_i^* = [s_x x_i - r_x(s_x - 1) \quad s_y y_i - r_y(s_y - 1) \quad s_z z_i - r_z(s_z - 1)]$$

If $s_x = s_y = s_z$, then uniform scaling is produced.

Symmetry and Reflection

There is a transformation $\mathbf{R}_f$ that produces the reflected or symmetric counterpart of a curve or surface. This can be done with respect to a plane, line, or point. For a Bézier curve,

$$\mathbf{p}^* = \sum_{i=0}^{n} \mathbf{p}_i \mathbf{R}_f B_{i,n} \qquad (10.19)$$

The transformation matrix $\mathbf{R}_f$ is a diagonal matrix whose elements are ± 1. A specific symmetric reflection is produced by appropriate choice of signs. The following combinations are possible

$$\mathbf{R}_f = \begin{bmatrix} \pm 1 & 0 & 0 \\ 0 & \pm 1 & 0 \\ 0 & 0 & \pm 1 \end{bmatrix}$$

$$\mathbf{R}_f = \begin{bmatrix} -1 & 0 & 0 \\ 0 & 1 & 0 \\ 0 & 0 & 1 \end{bmatrix} \quad \text{reflection through the } x = 0 \text{ plane.}$$

$$\mathbf{R}_f = \begin{bmatrix} 1 & 0 & 0 \\ 0 & -1 & 0 \\ 0 & 0 & 1 \end{bmatrix} \quad \text{reflection through the } y = 0 \text{ plane.}$$

$$\mathbf{R}_f = \begin{bmatrix} 1 & 0 & 0 \\ 0 & 1 & 0 \\ 0 & 0 & -1 \end{bmatrix} \quad \text{reflection through the } z = 0 \text{ plane.}$$

$$\mathbf{R}_f = \begin{bmatrix} 1 & 0 & 0 \\ 0 & -1 & 0 \\ 0 & 0 & -1 \end{bmatrix} \quad \text{reflection through the } x \text{ axis.}$$

$$\mathbf{R}_f = \begin{bmatrix} -1 & 0 & 0 \\ 0 & 1 & 0 \\ 0 & 0 & -1 \end{bmatrix} \quad \text{reflection through the } y \text{ axis.}$$

$$\mathbf{R}_f = \begin{bmatrix} -1 & 0 & 0 \\ 0 & -1 & 0 \\ 0 & 0 & 1 \end{bmatrix} \quad \text{reflection through the } z \text{ axis.}$$

$$\mathbf{R}_f = \begin{bmatrix} -1 & 0 & 0 \\ 0 & -1 & 0 \\ 0 & 0 & -1 \end{bmatrix} \quad \text{reflection through the origin.}$$

Reflection may be combined with differential scaling by using a modified transformation matrix $\mathbf{R}'_f$:

$$\mathbf{R}'_f = \begin{bmatrix} \pm s_x & 0 & 0 \\ 0 & \pm s_y & 0 \\ 0 & 0 & \pm s_z \end{bmatrix}$$

Symmetry in a Plane: Patterns

Rotation: For a repeated pattern or lattice of points in a plane there are only five possible rotational symmetries. If $\theta = 2\pi n$, where θ is the angle of rotational symmetry, then $n = 1, 2, 3, 4$, or 6. No other values are possible. Thus, it is not possible for a pattern to have fivefold rotational symmetry, or anything greater than sixfold symmetry.

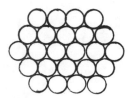

A 60° rotation of the array of circles about the center of any one brings the pattern back onto itself.

Inversion: An inversion requires a point r through which the transformation is taken. Then any point p at the vector displacement $\mathbf{p}$ from r is moved to $-\mathbf{p}$.

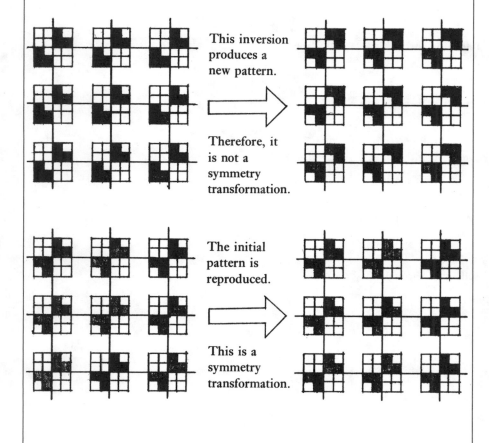

This inversion produces a new pattern.

Therefore, it is not a symmetry transformation.

The initial pattern is reproduced.

This is a symmetry transformation.

There are 17 distinct symmetries in the plane, including the five rotational symmetries, reflection, and inversion.

Patterns are assumed to extend indefinitely throughout the plane.

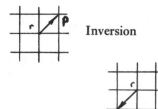

Inversion

The group of transformations that an object can undergo that leave its shape unchanged characterize the symmetries of the object.

"A thing is symmetrical if one can subject it to a certain operation and it appears exactly the same after the operation."

Hermann Weyl

Symmetry in a Plane: Polygons

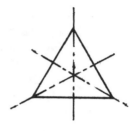

Equilateral triangle: six symmetry transforms
    three rotations (120°, 240°, 360°)
    three reflections

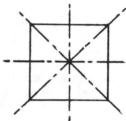

Square: nine symmetry transforms
    one inversion
    four rotations (90°, 180°, 270°, 360°)
    four reflections

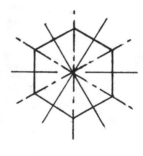

Hexagon: 13 symmetry transformations
    one inversion
    six rotations (60°, 120°, 180°, 240°, 300°, 360°)
    six reflections

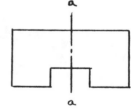

Symmetry reflection about *a-a*

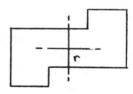

Symmetry inversion through point *r*

Inversion of an equilateral triangle produces a different figure.

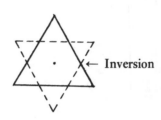

A regular polygon with *n* sides has *n* rotational symmetry transformations and *n* reflection symmetry transforms. If *n* is even, then it has an inversion.

Nonregular polygons may also have symmetry transformations.

Symmetry in 3D: Crystallographic

The geometrical problem of determining all possible regular arrangements of objects in three-dimensional space has its origin in the field of crystallography. It is usually sufficient to treat these objects as points (e.g., atoms in a crystal). Regular systems of points form a lattice of points in three dimensions.

An observer located at any lattice point of a symmetrical pattern cannot determine by any measurement at which point of the system he or she is located, since symmetry demands that every point relative to the other points is the same.

There are seven classes of crystallographic symmetry:

There are 230 different possible symmetries in three dimensions.

Triclinic: This arrangement has the least symmetry. Inversion through the vertex may produce a symmetry.

a, b, c are base (or primitive) vectors defining the crystal structure.

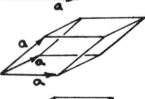

Trigonal: All the base vectors are of equal length, and the angles between them are equal. Inversion through the vertex and rotation about the long body diagonal produce symmetrical images.

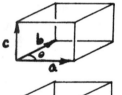

Monoclinic: A 180° rotation about **c** adds another symmetry transformation.

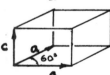

Hexagonal: Rotations of 60°, 120°, 180° about **c** add three more symmetry transforms.

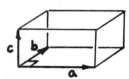

Orthorhombic: This lattice is symmetric for rotations of 180° about any of the three vectors.

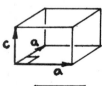

Tetragonal: Even higher-order symmetries are possible with this pattern.

Cubic: Forty-eight different symmetry transformations are possible for the cubic lattice. It has the highest symmetry of all the classes.

Symmetry in 3D: Polyhedra

A cube has 48 different symmetry transformations:

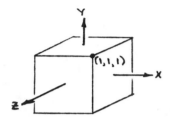

a. The identity transformation.

b. A rotation of 90°, 180°, and 270° about the x, y, and z axes (nine total).

c. A rotation of 120° and 240° about the four body diagonals (eight total).

d. A rotation of 180° about axes connecting the center of the cube with midpoints of each edge (six total).

e. Inversion through the cube's geometric center (origin in example).

f. Reflection through the planes $x = 0$, $y = 0$, and $z = 0$, followed by a rotation of 0°, 90°, or − 90° about a corresponding axis (e.g., following a reflection through the $x = 0$ plane, rotate about the x axis) (nine total).

g. Reflection along the four body diagonals followed by rotation of ±60° about that diagonal (eight total).

h. Reflection through the six planes: $x = \pm y$, $x = \pm z$, $y = \pm z$ (six total).

$$\mathbf{R}_f = \begin{bmatrix} 1 & 0 & 0 \\ 0 & 1 & 0 \\ 0 & 0 & 1 \end{bmatrix}$$

$$\mathbf{R}_f = \begin{bmatrix} -1 & 0 & 0 \\ 0 & -1 & 0 \\ 0 & 0 & -1 \end{bmatrix}$$

$$\mathbf{R}_f = \begin{bmatrix} -1 & 0 & 0 \\ 0 & 0 & 1 \\ 0 & -1 & 0 \end{bmatrix}$$

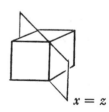

$x = z$

You can discover and work out the symmetry transformations for the other Platonic solids. An arbitrary polyhedron or more general solid may have a high or low degree of symmetry, or no symmetry at all. The use of symmetry transformations often facilitates both the geometric modeling and the computer graphic display of objects. There is a branch of mathematics called "group theory" that explores the subject of symmetry transformations in great detail.

Observe: there are three and only three nonzero elements in the 3×3 $\mathbf{R}_f$ symmetry matrix. Each nonzero element is located so that the only other elements in its row and column are zero. How many unique matrices are there like this?

$$\frac{9 \times 4 \times 1}{3 \times 2 \times 1} \times 2^3 = 48$$

Position–Direction Sweep

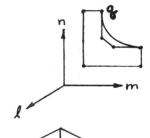

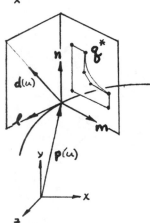

Given the outline of a cross section defined in the l,m,n coordinate system, sweep this shape through space to define a solid.

Define a parametric curve $p(u)$ that describes the successive positions of the cross section; and define another parametric function $d(u)$ that describes the directed orientation of the cross section. Then the orientation of the l,m,n coordinate system at any point $p(u)$ is given by the three mutually orthogonal unit vectors:

$p(u)$ and $d(u)$ are coordinated through their common parametric variable u. $d(u)$ determines the rotational orientation of m,n about an axis coincident with l.

$$l = \frac{p^u}{|p^u|} \quad m = \frac{d \times p^u}{|d \times p^u|} \quad n = l \times m$$

The unit vectors l,m,n form an orthogonal triad.

Thus, the sweep transformation of any point q in the initial l,m,n coordinate system onto the x,y,z system at $p(u)$ is given by

$$q^* = p(u) + q_l l + q_m m + q_n n$$

The complete cross section is thus reconstructed at any point $p(u)$. If parts of the cross section consist of curve segments, then the control points defining these curves are swept into their new position just like any other vertex point on the cross section. These curves are then regenerated as usual, but based on the relocated control points.

If it is desirable to continuously change the scale of the cross section as it sweeps along $p(u)$, then simply add an additional parametric function, say $s(u)$, constructed to yield the appropriate scale factors. Now all three functions $p(u)$, $d(u)$, and $s(u)$ operate in a coordinated fashion to position, direct, and scale the cross section.

$s(u)$ is also a vector function [as are $p(u)$ and $d(u)$, of course]. Therefore, it produces the three scale factors s_l, s_m, and s_n.

Nonlinear Deformations

Here are just a few of an unlimited number of nonlinear transformations that can be used to deform shapes in a controlled way.

Curvilinear:

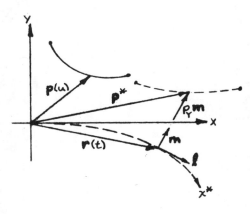

To deform a curve $\mathbf{p}(u)$, define a deformation of the *x* axis by $\mathbf{r}(t)$. Define a relationship between the parametric variables *u* and *t*:

$$t = t(u)$$

then the deformed curve is given by

$$\mathbf{p}^* = \mathbf{r}[t(u)] + p_y\mathbf{m}$$

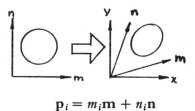

$$\mathbf{p}_i = m_i\mathbf{m} + n_i\mathbf{n}$$

$\mathbf{l} = \mathbf{r}^t$, $\mathbf{m} = \mathbf{z} \times \mathbf{l}$; where $\mathbf{z}$ is the unit vector in the *z* direction.

Bivariate Deformation:

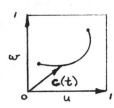

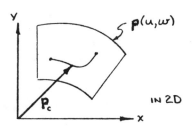

IN 2D

Define a curve $\mathbf{c}(t)$ and embed it in a normalized parametric plane *u,w*. Define a bivariate surface, $\mathbf{p}(u,w)$, in the plane *x,y* or space *x,y,z*. Then map the curve

$$\mathbf{p}_c = \mathbf{p}[u(t),w(t)]$$

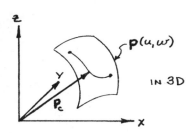

IN 3D

Deformation is defined by defining the embedding space (e.g., control points for a Bézier surface). This also is the means by which the deformed object is located, oriented, and scaled in *x,y,z* space.

Trivariate Deformation:

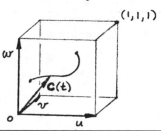

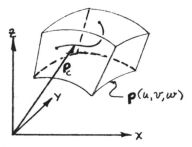

Define a curve $\mathbf{c}(t)$ and embed it in a normalized parametric space *u,v,w*. Define a trivariate solid $\mathbf{p}(u,v,w)$ and map $\mathbf{p}_c$:

$$\mathbf{p}_c = \mathbf{p}[u(t),v(t),w(t)]$$

Homogeneous Transformations

Homogeneous coordinates are used to facilitate many kinds of transformations, including projective and rigid body. The homogeneous coordinates of an ordinary point, $\mathbf{p}$, in three-dimensional space are $[hx \ \ hy \ \ hz \ \ h]$, denoted as $\mathbf{p}_h$, and whose ordinary coordinates are $x = hx/h$, $y = hy/h$, and $z = hz/h$. Thus, homogeneous points have four components. All transformations of homogeneous points are produced by matrix multiplication using a 4×4 transformation matrix $\mathbf{T}_h$. This approach allows the concatenation of any number of individual transformations into a single transformation matrix. Proceed as follows: First convert $\mathbf{p} = [x \ \ y \ \ z]$ into its equivalent homogeneous coordinates, the simplest being $\mathbf{p}_h = [x \ \ y \ \ z \ \ 1]$. Next, define the transformation matrix $\mathbf{T}_h$ and perform the matrix multiplication described in Eq. (10.20), below, producing $\mathbf{p}_h^*$. Finally, convert $\mathbf{p}_h^*$ to normal coordinates $\mathbf{p}^*$:

$$\mathbf{p}_h^* = \mathbf{p}_h \mathbf{T}_h \tag{10.20}$$

Here are some useful transformation matrices:

$$\text{Translation } \mathbf{T}_h = \begin{bmatrix} 1 & 0 & 0 & 0 \\ 0 & 1 & 0 & 0 \\ 0 & 0 & 1 & 0 \\ t_x & t_y & t_z & 1 \end{bmatrix}$$

$$\text{Rotation, } z \text{ Axis } \mathbf{T}_h = \begin{bmatrix} \cos\theta & \sin\theta & 0 & 0 \\ -\sin\theta & \cos\theta & 0 & 0 \\ 0 & 0 & 1 & 0 \\ 0 & 0 & 0 & 1 \end{bmatrix}$$

$$\text{Scaling } \mathbf{T}_h = \begin{bmatrix} s_x & 0 & 0 & 0 \\ 0 & s_y & 0 & 0 \\ 0 & 0 & s_z & 0 \\ 0 & 0 & 0 & 1 \end{bmatrix}$$

$$\text{General } \mathbf{T}_h = \begin{bmatrix} a & b & c & p \\ d & e & f & q \\ g & i & j & r \\ l & m & n & h \end{bmatrix}$$

Interpret the elements of the general transformation matrix as follows:

$a\text{–}j$:   rotations, reflection, scaling
l,m,n: translation
p,q,r: projection
h: the homogeneous coordinate

Julius Plücker (1801–1868): his rediscovery and work with homogeneous coordinates were an important step toward the arithmetization of geometry.

An affine transformation is composed of rotations, translations, and scalings.

Transformation and Evaluation of Curves and Surfaces

A curve or surface is usually subject to several modeling and viewing transformations prior to final display. Here is an effective approach to accomplish this:

Given a surface

$$\mathbf{p}(u,w) = \mathbf{UMPM}^T\mathbf{W}^T$$

where $\mathbf{P}$ is the matrix of control points $\mathbf{p}_{ij}$; first compute the net, or total, transformation $\mathbf{T}$. Then solve for the tensor

$$\mathbf{C} = [\mathbf{c}_{ij}] = \mathbf{M}[\mathbf{p}_{ij}\mathbf{T}]\mathbf{M}^T$$

The transformed surface equations

$$\mathbf{p}^*(u,w) = \mathbf{UCW}^T$$

are then evaluated after expansion and rearrangement of terms into a convenient polynomial expression. For example, for the bicubic Bézier surface

$$\begin{aligned}
\mathbf{p}^*(u,w) = \; & \mathbf{c}_{00} + u(\mathbf{c}_{10} + u(\mathbf{c}_{20} + \mathbf{c}_{30}u)) \\
& + w\{\mathbf{c}_{01} + u(c_{11} + u(\mathbf{c}_{21} + \mathbf{c}_{31}u)) \\
& + w\{\mathbf{c}_{02} + u(\mathbf{c}_{12} + u(\mathbf{c}_{22} + \mathbf{c}_{23}u)) \\
& + w\{\mathbf{c}_{03} + u(\mathbf{c}_{13} + u(\mathbf{c}_{23} + \mathbf{c}_{33}u))\}\}\}
\end{aligned}$$

It is more efficient to transform the relatively few control points and then scan, rather than to scan the curve or surface in object space and then subject each sample point to the viewing transformation. This implies

$$\mathbf{p}(u,w)\mathbf{T} = \mathbf{UM}[\mathbf{PT}]\mathbf{M}^T\mathbf{W}^T$$

This relationship does not hold if perspective transformations are included in $\mathbf{T}$.

For a bicubic Bézier surface:

$$\mathbf{U} = [u^3 \; u^2 \; u \; 1]$$
$$\mathbf{W} = [w^3 \; w^2 \; w \; 1]$$

$$\mathbf{M} = \begin{bmatrix} -1 & 3 & -3 & 1 \\ 3 & -6 & 3 & 0 \\ -3 & 3 & 0 & 0 \\ 1 & 0 & 0 & 0 \end{bmatrix}$$

The $\mathbf{c}_{ij}$, of course, are vectors with components $(c_{ij})_x, (c_{ij})_y, (c_{ij})_z$. Thus

$$\mathbf{c}_{ij} = [(c_{ij})_x \; (c_{ij})_y \; (c_{ij})_z]$$

$[\mathbf{p}_{ij}\mathbf{T}]$ and $[\mathbf{PT}]$ imply homogeneous transformations. Therefore, an appropriate conversion into and out of the 4D space of homogeneous transformations is required before subsequent pre- and postmultiplications are performed.

Orthographic Projection: Principal Planes

Projections are transformations that produce two-dimensional representations of three-dimensional objects. They are perhaps the most important kind of transformation in computer graphics, since they are necessary to construct the display image of a geometric object. The simplest of these is the orthographic projection. The orthographic projection of any point **p** onto an arbitrary plane is found by constructing a line through the point and perpendicular to the plane. The point of intersection of the line and plane is the projected point **p***.

The most trivial form of orthographic projection is that of a point **p** = [x y z] onto one of the three principal planes. For example, the orthographic projection of **p** onto the x,y plane is **p*** = [x y 0].

To project a curve or surface patch, merely project the defining control points. The curve or patch is then reconstructed from these projected points.

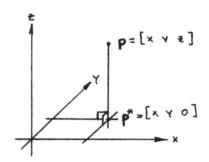
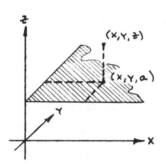

If the projection is onto a plane parallel to one of the principal planes, say $z = a$ (which is parallel to the x,y plane), then replace the appropriate coordinate with the constant defining the plane. Thus, for the projection plane defined by $z = a$, the point **p** = [x y z] projects as **p*** = [x y a]. This is easy to generalize for other planes parallel to any of the principal planes.

Orthographic Projection: Arbitrary Planes

Here are two algorithms showing some of the different approaches available when it is necessary to project points onto an arbitrary plane (i.e., one that is not necessarily parallel to a principal plane).

Projection Algorithm 1. Given the plane of projection and a point or set of points to be projected onto it, first compute the unit normal **n** to the plane. Next, find the rotation matrix or matrices that rotate **n** so that it is parallel to the z axis (i.e., compute θ and γ). Apply the rotation matrix to the points to be projected. Project the rotated points onto the $z = 0$ plane.

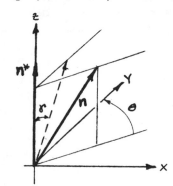

Rotate **n** into z axis, using θ and γ:

$$\theta = \tan^{-1}\left(\frac{n_x}{n_y}\right)$$

$$\gamma = \tan^{-1}\left(\frac{\sqrt{n_x^2 + n_y^2}}{n_z}\right)$$

Projection Algorithm 2. Given a plane $Ax + By + Cz + D = 0$, and a set of points $\mathbf{p}_i$ to be projected onto it, first compute **n**, the unit normal to the plane. Next, for each point $\mathbf{p}_i$, compute the directed distance d_i to the plane. Then,

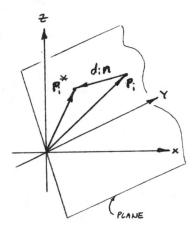

$$\mathbf{p}_i^* = \mathbf{p}_i + d_i\mathbf{n}$$

where

$$\mathbf{n} = [n_x \quad n_y \quad n_z]$$

$$n_x = A/\sqrt{A^2 + B^2 + C^2}$$

$$n_y = B/\sqrt{A^2 + B^2 + C^2}$$

$$n_z = C/\sqrt{A^2 + B^2 + C^2}$$

$$d_i = \frac{Ax_i + By_i + Cz_i + D}{\sqrt{A^2 + B^2 + C^2}}$$

$\mathbf{p}_i^*$ is on the plane.

Perspective Projection

The perspective projection of an object approximates the way an observer forms a visual image of it. The basic geometry of the perspective transformation includes the position of the viewer, the plane of projection, and λ, the normal distance from the viewer to the plane. If the viewer is on the z axis and the x,y plane is the plane of projection, then using the properties of similar triangles:

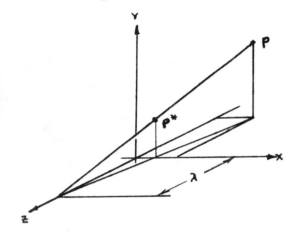

$$x^* = \frac{\lambda x}{\lambda - z}$$

$$y^* = \frac{\lambda y}{\lambda - z}$$

$$z^* = 0$$

If a left-hand coordinate system is used, then the denominator becomes $\lambda + z$ (assuming the viewer is on the $+ z$ axis).

This is expressed as a homogeneous transformation:

$$\mathbf{p}_h^* = \mathbf{p}_h \begin{bmatrix} 1 & 0 & 0 & 0 \\ 0 & 1 & 0 & 0 \\ 0 & 0 & 0 & r \\ 0 & 0 & 0 & 1 \end{bmatrix} \qquad (10.21)$$

If $\mathbf{p}_h = [x \ y \ z \ 1]$, then $\mathbf{p}_h^* = [x \ y \ 0 \ (rz + 1)]$, and

$$\mathbf{p}^* = \left[\frac{x}{rz + 1} \quad \frac{y}{rz + 1} \quad \frac{0}{rz + 1} \right]$$

and if $r = 1/\lambda$, then

$$\mathbf{p}^* = \left[\frac{\lambda x}{\lambda - z} \quad \frac{\lambda y}{\lambda - z} \quad 0 \right]$$

Two Straight Lines

Two straight lines in space may intersect in two different ways, if they intersect at all. First, they may intersect at a single point **r**. Second, they may be collinear and overlap either partially or completely.

If one line is given by $\mathbf{p}(u) = \mathbf{a} + u\mathbf{b}$ and the other by $\mathbf{q}(u) = \mathbf{c} + w\mathbf{d}$, then at their point of intersection $\mathbf{p}(u) = \mathbf{q}(u) = \mathbf{r}$, or

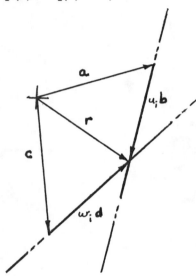

$$\mathbf{a} + u\mathbf{b} = \mathbf{c} + w\mathbf{d} \qquad (11.1)$$

If $u,w \in [0,1]$, then only solutions in this interval are valid solutions for line segments.

This yields three linear equations, one for each coordinate, with two unknowns, u and w. Solve for u and w using any two of these equations, and verify the results with the third. Finally, use either member of the solution pair (u_i, w_i) to compute **r**; that is, $\mathbf{r} = \mathbf{a} + u_i\mathbf{b}$ or $\mathbf{r} = \mathbf{c} + w_i\mathbf{d}$.

Vector algebra presents an alternative, direct solution. To solve for u, perform the following vector and scalar products on Eq. (11.1):

$$(\mathbf{c} \times \mathbf{d}) \cdot (\mathbf{a} + u\mathbf{b}) = (\mathbf{c} \times \mathbf{d}) \cdot (\mathbf{c} + w\mathbf{d})$$

Since $(\mathbf{c} \times \mathbf{d})$ is perpendicular to both **a** and **d**, the right-hand side of the equation is zero. So that

$$u = -\frac{(\mathbf{c} \times \mathbf{d}) \cdot \mathbf{a}}{(\mathbf{c} \times \mathbf{d}) \cdot \mathbf{b}}$$

Similarly for w:

$$w = -\frac{(\mathbf{a} \times \mathbf{b}) \cdot \mathbf{c}}{(\mathbf{a} \times \mathbf{b}) \cdot \mathbf{d}}$$

Straight Line and Plane

Define the points on a plane by $\mathbf{p}(u,w) = \mathbf{a} + u\mathbf{b} + w\mathbf{c}$, and points on a line by $\mathbf{q}(t) = \mathbf{d} + t\mathbf{e}$. The unit normal to the plane is given by $\mathbf{n} = (\mathbf{b} \times \mathbf{c})/|\mathbf{b} \times \mathbf{c}|$.

If $\mathbf{n} \cdot \mathbf{e} = 0$, then the line and plane are parallel. If $\mathbf{n} \cdot \mathbf{e} = 0$ and the point defined by $\mathbf{d}$ lies on the plane, then the line lies on the plane.

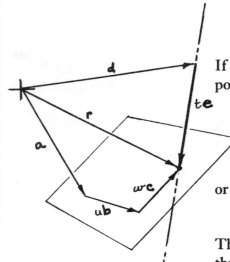

If the line and plane intersect at a point $\mathbf{r}$, then

$$\mathbf{r} = \mathbf{p}(u,w) = \mathbf{q}(t)$$

or

$$\mathbf{a} + u\mathbf{b} + w\mathbf{c} = \mathbf{d} + t\mathbf{e} \quad (11.2)$$

This vector equation produces three linear equations in three unknowns, t, u, and w. Using vector algebra

$$t = \frac{(\mathbf{b} \times \mathbf{c}) \cdot \mathbf{a} - (\mathbf{b} \times \mathbf{c}) \cdot \mathbf{d}}{(\mathbf{b} \times \mathbf{c}) \cdot \mathbf{e}}$$

$$u = \frac{(\mathbf{c} \times \mathbf{e}) \cdot \mathbf{d} - (\mathbf{c} \times \mathbf{e}) \cdot \mathbf{a}}{(\mathbf{c} \times \mathbf{e}) \cdot \mathbf{b}}$$

$$w = \frac{(\mathbf{b} \times \mathbf{e}) \cdot \mathbf{d} - (\mathbf{b} \times \mathbf{e}) \cdot \mathbf{a}}{(\mathbf{b} \times \mathbf{e}) \cdot \mathbf{c}}$$

Straight Line and Curve

Define points on the curve by $p(w) = au^3 + bu^2 + cu + d$, and points on the line by $q(t) = e + tf$. An intersection occurs wherever

$$au^3 + bu^2 + cu + d = e + tf \qquad (11.3)$$

Isolate u:

$$(e \times f) \cdot (au^3 + bu^2 + cu + d) = 0$$

There are three roots to this equation, which means there are three possible points of intersection. Use numerical methods to compute the roots.

Although a cubic is used here, the procedure is easily generalized.

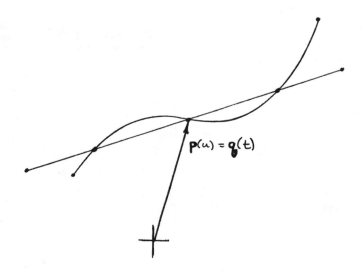

The curve may be composite, in which case each segment must usually be analyzed.

The curve may be closed.

Straight Line and Surface

Define points on the surface by $\mathbf{p}(u,w)$ and points on the line by $\mathbf{q}(t)$. Points of intersection occur when

$$\mathbf{p}(u,w) = \mathbf{q}(t) \qquad (11.4)$$

This vector equation represents three simultaneous, nonlinear equations in three unknowns. Their solution requires the application of numerical analysis methods.

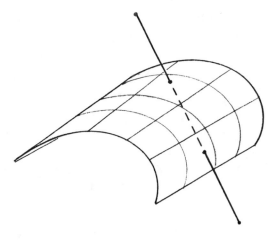

Anticipate multiple intersections.

Hint: Rotate and translate the line and surface as a group so that the line $\mathbf{q}(t)$ is coincident with the z axis. This simplifies the solution to

$$x(u,w) = 0$$
$$y(u,w) = 0$$
$$z(u,w) = z$$

Use the first two equations to solve for u and w, a procedure requiring numerical methods. Those solutions in the interval $u,w \in [0,1]$ are valid, and when they are substituted into $\mathbf{p}(u,w)$, the points of intersection are produced.

Two curves

Define two arbitrary curves in space by $\mathbf{p}(u)$ and $\mathbf{q}(t)$. Points of intersection occur if

$$\mathbf{p}(u) - \mathbf{q}(t) = 0 \tag{11.5}$$

Three nonlinear equations in two unknowns, u and t, are produced. Suppress one of the equations, say in z; then solve the remaining two equations for u and t. Verify by checking $p_z(u) - q_z(t) = 0$. Anticipate multiple roots.

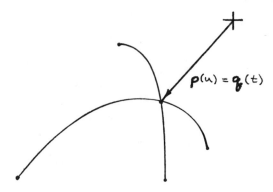

Before initiating a complex solution procedure, it is usually worthwhile to try to eliminate the more obviously nonintersecting pairs of curves from further computational consideration. Do this by determining if the projections of their respective control points $\mathbf{p}_i$ and $\mathbf{q}_i$ onto the coordinate axes overlap. This merely amounts to comparing the intervals $p_i\{\min,\max\}_x$ to $q_i\{\min,\max\}_x$, $p_i\{\min,\max\}_y$ to $q_i\{\min,\max\}_y$, and $p_i\{\min,\max\}_z$ to $q_i\{\min, \max\}_z$. If at least one disjoint interval is found, then the two curves do not intersect. If there are overlaps on all three axes, then an intersection is possible but not guaranteed. If this is true, then check for intersections between the projections of the curves onto the principal planes.

The guiding principle here is that if two curves intersect, then their projections also intersect. Clearly, the converse is also true.

Curve and Plane

If a curve and a plane intersect, then the scalar product of the normal vector **d** from the origin to the plane and the vector $[\mathbf{p}(u_i) - \mathbf{d}]$ lying in the plane must equal zero:

$$[\mathbf{p}(u_i) - \mathbf{d}] \cdot \mathbf{d} = 0 \qquad (11.6)$$

where $\mathbf{p}(u)$ defines points on the curve, $|\mathbf{d}| = D/\sqrt{A^2 + B^2 + C^2}$, and A, B, C, and D are the plane coefficients. The vector components of **d** are $[n_x|\mathbf{d}| \; n_y|\mathbf{d}| \; n_z|\mathbf{d}|]$, with $n_x = A/\sqrt{A^2 + B^2 + C^2}$, $n_y = B/\sqrt{A^2 + B^2 + C^2}$, $n_z = C/\sqrt{A^2 + B^2 + C^2}$.

u_i is the point on the curve corresponding to the point of intersection with the plane.

Check for multiple intersections.

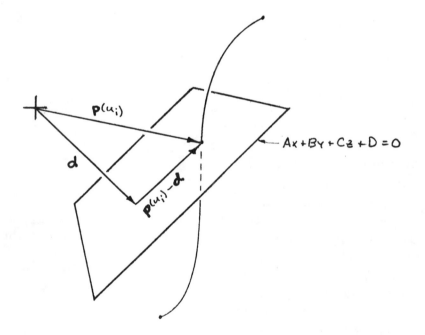

Hint: Rotate and translate the plane and curve as a group until the plane is coincident with the x,y plane and then solve $z(u) = 0$.

Curve and Surface —

If a curve and a surface intersect, then $\mathbf{r} = \mathbf{q}(t) = \mathbf{p}(u,w)$, and

$$\mathbf{p}(u,w) - \mathbf{q}(t) = 0 \tag{11.7}$$

At the point(s) of intersection. The equation produces three simultaneous, nonlinear equations in three unknowns. Numerical analysis methods are used to obtain solutions.

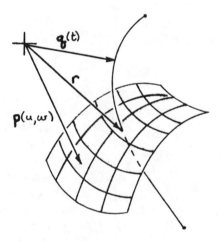

Multiple intersections are possible.

Two Planes

Given two planes defined by $\mathbf{p}(u,w) = \mathbf{a} + u\mathbf{b} + w\mathbf{c}$ and $\mathbf{q}(s,t) = \mathbf{d} + s\mathbf{e} + t\mathbf{f}$, the points on their intersection, if any, must satisfy $\mathbf{p}(u,w) - \mathbf{q}(s,t) = 0$, or

$$\mathbf{a} + u\mathbf{b} + w\mathbf{c} = \mathbf{d} + s\mathbf{e} + t\mathbf{f} \qquad (11.8)$$

This produces three simultaneous linear equations in four unknowns (u, w, s, and t). The extra degree of freedom (the fourth independent variable) implies that the intersection is a curve (a straight line in this case) and not a point. So, an additional constraint is introduced, for example: $u = u_i$, where u_i is some constant (say $u_i = 0$).

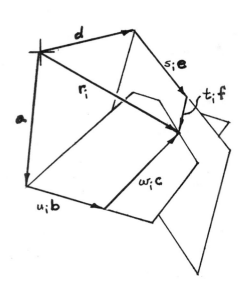

The additional constraint reduces the number of unknowns to three, and now those three simultaneous linear equations can be solved. The solution produces a point $\mathbf{r}_i$ on the line of intersection.

Next, select another constraint, such as $u = u_j$, where $u_i \neq u_j$ (say $u_j = 1$), and solve the three equations, again, to produce a second point $\mathbf{r}_j$.

The two points $\mathbf{r}_i$ and $\mathbf{r}_j$ are sufficient to define the line of intersection.

Two polyhedra intersect if one or both contain vertex points of the other. Any edge radiating from a contained vertex and joining a noncontained vertex must intersect a face of the containing polyhedron. From these conditions it is possible to determine the proper face–face intersections.

The intersection of three planes is given by

$$\mathbf{p} = \frac{d_1(\mathbf{n}_2 \times \mathbf{n}_3) + d_2(\mathbf{n}_3 \times \mathbf{n}_1) + d_3(\mathbf{n}_1 \times \mathbf{n}_2)}{\mathbf{n}_1 \cdot \mathbf{n}_2 \times \mathbf{n}_3}$$

where $\mathbf{n}_1, \mathbf{n}_2, \mathbf{n}_3$ are unit normals to each of the three planes, and d_1, d_2, d_3 are the respective distances of each from the origin.

This equation is verified by demonstrating that it satisfies the equation for each plane: $\mathbf{p} \cdot \mathbf{n}_1 = d_1$, $\mathbf{p} \cdot \mathbf{n}_2 = d_2$, and $\mathbf{p} \cdot \mathbf{n}_3 = d_3$.

Plane and Surface

If a plane and a surface patch intersect, then the scalar product of the normal vector **d** from the origin to the plane and the vector $[\mathbf{p}(u,w) - \mathbf{d}]$ lying in the plane must equal zero:

$$[\mathbf{p}(u,w) - \mathbf{d}] \cdot \mathbf{d} = 0 \qquad (11.9)$$

where $\mathbf{p}(u,w)$ defines points on the patch. A single nonlinear equation in two unknowns, u and w, must be solved. The extra degree of freedom implies that the solution is a curve. To find points on this curve of intersection, fix one of the parametric variables, u or w, at discrete intervals, say $u = 0, 0.1, 0.2, \ldots, 1.0$, and solve for the other, w, at each of these u values. This produces pairs of u,w values corresponding to a sequence of points on the intersection curve.

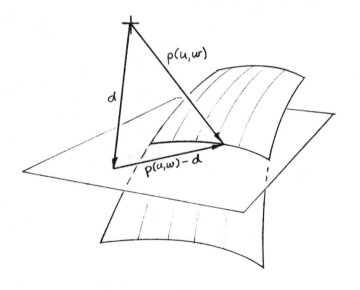

Here is another approach. Rotate and translate the plane and surface as a group so that the plane is coincident with the x,y plane (the $z = 0$ plane). Then solve

$$z(u,w) = 0$$

fixing successive values of either u or w.

"The science of pure mathematics, in its modern developments, may claim to be the most original creation of the human spirit."

Alfred North Whitehead

Two Surfaces ___

The most complex and computationally most difficult intersection problem is that of finding the intersection of two surfaces. Many successful techniques exist for finding this intersection. Here is a brief description of one of them, a simple approach to describe, but subtle and requiring some sophisticated mathematics to implement efficiently.

In general a solution is represented by three simultaneous, nonlinear equations in four unknowns (u, w, s, and t). The extra degree of freedom indicates that the intersection is a curve:

$$\mathbf{p}(u,w) - \mathbf{q}(s,t) = 0 \qquad (11.10)$$

The solution is obtained by finding the intersection between each of a series of isoparametric curves lying on one of the patches and the other patch (the curve and patch intersection problem). The points obtained lie on and define the curve of intersection between the two surfaces.

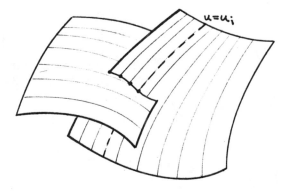

Curves: Tangent Vector

The tangent vector at a point $\mathbf{p}_i$ on a curve is denoted by $\mathbf{p}_i^u$. The unit tangent vector is

$$\mathbf{t}_i = \mathbf{p}_i^u / |\mathbf{p}_i^u| \tag{12.1}$$

The equation of a straight line through $\mathbf{p}_i$ and parallel to $\mathbf{t}_i$ is

$$\mathbf{r}(v) = \mathbf{p}_i + v\mathbf{t}_i \tag{12.2}$$

where v is some parametric variable.

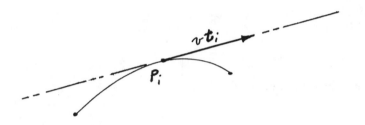

$\mathbf{p}^u = d\mathbf{p}(u)/du$

Local properties are those associated with and computed at a point on a curve, surface, or other analytic geometric object. Differential geometry is largely addressed to characterizing these properties.

Curves: The Normal Plane

The normal plane at any point $\mathbf{p}_i$ on a curve is that plane through $\mathbf{p}_i$ and perpendicular to the local tangent vector $\mathbf{p}_i^u$. If $\mathbf{q}$ is any point on the plane, then

$$(\mathbf{q} - \mathbf{p}_i) \cdot \mathbf{p}_i^u = 0 \tag{12.3}$$

Let (x, y, z) denote the coordinates of $\mathbf{q}$, then

$$\begin{bmatrix} x - x_i \\ y - y_i \\ z - z_i \end{bmatrix}^T \begin{bmatrix} x_i^u \\ y_i^u \\ z_i^u \end{bmatrix} = 0$$

When the matrix algebra is performed and the terms are rearranged, find

$$x_i^u x + y_i^u y + z_i^u z - (x_i x_i^u + y_i y_i^u + z_i z_i^u) = 0$$

This is analogous to the conventional algebraic equation for a plane: $Ax + By + Cz + D = 0$.

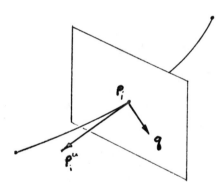

Curves: Principal Normal Vector

The principal normal vector $\mathbf{n}_i$ at any point $\mathbf{p}_i$ on a curve lies in the normal plane and points in the direction the curve is turning: that is, toward the center of curvature associated with that point. It is given by

$$\mathbf{n}_i = \mathbf{p}_i^{uu} - \frac{\mathbf{p}_i^{uu} \cdot \mathbf{p}_i^{u}}{|\mathbf{p}_i^{u}|^2} \mathbf{p}_i^{u} \tag{12.4}$$

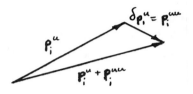

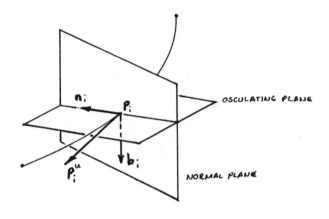

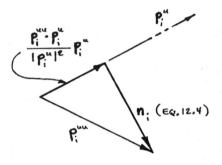

The binormal vector $\mathbf{b}_i$ at a point $\mathbf{p}_i$ on a curve also lies in the normal plane and is computed as the vector product:

$$\mathbf{b}_i = \mathbf{p}_i^{u} \times \mathbf{n}_i \tag{12.5}$$

The absolute values of $\mathbf{n}_i$ and $\mathbf{b}_i$ are meaningless. It is usually more convenient to work with the unit vectors $\hat{\mathbf{n}}_i$ and $\hat{\mathbf{b}}_i$.

Curves: Osculating Plane

The osculating plane at a point p_i on a curve is the limiting position of the plane defined by p_i and two neighboring points on the curve, p_h and p_j, as these points approach p_i. The equation of the osculating plane is most simply expressed in the form of a determinant:

$$\left| (q - p_i) \; p_i^u \; p_i^{uu} \right| = 0 \tag{12.6}$$

where q is an arbitrary point on the plane. In terms of the vector components, Eq. (12.6) becomes:

$$\begin{vmatrix} x - x_i & x_i^u & x_i^{uu} \\ y - y_i & y_i^u & y_i^{uu} \\ z - z_i & z_i^u & z_i^{uu} \end{vmatrix} = 0$$

If the determinant is expanded, then find

$$(x - x_i)(y_i^u z_i^{uu} - y_i^{uu} z_i^u) - (y - y_i)(x_i^u z_i^{uu} - x_i^{uu} z_i^u)$$
$$+ (z - z_i^u)(x_i^u y_i^{uu} - x_i^{uu} y_i^u) = 0$$

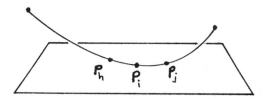

The three points must not be collinear (i.e., the osculating plane of a straight line is undefined).

The tangent and principal normal vectors lie in this plane.

Curves: Rectifying Plane

The rectifying plane at a point $\mathbf{p}_i$ on a curve is the plane through $\mathbf{p}_i$ and perpendicular to the principal normal $\mathbf{n}_i$. Thus,

$$(\mathbf{q} - \mathbf{p}_i) \cdot \mathbf{n}_i = 0 \qquad (12.7)$$

where $\mathbf{q}$ is an arbitrary point on the plane.

Here is another way to describe the rectifying plane:

$$\mathbf{q} = \mathbf{p}_i + u\hat{\mathbf{p}}_i^u + w\hat{\mathbf{b}}_i$$

where $\hat{\mathbf{b}}_i$ is the unit binormal vector.

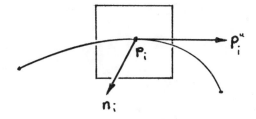

Curves: The Moving Trihedron

There are three characteristic vectors and three characteristic planes associated with each point p_i on any analytic curve. They are local or intrinsic properties: the tangent, principal normal, and binormal vectors, and the normal, osculating, and rectifying planes. These properties vary from point to point along a curve. When assembled, these vectors and planes form a convenient local coordinate system: the vectors define the coordinate axes and the planes define the three principal coordinate planes. It is a right-handed orthogonal coordinate system.

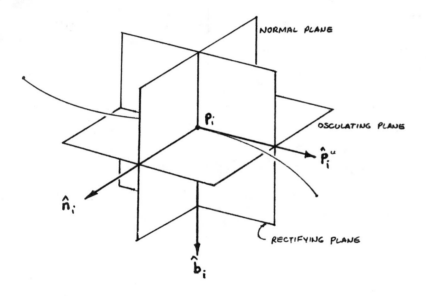

Curves: Curvature ——

The curvature $1/\rho_i$ at a point $\mathbf{p}_i$ on a curve is

$$\frac{1}{\rho_i} = \frac{\left| \mathbf{p}_i^u \times \mathbf{p}_i^{uu} \right|}{\left| \mathbf{p}_i^u \right|^3} \tag{12.8}$$

where ρ_i is the radius of curvature. The radius of curvature is measured in the osculating plane along the principal normal vector $\hat{\mathbf{n}}_i$. The radius of curvature vector $\mathbf{k}_i$ is the vector from $\mathbf{p}_i$ to the center of curvature:

$$\mathbf{k}_i = \rho_i \hat{\mathbf{n}}_i$$

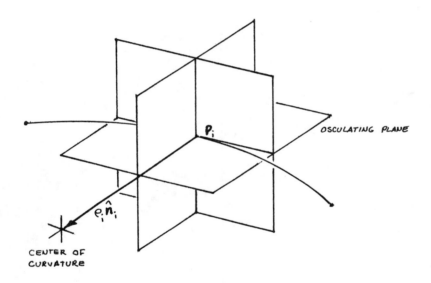

The curvature at a point $\mathbf{p}_i$ on a curve is the limit of the ratio of the angle $\Delta\theta$ between the tangent at $\mathbf{p}_i$ and the tangent at a neighboring point $\mathbf{p}_j$, to the arc $\widehat{\mathbf{p}_i\mathbf{p}_j}$ as $\mathbf{p}_j$ approaches $\mathbf{p}_i$ along the curve:

$$\frac{1}{\rho} = \lim_{\Delta s \to 0} \left(\frac{\Delta\theta}{\Delta s} \right)$$

where $\Delta s = \widehat{\mathbf{p}_i\mathbf{p}_j}$.

The classic curvature formula from analytic geometry for a plane curve is

$$\frac{1}{\rho} = \frac{d^2 y/dx^2}{[1 + (dy/dx)^2]^{3/2}}$$

In parametric form this becomes

$$\frac{1}{\rho} = \frac{x^u y^{uu} - x^{uu} y^u}{[(x^u)^2 + (y^u)^2]^{3/2}}$$

Curves: Torsion _____

The torsion τ_i at a point $\mathbf{p}_i$ on a curve is

$$\tau_i = \frac{[\mathbf{p}_i^u \ \mathbf{p}_i^{uu} \ \mathbf{p}_i^{uuu}]}{|\mathbf{p}_i^u \times \mathbf{p}_i^u|^2} \tag{12.9}$$

where $[\mathbf{p}_i^u \ \mathbf{p}_i^{uu} \ \mathbf{p}_i^{uuu}]$ is the triple scalar product.

Torsion amounts to a rotation or twist of the binormal vector about the tangent vector. It is the limit of the ratio of the angle between the binormal at $\mathbf{p}_i$ and the binormal at an adjacent point $\mathbf{p}_j$ to the arc $\widehat{ij}$ as $\mathbf{p}_j$ approaches $\mathbf{p}_i$ along the curve.

Curvature and torsion are related as follows

$$\tau_i = \frac{[\mathbf{p}_i^u \ \mathbf{p}_i^{uu} \ \mathbf{p}_i^{uuu}]}{|\mathbf{p}_i^u|^6}\rho_i^2$$

This expression holds if $1/\rho \neq 0$.

For a plane curve $\tau = 0$.

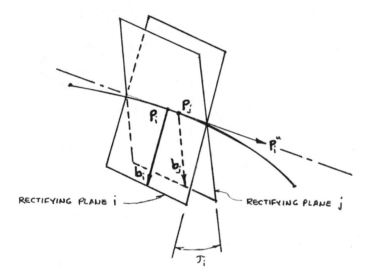

"The geometrical mind is not so closely bound to geometry that it cannot be drawn aside and transferred to other departments of knowledge. A work of morality, politics, criticism, perhaps even eloquence will be more elegant, other things being equal, if it is shaped by the hand of geometry."

Bernard Le Bovier de Fontenelle

Curves: Inflection Points

Inflection points are those points on a curve where curvature equals zero. This is true when

$$\left| \mathbf{p}^u \times \mathbf{p}^{uu} \right| = 0 \qquad (12.10)$$

This equation can also be written as $(\mathbf{p}^u \times \mathbf{p}^{uu}) \cdot (\mathbf{p}^u \times \mathbf{p}^{uu}) = 0$. Here is the result of performing the indicated scalar and vector operations:

$$(y^u z^{uu} - z^u y^{uu})^2 + (z^u x^{uu} - x^u z^{uu})^2$$
$$+ (x^u y^{uu} - y^u x^{uu})^2 = 0$$

Each of these terms must be zero; thus

i. $y^u z^{uu} - z^u y^{uu} = 0$
ii. $z^u x^{uu} - x^u z^{uu} = 0$
iii. $x^u y^{uu} - y^u x^{uu} = 0$

For a parametric cubic curve (Hermitian), Eq. iii becomes

$$3(b_x a_y - a_x b_y)u^2 + 3(c_x a_y - a_x c_y)u$$
$$+ (c_x b_y - b_x c_y) = 0$$

Similar equations obtain for i and ii. Three quadratic equations in u are produced. Only roots common to all three equations, and within the unit interval, determine a valid point of inflection.

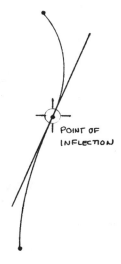

POINT OF
INFLECTION

Surfaces: Normals

The unit normal vector $\mathbf{n}(u,w)$ at any point $\mathbf{p}(u,w)$ on a surface patch is

$$\mathbf{n}(u,w) = \frac{\mathbf{p}^u \times \mathbf{p}^w}{\left| \mathbf{p}^u \times \mathbf{p}^w \right|} \qquad (12.11)$$

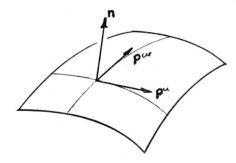

The unit normal is applicable to many computer graphics display problems involving solid geometric models; silhouette curves, hidden surfaces, and lighting and shading effects are examples.

Surfaces: Tangent Plane

The vector equation of the plane tangent to any point, $\mathbf{p}_i$, on a surface patch is

$$\mathbf{q}(s,t) = \mathbf{p}_i + s\mathbf{p}_i^u + t\mathbf{p}_i^w \qquad (12.12)$$

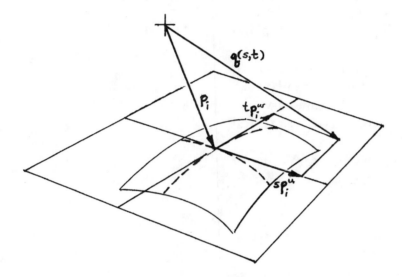

In a more general form, expressed as a determinant, find

$$\begin{vmatrix} x - x_i & x_i^u & x_i^w \\ y - y_i & y_i^u & y_i^w \\ z - z_i & z_i^u & z_i^w \end{vmatrix} = 0 \qquad (12.13)$$

Surfaces: Principal Curvature

The principal curvature at any point $\mathbf{p}$ on a surface is described and defined as follows. At any point $\mathbf{p}(u,w)$ on a surface S construct the tangent plane T, and any line t through $\mathbf{p}$ that also lies in T (the direction of t is given in terms of du/dw). All planes P intersecting T and containing t cut S in a one-parameter family of plane curves c, all passing through $\mathbf{p}$ and tangent to t.

There is an infinite number of nonplanar curves on S, through $\mathbf{p}$ and tangent to t, with P as their osculating plane; all have the same radius and center of curvature, the same curvature vector $\mathbf{k}$, and the same principal normal $\mathbf{n}$. Curve c is a typical example.

The normal curvature vector $\mathbf{k}_n$ at $\mathbf{p}$ is the vector projection of $\mathbf{k}$ onto the unit normal $\mathbf{n}$. Thus, $\mathbf{k}_n = (\mathbf{k} \cdot \mathbf{n})\mathbf{n}$, or $\kappa_n = \mathbf{k} \cdot \mathbf{n}$, where

$$\kappa_n = \frac{L(du/dt)^2 + 2M(du/dt)(dw/dt) + N(dw/dt)^2}{E(du/dt)^2 + 2F(du/dt)(dw/dt) + G(dw/dt)^2} \quad (12.14)$$

κ_n depends only on the direction of the tangent line t. All curves through a point on a surface, tangent to the same line through $\mathbf{p}$, have the same normal curvature at $\mathbf{p}$. Thus, all possible values for curvature of a curve through $\mathbf{p}$ are obtained by considering only the intersection curves of planes through $\mathbf{p}$. Among these intersection curves one is of special interest: that curve cut by the plane containing the normal $\mathbf{n}$. As the plane is rotated about the normal, the curvature κ_n varies and exhibits a maximum and minimum in two perpendicular directions. These extreme values are the principal normal curvatures, κ_1 and κ_2, and they are the roots of the following equation:

$$(EG - F^2)\kappa^2 - (EN + GL - 2FM)\kappa + (LN - M^2) = 0 \quad (12.15)$$

Another curvature is Gaussian curvature K:

$$K = \kappa_i \kappa_2 = \frac{LN - M^2}{EG - F^2}$$

The mean curvature H is

$$H = \tfrac{1}{2}(\kappa_1 + \kappa_2) = \frac{EN + GL - 2FM}{2(EG - F^2)}$$

From differential geometry, the coefficients of the first and second fundamental forms are

$$E = \mathbf{p}^u \cdot \mathbf{p}^u$$
$$F = \mathbf{p}^u \cdot \mathbf{p}^w$$
$$G = \mathbf{p}^w \cdot \mathbf{p}^w$$

$$L = \mathbf{p}^{uu} \cdot \mathbf{n}$$
$$M = \mathbf{p}^{uw} \cdot \mathbf{n}$$
$$N = \mathbf{p}^{ww} \cdot \mathbf{n}$$

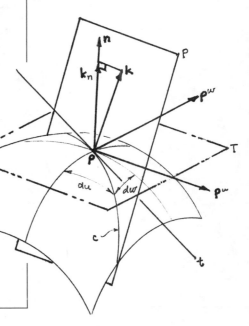

Surfaces: Curvature Approximation

A surface with continuously varying curvature can be approximated arbitrarily closely by a polyhedron with triangular faces, on condition that the number of faces is made sufficiently large and the size of each sufficiently small. The curvature at any point on the surface is then measured at the appropriate vertex as the deficit angle ϕ.

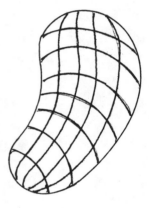 

Subdivide the surface with an isoparametric grid or mesh. Then triangulate it.

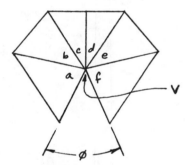

Lay out all faces around the vertex V in a plane. Then sum the face angles at V:

$$\phi = 2\pi - (a + b + c + d + e + f)$$

Characteristic Tests

There are several tests applied to curves and surfaces to detect the presence of certain geometric characteristics.

A curve is a plane curve if and only if it has zero torsion throughout, $\tau = 0$. This means that the numerator of Eq. (12.9) must equal zero:

$$|\mathbf{p}^u \ \mathbf{p}^{uu} \ \mathbf{p}^{uuu}| = 0$$

or

$$\begin{vmatrix} x^u & x^{uu} & x^{uuu} \\ y^u & y^{uu} & y^{uuu} \\ z^u & z^{uu} & z^{uuu} \end{vmatrix} = 0$$

A straight line has zero curvature. Thus, the numerator of Eq. (12.8) must equal zero for all values of the parametric variable, u:

$$|\mathbf{p}^u \times \mathbf{p}^{uu}| = 0$$

A surface is planar if $\kappa_n = 0$ at all points on it, and spherical if $\kappa_n = $ constant.

If the Gaussian curvature K of a surface is zero everywhere, then the surface is developable.

$$K = \kappa_1 \kappa_2 = \frac{LN - M^2}{EG - F^2} = 0$$

Or, more simply, $K = 0$ if $LN - M^2 = 0$.

Triple scalar product. Interpret in determinant form.

Arc Length

There are several ways to compute the arc length of a parametrically defined curve. Here is the simplest, although least elegant approach.

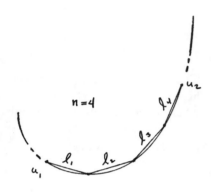

To compute the arc length between u_1 and u_2, first divide the curve segment into n equal parametric intervals. Next, compute the endpoint coordinates of each interval. Finally, compute the sum of the successive straight-line distances between these points:

$$L = \sum_{i=1}^{n} l_i$$

This, obviously, only approximates the "true" length. To improve the accuracy, divide each interval in half and repeat the computations, now for twice the original number of intervals. Compare this new length to the initially computed length. If the difference is negligible (according to some specified criteria), then the solution is acceptable. Otherwise, subdivide again and repeat the computation. This approach is not usually the most efficient, nor particularly accurate unless n is large (the procedure always returns a somewhat shorter-than-true length).

Here is another approach. The arc length between u_1 and u_2 is

$$L = \int_{u_1}^{u_2} \sqrt{\mathbf{p}^u \cdot \mathbf{p}^u} \, du \text{ where } u_2 > u_1$$

Use Gaussian quadrature (or some other appropriate scheme) to reduce this integral to

$$\int_{u_1}^{u_2} f_L(u) \, du = \sum_{i=1}^{n} w_i f_L(u_i)$$

where n is the number of points used, w_i are the weight values, and u_i are the Gaussian abcissas.

Global properties depend on overall characteristics of a geometric object, such as length, area, volume, geometric center (center of gravity), section modulus, and moments of inertia. The minimum distance between two objects can be thought of as a global property, more specifically a spatial relationship between two objects. And, of course, topology is a global characteristic.

$$l_i = [(x_i - x_{i-1})^2 + (y_i - y_{i-1})^2 + (z_i - z_{i-1})^2]^{1/2}$$

Surface Area

The surface area of a parametrically defined patch is computed from

$$dA = |\mathbf{n}|\,du\,dw = f(u,w)\,du\,dw$$

where $\mathbf{n}(u,w)$ is a vector function defining the patch normals, and dA is the scalar element of area. Thus,

$$A = \int_0^1 \int_0^1 f_A(u,w)\,du\,dw$$

Use Gaussian quadrature (or some other scheme) to evaluate the double integral. Thus,

$$A = \sum_{i=0}^n \sum_{j=0}^n g_i h_j f_A(u_i,w_j)$$

where g_i and h_j are the weight values associated with a specific n-point quadrature formula.

The limits of integration shown here cover the entire patch, where $u,w \in [0,1]$. More generally,

$$A = \int_{u_1}^{u_2} \int_{w_1}^{w_2} f(u,w)\,du\,dw$$

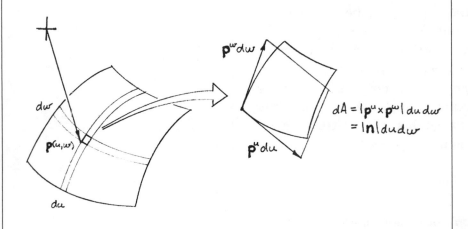

"To find the length of an object, we have to perform certain physical operations. The concept of length is therefore fixed when the operations by which length is measured are fixed: that is, the concept of length involves as much as and nothing more than the sets of operations by which length is determined."

Percy Williams Bridgman

Volume

The volume of a closed region whose surface is defined parametrically is

$$dV = \tfrac{1}{3}[\mathbf{p}(u,w) \cdot \mathbf{n}(u,w)]du\,dw$$
$$= f_v(u,w)du\,dw$$

where $\mathbf{p}(u,w)$ is the parametric equation of points defining the patch, and $\mathbf{n}(u,w)$ defines the unit normals. dV is the scalar element of volume. The factor "$\tfrac{1}{3}$" arises from the formula for a pyramid. The dot product of the two vector functions satisfies the requirement of perpendicularity between the base of a pyramid and its height (altitude) in the formula. Thus,

$$V = \int_0^1 \int_0^1 f_V du\,dw$$

Use Gaussian quadrature (or some other scheme) to evaluate this double integral.

This method is shown for a single patch. However, most objects will be defined by many patches forming the closed surface of the object's boundary. The integration is carried out over each and every patch to produce the total volume.

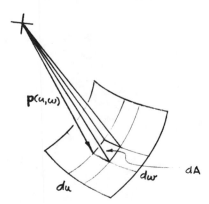

"I am coming more and more to the conviction that the necessity of our geometry cannot be demonstrated, at least neither by, nor for, the human intellect. . . . Geometry should be ranked, not with arithmetic, which is purely aprioristic, but with mechanics."

Carl Friedrich Gauss

Distance between a Point and Line

The minimum distance between any point $\mathbf{q}$ and any line $\mathbf{p}(u) = \mathbf{p}_0 + u(\mathbf{p}_1 - \mathbf{p}_0)$ is

$$d_{\min} = |\mathbf{p} - \mathbf{q}|$$

where

$$(\mathbf{p} - \mathbf{q}) \cdot \mathbf{p}^u = 0$$

For a straight line $\mathbf{p}^u = \mathbf{p}_1 - \mathbf{p}_0$, and the above equation reduces to a single linear equation in u:

$$u = \frac{(x_1 - x_0)(x - x_0) + (y_1 - y_0)(y - y_0) + (z_1 - z_0)(z - z_0)}{[(x_1 - x_0)^2 + (y_1 - y_0)^2 + (z_1 - z_0)^2]^{1/2}}$$

where x, y, z are the coordinates of $\mathbf{q}$. Knowing u, $\mathbf{p}(u)$ is easy to compute.

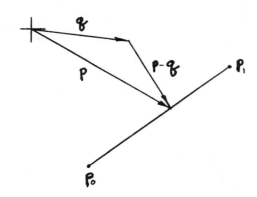

"Mathematics is the science which draws necessary conclusions."

Benjamin Pierce

Distance between a Point and Curve

Computing the minimum distance between a point **q** and a curve **p**(u) requires finding a vector (**p** − **q**) from the point to the curve that is perpendicular to the tangent vector **p**^{u} at **p**. Thus

$$d_{\min} = |\mathbf{p} - \mathbf{q}|$$

where

$$(\mathbf{p} - \mathbf{q}) \cdot \mathbf{p}^u = 0$$

If the curve is a parametric cubic, then a quintic polynomial is produced by the above equation. A variety of numerical methods is available for finding the roots of this equation.

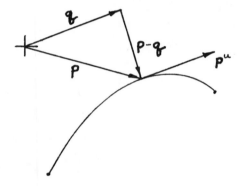

Distance between a Point and Plane

Given a plane $Ax + By + Cz + D = 0$, and any point $\mathbf{p}_i$, the minimum distance between them is

$$d_{\min} = |c\mathbf{u}_3| = c$$

and the closest point on the plane $\mathbf{p}_i$ is $\mathbf{p}_i^*$. Use the coefficients of the plane, A,B,C,D, to compute $\mathbf{p}_0$ (any arbitrary point on the plane), and $\mathbf{n}$, the unit normal to the plane. Next, compute

$$\mathbf{u}_1 = \frac{\mathbf{n} \times \mathbf{p}_0}{|\mathbf{n} \times \mathbf{p}_0|}$$

$$\mathbf{u}_2 = \mathbf{n} \times \mathbf{u}_1$$
$$\mathbf{u}_3 = \mathbf{n}$$

where $\mathbf{u}_1, \mathbf{u}_2, \mathbf{u}_3$ define a triad of mutually orthogonal unit vectors. Compute a,b,c, from $\mathbf{p}_i = \mathbf{p}_0 + a\mathbf{u}_1 + b\mathbf{u}_2 + c\mathbf{u}_3$, which produces three linear equations in three unknowns. Thus,

$$\mathbf{p}_i^w = \mathbf{p}_0 + a\mathbf{u}_1 + b\mathbf{u}_2$$

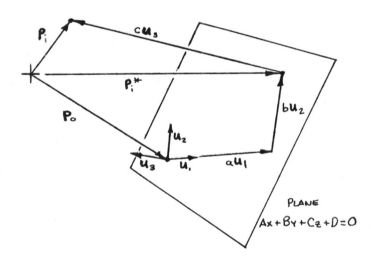

Distance between a Point and Surface

Computing the minimum distance between any point **q** and a surface patch **p**(*u*,*w*) requires finding a vector (**p** − **q**) from the point to the patch that is normal to the patch at **p**. Since the normal at any point on the patch is given by $\mathbf{p}^u \times \mathbf{p}^w$, there are two valid expressions of the solution:

$$(\mathbf{p} - \mathbf{q}) \times (\mathbf{p}^u \times \mathbf{p}^w) = 0$$

or

$$(\mathbf{p} - \mathbf{q}) = a(\mathbf{p}^u \times \mathbf{p}^w)$$

Numerical methods must be used to obtain a solution.

Although three equations are produced, only two of them are independent, since the unit normal would suffice in either case.

The solution may take one of many forms. For example, there may be no normal between the point and a patch (at least within the interval $u,w \in [0,1]$); this means the point **q** must be examined with respect to the patch boundary curves. However, there may be more than one normal from the point to the patch, and the distances of each must be compared.

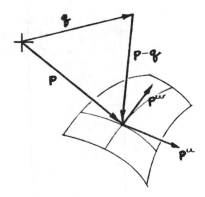

Distance between a Line and Curve

Given a straight line $\mathbf{p}(u) = \mathbf{p}_0 + u(\mathbf{p}_1 - \mathbf{p}_0)$ and a curve $\mathbf{q}(s)$, the minimum distance between them is

$$d_{\min} = |\mathbf{p} - \mathbf{q}|$$

where

$$(\mathbf{p} - \mathbf{q}) \cdot \mathbf{q}^s = 0$$

and

$$(\mathbf{p} - \mathbf{q}) \cdot (\mathbf{p}_1 - \mathbf{p}_0) = 0$$

Two nonlinear simultaneous equations in u and s are produced and must be solved.

In a plane, $\mathbf{p}_1 - \mathbf{p}_0$ and $\mathbf{q}^s$ are parallel, but in three-dimensional space they may be skewed.

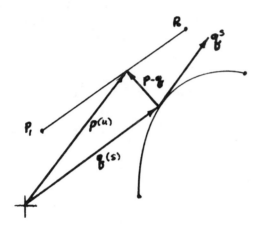

Given two straight lines, find the minimum distance between them.

Let

$$\mathbf{a} = \frac{\mathbf{p}_1 - \mathbf{p}_0}{|\mathbf{p}_1 - \mathbf{p}_0|}$$

$$\mathbf{b} = \frac{\mathbf{q}_1 - \mathbf{q}_0}{|\mathbf{q}_1 - \mathbf{q}_0|}$$

then

$$|\mathbf{d}| = \left| \frac{(\mathbf{q}_0 - \mathbf{p}_0) \cdot (\mathbf{a} \times \mathbf{b})}{|\mathbf{a} \times \mathbf{b}|} \right|$$

$$\mathbf{p}(u) = \mathbf{p}_0 + u(\mathbf{p}_1 - \mathbf{p}_0)$$
$$\mathbf{q}(v) = \mathbf{q}_0 + v(\mathbf{q}_1 - \mathbf{q}_0)$$

Distance between two skew lines in space:

$$u_d = \frac{BF - CE}{AE - BD}, \quad v_d = \frac{CD - AF}{AE - BD}$$

$A = p_{x_1} - p_{x_0}$
$B = q_{x_1} - q_{x_0}$
$C = p_{x_0} - q_{x_0} - d_x$
$D = p_{y_1} - p_{y_0}$
$E = q_{y_1} - q_{y_0}$
$F = p_{y_0} - q_{y_0} - d_y$

Distance between a Line and Surface

Given a straight line, $\mathbf{p}(u) = \mathbf{p}_0 + u(\mathbf{p}_1 - \mathbf{p}_0)$ and a surface patch, $\mathbf{q}(s,t)$, the minimum distance between them is

$$d_{\min} = |\mathbf{p} - \mathbf{q}|$$

where

    i. $(\mathbf{p} - \mathbf{q}) \times (\mathbf{q}^s \times \mathbf{q}^t) = 0$

and

    ii. $(\mathbf{p} - \mathbf{q}) \cdot (\mathbf{p}_1 - \mathbf{p}_0) = 0$

This immediately follows from the observation that if $|\mathbf{p} - \mathbf{q}|$ is the minimum distance, then $(\mathbf{p} - \mathbf{q})$ is parallel to $(\mathbf{q}^s \times \mathbf{q}^t)$ and perpendicular to $(\mathbf{p}_1 - \mathbf{p}_0)$.

Four nonlinear simultaneous equations are produced in three unknowns, u, s, and t. The ambiguity of the extra equation is resolved as follows: Rewrite expression i as the equally valid $(\mathbf{p} - \mathbf{q}) \times (\mathbf{q}^s \times \mathbf{q}^t)/|\mathbf{q}^s \times \mathbf{q}^t| = (\mathbf{p} - \mathbf{q}) \times \mathbf{n}(s,t) = 0$. Since a definite relationship exists between the components of $\mathbf{n}(s,t)$, namely: $n_x^2 + n_y^2 + n_z^2 = 1$, then the vector expression i produces only two independent equations. Hence, there are three independent, nonlinear, simultaneous equations to be solved, returning values for u, s, and t. Again, numerical methods must be used.

Caution: check for no solution or multiple solutions.

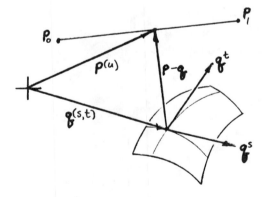

Distance between Two Curves

Given two parametric curves, $\mathbf{p}(u)$ and $\mathbf{q}(t)$, the minimum distance between them is

$$d_{\min} = |\mathbf{p} - \mathbf{q}|$$

where

$$(\mathbf{p} - \mathbf{q}) \cdot \mathbf{p}^u = 0$$

and

$$(\mathbf{p} - \mathbf{q}) \cdot \mathbf{q}^t = 0$$

Two nonlinear simultaneous equations are produced, whose solution returns values for u and t.

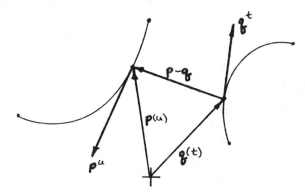

Two curves are parallel if it is possible to establish a one-to-one correspondence between their points so that corresponding points are equidistant and corresponding tangents are parallel.

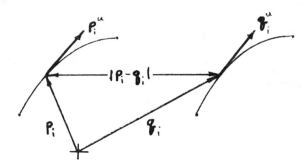

If $\mathbf{p}(u), \mathbf{q}(u)$ are parallel, then $\begin{cases} |\mathbf{p}_i - \mathbf{q}_i| = \text{constant, } \forall i \\ \mathbf{p}_i^u \times \mathbf{q}_i^u = 0 \end{cases}$

Distance between a Curve and Surface

Given a curve $\mathbf{q}(t)$ and a surface patch $\mathbf{p}(u,w)$, then the minimum distance between them is

$$d_{\min} = |\mathbf{p} - \mathbf{q}|$$

where

i. $(\mathbf{p} - \mathbf{q}) \times \dfrac{(\mathbf{p}^u \times \mathbf{p}^w)}{|\mathbf{p}^u \times \mathbf{p}^w|} = (\mathbf{p} - \mathbf{q}) \times \mathbf{n}(u,w) = 0$

and

ii. $(\mathbf{p} - \mathbf{q}) \cdot \mathbf{q}^t = 0$

Three independent, nonlinear, simultaneous equations are produced (note: expression i produces only two, since $n_x^2 + n_y^2 + n_z^2 = 1$), whose solution returns values for t, u, and w.

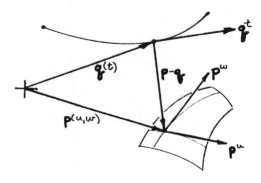

Distance between Two Surfaces

Given two surface patches, $\mathbf{p}(u,w)$ and $\mathbf{q}(s,t)$, the minimum distance between them is

$$d_{\min} = |\mathbf{p} - \mathbf{q}|$$

where

$$(\mathbf{p} - \mathbf{q}) \times \frac{(\mathbf{p}^u \times \mathbf{p}^w)}{|\mathbf{p}^u \times \mathbf{p}^w|} = (\mathbf{p} - \mathbf{q}) \times \mathbf{n}(u,w) = 0$$

and

$$(\mathbf{p} - \mathbf{q}) \times \frac{(\mathbf{q}^s \times \mathbf{q}^t)}{|\mathbf{q}^s \times \mathbf{q}^t|} = (\mathbf{p} - \mathbf{q}) \times \mathbf{m}(s,t) = 0$$

Four independent, nonlinear, simultaneous equations are produced (note: $n_x^2 + n_y^2 + n_z^2 = m_x^2 + m_y^2 + m_z^2 = 1$), whose solution returns values for u, w, s, and t.

As with all problems of this type, check for no solution and multiple solutions.

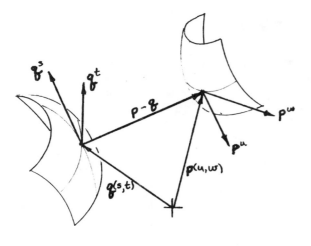

"Philosophy is written in this grand book—I mean the universe—which stands continually open to our gaze, but it cannot be understood unless one first learns to comprehend the language and interpret the characters in which it is written. It is written in the language of mathematics, and its characters are triangles, circles, and other geometrical figures, without which it is humanly impossible to understand a single word of it; without these, one is wandering about in a dark labyrinth."

Galileo Galilei

Display Coordinate Systems

Computer graphics systems use a variety of both two- and three-dimensional coordinate systems. Each system is identified by name and a unique set of coordinate axes. Here are five common, interrelated systems.

○ The **global** (or **world**) coordinate system: this is the principal three-dimensional frame of reference for defining and locating in space all objects in a computer graphics scene and the observer's viewpoint.

○ The **local** coordinate system: this is often used to define an object independently of the global system, and without giving a specific location in the global system.

○ The **view** coordinate system: this locates objects relative to the observer. It often simplifies the mathematics of projecting the image of an object onto the picture plane. The location and orientation of the view coordinate system changes each time the view changes.

○ The **picture-plane** coordinate system: this is a two-dimensional system and locates points on the picture plane (sometimes called the **projection plane**).

○ The **display screen** coordinate system: this locates points on the surface of a particular computer graphic display device.

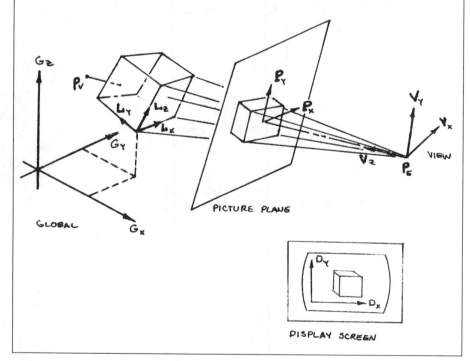

p_E = eyepoint of observer

p_V = point on line-of-sight, viewpoint

V_z = line-of-sight

"Histories make men wise; poets, witty; the mathematics subtile, . . ."

Francis Bacon

Window and Viewport

The picture plane is unbounded, so only those images projected onto a finite portion of it are displayed. A rectangular, bounded area called a **window** is specified, and it defines that portion of the scene on the picture plane to be displayed. The scene or image within this window is then mapped to another bounded area called the **viewport**. The viewport defines a rectangular area on the screen coordinate system. The image in the viewport is the one that is actually displayed.

Given a point **p**, whose coordinates are x,y in the picture plane, find its display screen coordinates, say $\mathbf{p}_s$ with coordinates x_s and y_s. Assume the display is an $H \times V$ pixel screen. The selected image (the point **p** in this case) lies within the window whose boundaries are described by Wx_L, Wx_R, Wy_T, and Wy_B, and is to be displayed within the viewport whose boundaries are described by Vx_L, Vx_R, Vy_T, and Vy_B. Here are the transformation equations:

$$x_s = \frac{x - Wx_L}{Wx_R - Wx_L} (Vx_R - Vx_L) + Vx_L$$

$$y_s = \frac{y - Wy_B}{Wy_T - Wy_B} (Vy_T - Vy_B) + Vy_B \qquad (14.1)$$

The terms **object space** and **image space** are often used. Object space corresponds to the world coordinate system, and image space corresponds to the display screen system.

The window–viewport transformation establishes a one-to-one correspondence between points in the picture plane window and points in the display screen viewport. This transformation "maps" points from the world system onto the display screen.

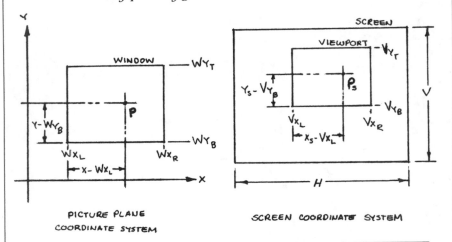

PICTURE PLANE COORDINATE SYSTEM

SCREEN COORDINATE SYSTEM

Equations (14.1) return real, noninteger numbers for x_s and y_s. These values must be truncated or rounded to produce the required integer screen coordinates.

The window and viewport images are related by scale factors s_x and s_y, where

$$s_x = \frac{Vx_R - Vx_L}{Wx_R - Wx_L} \quad \text{and} \quad s_y = \frac{Vy_T - Vy_B}{Wy_T - Wy_B}$$

There is no horizontal/vertical distortion if $s_x = s_y$.

Normalized Coordinates

To accommodate the variety of display screen sizes possible in an extensive graphics network, a mathematical technique called **normalization** is used. Coordinates are computed for an imaginary, or hypothetical, screen whose horizontal and vertical dimensions are $H = 1$, $V = 1$. This is a unit, or normalized, screen.

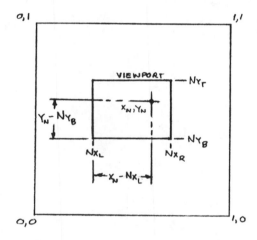

Here are the transformation equations for mapping from an arbitrary window on the picture plane onto a viewport on a normalized screen:

$$x_N = \frac{x - Wx_L}{Wx_R - Wx_L}(Nx_R - Nx_L) + Nx_L$$

$$y_N = \frac{y - Wy_B}{Wy_T - Wy_B}(Ny_T - Ny_B) + Ny_B$$

(14.2)

where x_N and y_N are the normalized coordinates. These coordinates are transmitted and finally transformed locally to suit the particular display screen, so that

$$x_s = Hx_N$$
$$y_s = Vy_N$$

(14.3)

Pixels and Point Resolution

It is not always possible to resolve every point in a set of points to be displayed. Consider, for example, the three points p_1, p_2, and p_3, arranged, for simplicity, on a common horizontal line so that $y_1 = y_2 = y_3$. This means that only the x coordinates determine their separation.

If the number of pixels between p_1 and p_3, say $\Delta H_{1,3}$, is less than the ratio of the separations of p_1 and p_3 to p_1 and p_2, then p_1 and p_2 cannot be resolved. That is, p_1 and p_2 will not be displayed as two separate and distinct points. This relationship is expressed by the inequality

$$\frac{x_3 - x_1}{x_2 - x_1} > \Delta H_{1,3}$$

If this inequality is true, then p_1 and p_2 cannot be resolved.

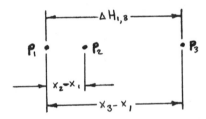

"It may be that man has introduced limited and even artificial concepts and only in this way has managed to institute some order in nature. Man's mathematics may be no more than a workable scheme. Nature itself may be far more complex or have no inherent design. Nevertheless, mathematics remains the method 'par excellence' for the investigation, representation, and mastery of nature. In those domains where it is effective, it is all we have; if it is not reality itself, it is the closest to reality we can get."

Morris Kline

Line Containment and Clipping

Only line segments within the window are displayed. If a line segment is given by $\mathbf{p}(u) = \mathbf{p}_0 + u(\mathbf{p}_1 - \mathbf{p}_0)$ where $u \in [0,1]$, then it is completely within the window if, and only if, all the following inequalities are true

$$Wx_L \leq x_0, x_1 \leq Wx_R \quad \text{and} \quad Wy_B \leq y_0, y_1 \leq Wy_T \quad (14.4)$$

If $\mathbf{p}_0$ and $\mathbf{p}_1$ are both inside the window, then the line segment is inside the window.

A line is completely outside the window if any one of the following sets of inequalities is true:

$$\begin{array}{ll} x_0, x_1 < Wx_L, & x_0, x_1 > Wx_R \\ y_0, y_1 < Wy_B, & y_0, y_1 > Wy_T \end{array} \quad (14.5)$$

These containment tests presume that $\mathbf{p}_0$ and $\mathbf{p}_1$ have been transformed or projected or both onto the picture plane and that their coordinates are given in terms of the picture plane coordinate system.

Otherwise, part of the line lies within the window, and part outside, so that intersection computations are required to determine how to clip the line.

Expressing the window boundaries as parametric line segments somewhat simplifies the clipping procedure, since all valid points of intersection between them and lines to be clipped must be within the unit interval.

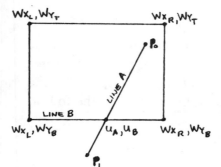

The parametric equations for line B are

$$x = Wx_L + u(Wx_R - Wx_L)$$
$$y = Wy_B$$

The intersection between line A and line B is found by solving the appropriate simultaneous equations for u_A and u_B, obtaining

$$u_A = \frac{Wy_B - y_0}{y_1 - y_0}$$

$$u_B = \left(\frac{x_1 - x_0}{y_1 - y_0}\right)\left(\frac{Wy_B - y_0}{Wx_R - Wx_L}\right) + \left(\frac{x_0 - Wx_L}{Wx_R - Wx_L}\right) \quad (14.6)$$

If $u_A, u_B \in [0,1]$, then the intersection is valid. u_A then divides the line A into two segments, one segment inside and the other outside the window. Test each segment to determine which to keep and which to clip off by using Eqs. (14.4) and (14.5).

Window Point Containment

A point $\mathbf{p}_i$ is contained within the window if and only if the following inequalities are true:

$$Wx_L \le x_i \le Wx_R \quad \text{and} \quad Wy_B \le y_i \le Wy_T$$

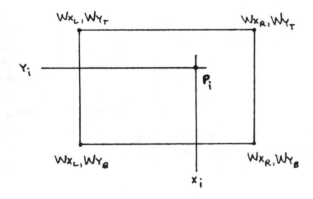

Wx_L, Wy_T are the picture plane coordinates of the upper left-hand corner of the window, and similarly for the other corners.

Note: a similar test applies to determine if a point lies within a given rectangular volume or box whose min/max corner coordinates are $(x_{max}, y_{max}, z_{max})$ and $(x_{min}, y_{min}, z_{min})$. A point $\mathbf{p}_i$ is inside a rectangular volume if and only if all the following inequalities are true:

$$x_{min} \le x_i \le x_{max}$$
$$y_{min} \le y_i \le y_{max}$$
$$z_{min} \le z_i \le z_{max}$$

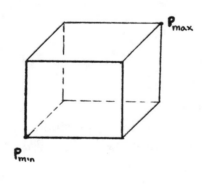

There is the assumption that both the window and the box boundary lines and planes are aligned parallel to the principal axes and planes of their embedding coordinate system.

Polygon Clipping

Given a polygon in the picture plane, defined as a consecutive sequence of its vertex points $(p_1, p_2, \ldots, p_i, \ldots, p_n)$, apply the window point containment test to each vertex point. If the containment status (in/out) changes between two consecutive points, then polygon edges connecting those vertices must intersect a window boundary. When all intersections have been found, clip the polygon by deleting those edges and edge segments lying outside the window. A new sequence of vertices is established, defining the clipped polygon.

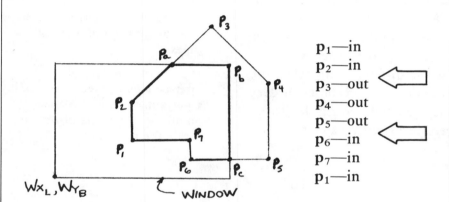

p_1—in
p_2—in
p_3—out   ⇐ intersection
p_4—out
p_5—out
p_6—in   ⇐ intersection
p_7—in
p_1—in

Delete p_3, p_4, p_5;
add p_a, p_b, p_c

It is quite possible that a polygon edge joining two vertices not themselves inside the window might nonetheless pass through the window. For example, imagine slightly adjusting the position of vertices 3 and 4 (moving each toward the lower left) so that they remain outside the window but part of the edge joining them passes through the window. This simply requires that all edges joining sequential pairs of vertices outside the window be tested using a line containment and clipping algorithm.

Polygon Filling

Given a polygon, find the intersections between it and a series of horizontal lines. This is an important part of the polygon-filling problem, to turn on the pixels on those segments of the raster scan lines that are inside the polygon. One way to solve this problem is described as follows:

Assume that the polygon is defined in the display-screen coordinate system. Let lines A and B represent typical horizontal scan lines. The x coordinates of these lines range from $x = 0$ to $x = x_H$, where x_H is the display width and the y coordinate is constant for each line. Represent each polygon edge as a parametric line segment. Search for and compute all intersections between each scan line, say, for example, line A, and each edge of the polygon, a through j of the polygon below.

Line A intersects the polygon at four different points. Pair off the x coordinates of these intersections in ascending order: $(x_j, x_b), (x_d, x_f)$. The scan line segments delimited by these values are in the "on" state. Proceed in a similar way for all scan lines known to intersect the polygon.

A straight line intersects a polygon an even number of times.

If n_i, is the number of intersections between a line and a polygon, then $n_i/2$ is the number of segments of the line inside the polygon.

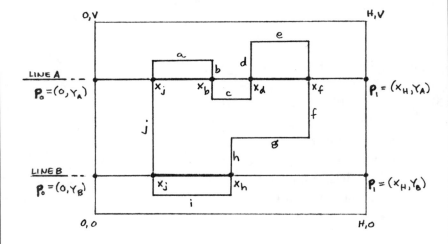

The search for intersections is expedited by considering only those polygon edges whose end point y coordinates are such that one is greater than and one is less than the y coordinate of the scan line.

Computing Points on a Line

Points that occur at equal intervals along a line segment are frequently required in both geometric modeling and computer graphics. Here are two ways to compute these points, one much faster than the other.

Given a line $\mathbf{p}(u) = \mathbf{p}_0 + u(\mathbf{p}_1 - \mathbf{p}_0)$, find the coordinates of points on it at n equal intervals. Since the end points $\mathbf{p}_0$ and $\mathbf{p}_1$ are given, there remain $n - 1$ intermediate points to compute. One approach is to compute $x_i = x_0 + u_i(x_1 - x_0)$ for each intermediate point $\mathbf{p}_i$ (similarly for y_i and z_i). There are $n - 1$ values to compute of the parametric variable:

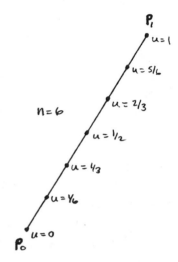

$$u = \frac{1}{n}, \frac{2}{n}, \frac{3}{n}, \ldots, \frac{n-1}{n}$$

For the x coordinates there are $n - 1$ multiplications and n additions (including finding $x - x_0$ once). The total for all coordinates are: $3n$ additions, $3(n - 1)$ multiplications, and $n - 1$ divisions.

Here is the faster method: The parametric variable always changes (is incremented) by a constant amount, $\Delta u = 1/n$. For x_{i+1}:

$$x_{i+1} = x_0 + u_{i+1}(x_1 - x_0)$$

But $u_{i+1} = u_i + \Delta u$, so that $x_{i+1} = x_0 + (u_i + \Delta u)(x_1 - x_0)$, or

$$x_{i+1} = x_i + \Delta u(x_1 - x_0)$$

Since $\Delta u(x_1 - x_0)$ is a constant, where $\Delta x = \Delta u(x_1 - x_0)$, then

$$x_{i+1} = x_i + \Delta x$$

This equation says that each successive x coordinate is obtained by adding a constant to the previous value. To compute Δu requires one division. To compute Δx requires one addition and one multiplication. For the x coordinate there are $n - 1$ additions. The totals for all coordinates are: $3n$ additions, 3 multiplications, and 1 division.

Origin of the Picture-Plane Coordinate System

The origin of the picture-plane coordinate system lies on the intersection of the plane with the normal vector to it from the eyepoint of the observer $\mathbf{p}_E$. This normal also establishes one of the three picture-plane coordinate system axes $\mathbf{u}_3$. The other two axes, $\mathbf{u}_1$ and $\mathbf{u}_2$, lie in the plane, and their orientation may be arbitrary.

Specify the eyepoint $\mathbf{p}_E$, the unit normal in the viewing direction $\mathbf{u}_3$, and the distance from $\mathbf{p}_E$ to the picture plane λ. Then

$$\mathbf{p}_0 = \mathbf{p}_E - \lambda\mathbf{u}_3$$

Note: the orthogonal triad of unit vectors, $\mathbf{u}_1$, $\mathbf{u}_2$, and $\mathbf{u}_3$, form a right-hand coordinate system. Change the sign of $\mathbf{u}_3$ to form a left-hand system.

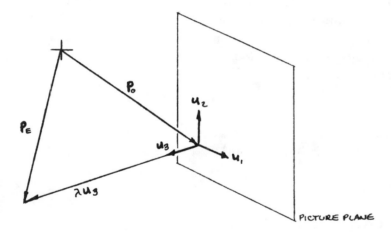

General Orthographic Projection

Compute the global and picture-plane coordinates of the orthographic projection p_i^* of any point p_i. Points in the picture plane must satisfy $p_0 + au_1 + bu_2$. The triad of mutually orthogonal unit normals, u_1, u_2, and u_3, describes the picture-plane coordinate system.

Assume that the picture plane and its coordinate system are defined; that is, p_0, u_1, u_2, and u_3 are given. So, given p_i, find (x_i^*, y_i^*, z_i^*) and (a,b,c). First, compute a, b, and c from

$$p_i = p_0 + au_1 + bu_2 + cu_3$$

which produces three simultaneous linear equations in three unknowns.

Finally, compute x_i^*, y_i^*, and z_i^* from

$$p_i^* = p_0 + au_1 + bu_2$$

This procedure is similar to finding the minimum distance between a point and a plane.

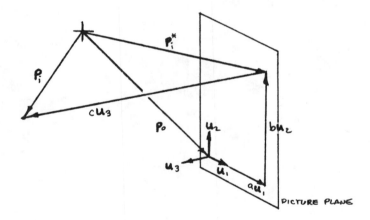

General Perspective Projection

Compute the perspective projection $\mathbf{p}_i^*$ of any point $\mathbf{p}_i$ onto the picture plane $\mathbf{p}_0 + a\mathbf{u}_1 + b\mathbf{u}_2$ with the eyepoint at $\mathbf{p}_E$. Since

$$\mathbf{p}_i^* = \mathbf{p}_0 + a\mathbf{u}_1 + b\mathbf{u}_2$$

and, also,

$$\mathbf{p}_i^* = \mathbf{p}_E + c(\mathbf{p}_i - \mathbf{p}_E)$$

then

$$\mathbf{p}_0 + a\mathbf{u}_1 + b\mathbf{u}_2 = \mathbf{p}_E + c(\mathbf{p}_i - \mathbf{p}_E)$$

Rearrange and note that $\mathbf{p}_E - \mathbf{p}_0 = \lambda\mathbf{u}_3$, so that

$$a\mathbf{u}_1 + b\mathbf{u}_2 - \lambda\mathbf{u}_3 - c(\mathbf{p}_i - \mathbf{p}_E) = 0$$

This equation produces three simultaneous linear equations in three unknowns, a, b, and c. From the solution compute $\mathbf{p}_i^*$.

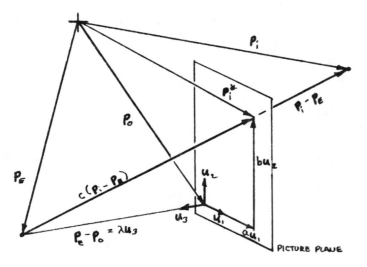

"In any particular theory there is only as much real science as there is mathematics."

Immanuel Kant

Display and Scene Transformations

The distinction between display and scene transformations is this: Scene transformations are characteristically three dimensional and operate on model data to alter the viewing orientation. Display transformations operate on the two-dimensional display data to change the display scale or rotate the displayed objects around the line-of-sight. Display transforms do not affect the projected view, only the viewer's relationship to the plane of the display.

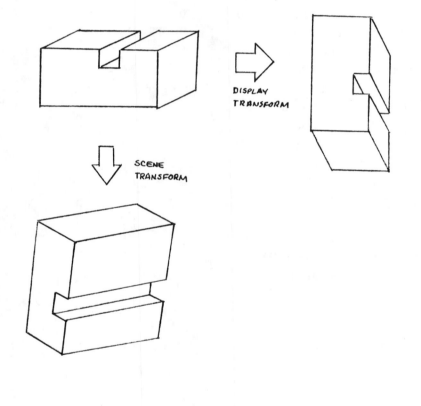

DISPLAY TRANSFORM

SCENE TRANSFORM

"Nothing puzzles me more than time and space; and yet nothing troubles me less, as I never think about them."

Charles Lamb

Orbit Scene Transformation

If the objects and the viewpoint in a scene remain in fixed positions, and the eyepoint "orbits" about the viewpoint, then an orbit scene transformation is produced. Assuming that the geometric objects comprising a display scene have been defined, proceed as follows: First, define the observer's location, or eyepoint, p_E. Next, define the point toward which the observer looks, the viewpoint p_V. Then $p_V - p_E$ is the line-of-sight vector. An orbit scene transformation produces a new location for p_E by rotating the line-of-sight about any axis through p_V.

To produce the initial view, construct u_1, u_2, u_3 at the origin of the world coordinate system, aligned with the positive x, y, z axes. Translate this system to p_V using T_V. Connect to a left-hand system using T_{RL}. Compute the angles of rotation that will align u_3 with $p_V - p_E$, and apply the necessary rotation transformations T_θ and T_ϕ (usually, only two rotations are necessary). Translate the system to p_0 using T_0. The perspective projection transformation is T_P. Finally, concatenate all these into a single expression giving the transformation of points in the world system into the picture plane:

$$p^* = pT_V T_{RL} T_\theta T_\phi T_0 T_P$$

Generate new views by orbiting about p_V. The line-of-sight is always toward p_V, which remains fixed. New transformation matrices must be constructed, reflecting changes in the position of p_E.

This transformation can be combined with either orthogonal or perspective projection.

u_1, u_2, u_3 form a triad of orthogonal unit vectors.

$$T_V = \begin{bmatrix} 1 & 0 & 0 & 0 \\ 0 & 1 & 0 & 0 \\ 0 & 0 & 1 & 0 \\ -x_V & -y_V & -z_V & 1 \end{bmatrix}$$

$$T_{RL} = \begin{bmatrix} 1 & 0 & 0 & 0 \\ 0 & 1 & 0 & 0 \\ 0 & 0 & -1 & 0 \\ 0 & 0 & 0 & 1 \end{bmatrix}$$

$$T_0 = \begin{bmatrix} 1 & 0 & 0 & 0 \\ 0 & 1 & 0 & 0 \\ 0 & 0 & 1 & 0 \\ 0 & 0 & r & 1 \end{bmatrix}$$

where $r = |p_V - p_0|$

$$T_P = \begin{bmatrix} 1 & 0 & 0 & 0 \\ 0 & 1 & 0 & 0 \\ 0 & 0 & 1 & 1/d \\ 0 & 0 & 0 & 1 \end{bmatrix}$$

where $d = |p_0 - p_E|$

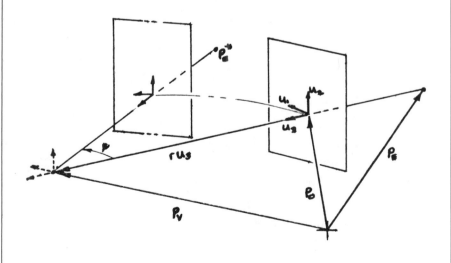

Pan Scene Transformation

Produce pan scene transformations of the initial display by imposing an equal vector translation **t** to both the eyepoint and the viewpoint:

$$\mathbf{p}_E^* = \mathbf{p}_E + \mathbf{t}$$
$$\mathbf{p}_V^* = \mathbf{p}_V + \mathbf{t}$$

Note that the triad $\mathbf{u}_1, \mathbf{u}_2, \mathbf{u}_3$ is translated parallel to its initial orientation. This means that the picture plane is translated in a similar way.

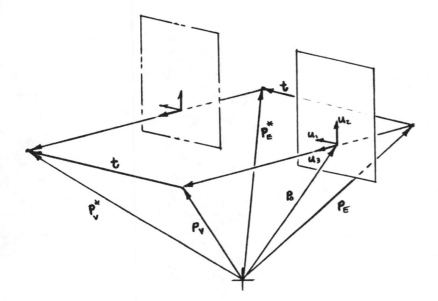

Results of Pan Transformations

Here are the results of some pan scene transformations on the display of a simple geometric object. The initial display is in the center. Note that pan transformations never generate a view of the rear of the object, and also that a large enough pan motion will move the object out of the display in the opposite direction.

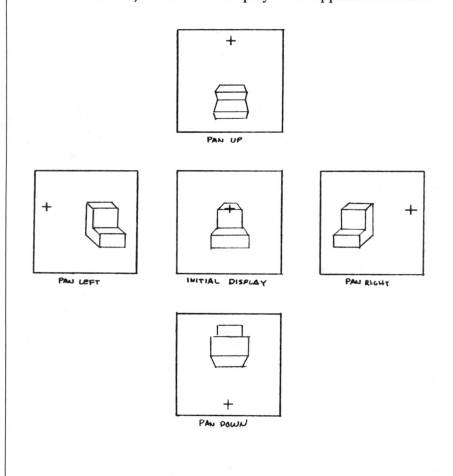

Aim Scene Transformation

Aim scene transformations are used to describe the effect on the display when the observer looks in various directions from a fixed position in space relative to the geometric objects comprising the scene. The line-of-sight $\mathbf{p}_V - \mathbf{p}_E$ is changed by moving $\mathbf{p}_V$.

Here is an example. After constructing the initial display, change the viewpoint by applying a sequence of rotations to the line-of-sight, $\mathbf{p}_V - \mathbf{p}_E$, about an axis through $\mathbf{p}_E$ (specify an axis and an angle of rotation ψ). The example shows a rotation ψ about the $\mathbf{u}_2$ axis. First, translate $\mathbf{u}_1, \mathbf{u}_2, \mathbf{u}_3$ into $\mathbf{p}_E$, then rotate this triad and $\mathbf{p}_V - \mathbf{p}_E$ through ψ about $\mathbf{u}_2$, Finally, reverse the translation of $\mathbf{u}_1, \mathbf{u}_2, \mathbf{u}_3$. Now all the vector elements are in place for a new projection.

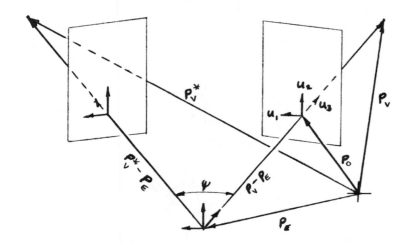

Polyhedra Edge Visibility

Each face of a polyhedron is a polygon. To project a polyhedron, simply project each face polygon onto the picture plane (and ultimately onto the display screen). If nothing more is done, then each edge is visible in the display, as if the polyhedron's faces were transparent . . . or as if the polyhedron were a wire-framework construction, a so-called wireframe model. The all-edges-visible wireframe projection gives some idea of the polyhedron's shape, but a more realistic image distinguishes between visible and hidden edges.

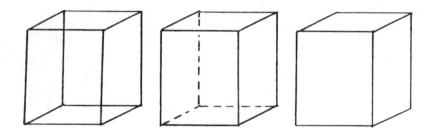

Three different conditions of edge visibility.

Convex Polyhedron Edge Visibility

To determine the edge visibility of a convex polyhedron, first determine the visibility of each vertex.

1. Project the face polygons onto the picture plane (for simplicity assume it's the x,y plane).
2. Write the plane equation for each face (i.e., find the plane coefficients A,B,C,D), using the world coordinates of any three vertex points of the face polygon.
3. Write the parametric equation (in the world system) of the line segment between each vertex point p_i and the eyepoint p_E. Assume $u = 0$ at p_E and $u = 1$ at p_i. These are called the vertex projection lines.
4. Compute for each vertex projection line the intersection, if any, with each face plane, excluding the faces bounding the vertex itself. If a vertex projection line intersects any face such that the point of intersection lies between p_E and p_i (i.e., $0 < u < 1$), then p_i is hidden. Otherwise, p_i is visible.
5. If a vertex is hidden, then all edges radiating from it are also hidden.

For any convex polyhedron, an edge is either completely hidden or completely visible.

Not only must the line intersect the plane of the face in the world coordinate system, but the point of intersection must be inside the projected polygon defining the boundary of the face in the picture plane. This requires a containment test in the picture plane.

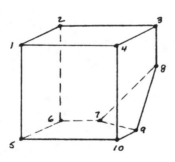

"We must confess in all humility that, while number is a product of our mind alone, space has a reality beyond the mind whose rules we cannot completely prescribe."

Carl Friedrich Gauss

Concave Polyhedron Edge Visibility

To determine the edge visibility of a concave polyhedron, begin by testing the visibility of each vertex. Note that for concave polyhedra an edge may be partially visible.

1. Test vertex visibility as for convex polyhedra. If a vertex is hidden, then at least some portion of each edge radiating from it is hidden. Mark these as "$H?$" edges. All other edges are entirely visible.

2. Compute intersections (in the picture plane) of each $H?$ edge with all other edges (including other $H?$ edges). Preserve those intersections within the $H?$ edge unit interval. Those $H?$ edges with no valid intersections are completely hidden.

3. Segment each remaining $H?$ edge at the intersection points on it, and test the visibility of each segment. For example, test the visibility of the midpoint of each of these segments.

4. Observe that the visibility of an edge changes only at the intersection with another edge.

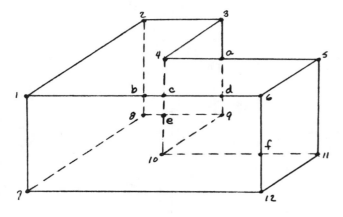

Edge 3,9 is partially visible. Its state-of-visibility changes at a.

"Mathematics, rightly viewed, possesses not only truth, but supreme beauty—a beauty cold and austere, like that of sculpture, without appeal to any part of our weaker nature, without the gorgeous trappings of painting or music, yet sublimely pure, and capable of a stern perfection such as only the greatest art can show."

Bertrand Russell

Directed Polyhedron Faces

An outward-pointing normal vector can be computed for each face of a convex polyhedron. This is possible if each face is consistently defined by its vertices listed sequentially in a counterclockwise order. Use any three vertices, in sequence, to define the two edges they (the vertex points) bound as two vectors. The vector product of these two vectors (taken in the same sequential order) produces an outward-pointing vector normal to the face. Use this normal to determine if the face points toward or away from the observer. An edge is hidden if both its bounding faces point away from the observer; otherwise, it is visible.

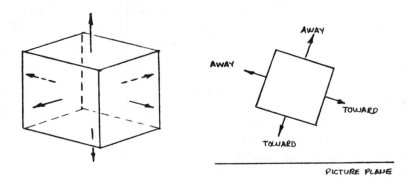

Silhouette of a Convex Polyhedron

Given a convex polyhedron, find the set of edges defining its silhouette.

1. Project the polyhedron onto the picture plane (for simplicity, the x,y plane).
2. Compute the implicit equation of each edge: $f_i(x,y) = 0$. Do this in the picture plane (transformed so it coincides with the x,y plane).
3. Test each edge equation for all vertices (except for the vertices bounding the edge being tested). If $f_i(x,y)$ is the same sign, or zero, for all vertices, then that edge is on the silhouette.

All silhouette edges are visible and so are the silhouette vertices.

Silhouette edges are those separating front-facing and back-facing polygons.

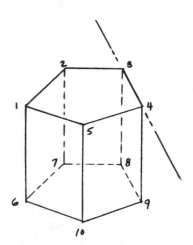

Edge 3,4 is on the silhouette because, in the plane of projection (this page), all the vertices lie on one side of it.

Silhouette Curve

The silhouette of a geometric object with a curved surface has these characteristics: All normals to the surface are also normal to the line-of-sight if they are on the silhouette curve. For simplicity, place the observer at the origin of the world coordinate system (transform observer's eyepoint, viewpoint, and all objects in the scene, as necessary, to achieve this). Then the silhouette curve is the locus of points satisfying

$$\mathbf{p} \cdot (\mathbf{p}^u \times \mathbf{p}^w) = 0$$

This is a nonlinear (eighth degree!) equation in two unknowns. The solution is a curve—the silhouette curve. Numerical methods are needed to obtain the solution.

If the picture plane corresponds to the x,y plane, and an orthogonal projection is sought, then some reduction in the degree of the nonlinear equation is achieved. Here, all lines of projection are parallel to the z axis, and the silhouette curve is the locus of points satisfying

$$\mathbf{p}_z \cdot (\mathbf{p}^u \times \mathbf{p}^w) = 0$$

where $\mathbf{p}_z = [0 \ \ 0 \ \ 1]$.

(Obviously!) the silhouette curve depends on the observer's position with respect to the object.

There are other ways to determine the silhouette curve, somewhat less analytic. A variation of the "painter's algorithm" will do, if only display-realism objectives are to be met. Or, approximating the curved surface with a mesh of plane polygonal faces also works.

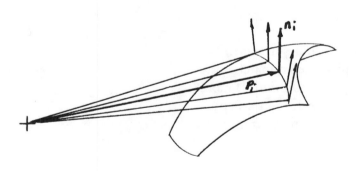

"Really, universally, relations stop nowhere, and the exquisite problem of the artist is eternally but to draw, by a geometry of his own, the circle within which they shall happily appear to do so."

Henry James

Hidden Surfaces

There are so many approaches to solving the hidden surface problem, and the methods are generally so sophisticated that only two relatively simple-to-describe procedures are given here.

Given a geometric object whose boundary surfaces are defined parametrically:

i. Approximate the bounding surface with plane polygonal faces derived from the parametric grid. Since it is unlikely that the four points defining the corners of a quadrilateral grid element will be coplanar, it is suggested that each quadrilateral be divided into two triangular elements. Then use the techniques applied to polyhedron edge and face visibility.

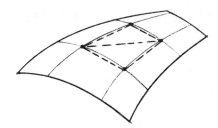

ii. Create a u,w grid on each forward facing surface in the display. Size the grid so that when projected it matches the size of the pixel that defines the display resolution. If more than one surface is projected onto a pixel, then a depth-checking algorithm is invoked to determine visibility.

Reflection and Light

The way a real object reflects light is a function of its surface material, the strength or intensity of the light source, and the angle between the light source and the surface normal. Dull surfaces produce a diffuse reflection, scattering light equally in all directions, and thus appear equally bright from any viewing angle. Assuming a point source of light, the intensity of light, I_d, reaching the observer's eye is

$$I_d = k_d I_p \cos \theta$$

or

$$I_d = k_d I_p (1 \cdot n)$$

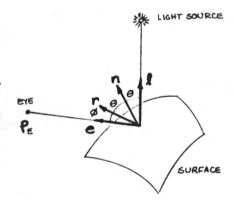

where k_d is the reflection coefficient of the surface material (it varies between 0 and 1, depending on the material), I_p is the intensity of the point source of light, and θ is the angle between the surface normal n and the direction l to the light source. l and n are unit vectors.

A shiny surface produces specular reflection, high-lights or bright spots the same color as the light source. The image is, of course, distorted by the curvature of the surface and its texture. Specular reflection is visible only when ϕ is close to zero. (Note: l,n,r are coplanar.)

Bubbles: A Display Challenge

Here is an example from Nature of modest physical complexity. The form and physics are straightforward. A display must capture these attributes to convince us of its reality.

Nature decrees that a free-floating bubble, such as a soap bubble, assumes a spherical shape. If it comes to rest on a flat surface, it deforms into a hemisphere. The bubble's volume remains the same, so that the ratio of their radii is:

$$V = \left(\frac{4\pi}{3}\right)r_s^3 = \left(\frac{1}{2}\right)\left(\frac{4\pi}{3}\right)r_h^3$$

$$\frac{r_s}{r_h} = \sqrt[3]{\frac{1}{2}}$$

Two equal hemispherical bubbles set into random contact slowly readjust their junction until they reach a stable configuration, joining to form an angle of 120° along their common boundary. The intermediate partitioning film is planar.

Here is the geometry that results when two bubbles of unequal size coalesce into a double bubble. The features to observe are these: The partitioning film assumes a spherical curvature (as pressure is equalized between the two bubbles), and the three centers of curvature are collinear. The 60° angles are no accident; the physics of Mother Nature just happens to work out that way. The distance between the centers of the bubbles

$$d = \sqrt{r_1^2 + r_2^2 - r_1 r_2}$$

The radius of the partition is

$$r_p = \frac{r_1 r_2}{r_2 - r_1}$$

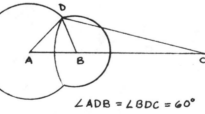

∠ADB = ∠BDC = 60°

Granted, any bubble can be perturbed and its shape caused to oscillate in a variety of modes, but that is another subject.

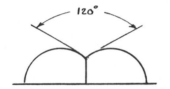

Using just these geometric properties you can work out the geometry of larger clusters.

"Form is born of the formless struggle of molecules."

Peter S. Stevens,
Patterns in Nature

Index